W9-AUZ-313

Cash and Credit Information for Teens

TEEN FINANCE SERIES

First Edition

Cash and Credit Information for Teens

Tips for a Sucessful Financial Life

Including Facts about Earning, Spending, and Borrowing Money, with Topics Such as Budgeting, Consumer Rights, Banks, Paychecks, Taxes, Loans, Credit Cards, and More

◆

Edited by Kathryn R. Deering

615 Griswold Street • Detroit, MI 48226

Bibliographic Note

Because this page cannot legibly accommodate all the copyright notices, the Bibliographic Note portion of the Preface constitutes an extension of the copyright notice.

Edited by Kathryn R. Deering

Teen Finance Series

Karen Bellenir, *Managing Editor*
Elizabeth Barbour, *Research and Permissions Coordinator*
Cherry Stockdale, *Permissions Assistant*
Laura Pleva Nielsen, *Index Editor*
EdIndex, Services for Publishers, *Indexers*

* * *

Omnigraphics, Inc.

Matthew P. Barbour, *Senior Vice President*
Kay Gill, *Vice President—Directories*
Kevin Hayes, *Operations Manager*
Leif Gruenberg, *Development Manager*
David P. Bianco, *Marketing Director*

* * *

Peter E. Ruffner, *Publisher*

Frederick G. Ruffner, Jr., *Chairman*

Copyright © 2005 Omnigraphics, Inc.

ISBN 0-7808-0780-4

Library of Congress Cataloging-in-Publication Data

Cash and credit information for teens : tips for a successful financial life including facts about earning, spending, and borrowing money, with topics such as budgeting, consumer rights, banks, paychecks, taxes, loans, credit cards, and more / edited by Kathryn R. Deering.
    p. cm. -- (Teen finance series)
    Summary: "Provides information for teens about basic money management and personal finance"--Provided by publisher.
    Includes bibliographical references and index.
    ISBN 0-7808-0780-4 (hardcover : alk. paper)
    1. Teenagers--Finance, Personal. I. Deering, Kathryn R. II. Series.
    HG179.C346 2005
    332.024'00835--dc22
                                                                  2005016285

Table Of Contents

Part IV: You And Your Job

Part V: Understanding Loans And Credit Cards

Part VI: Avoiding Financial Risks

Part VII: If You Need More Information

Preface

About This Book

For teens, financial literacy has become a topic that cannot be ignored. Without adequate guidance or information, most young adults must learn how to manage their money by trial and error, and they often join the workforce without knowing how to balance their checkbooks or control their credit card spending.

Cash And Credit Information For Teens provides a complete overview of personal finances. It includes helpful practical information such as how to keep track of personal finances and how to create a personal budget; how to choose banking services; how to manage a checkbook, ATM, debit and credit cards; how to avoid credit problems; and what to look for in a school or automobile loan. This book also explains how to find a job and how to understand paycheck deductions; what to do about paying taxes; how to avoid unsafe financial practices; and how to make good consumer choices, including how to purchase cell phones and that special first car. Directories of helpful websites and financial organizations direct readers to sources of additional information.

How To Use This Book

This book is divided into parts and chapters. Parts focus on broad areas of interest; chapters are devoted to single topics within a part.

Part I: You And Your Money discusses a brief history of money and introduces the Federal Reserve, the U.S. banking system, and monetary policy. It also explains the basics of personal money management: how to keep track of your income and how to create a personal budget.

Part II: You Are A Consumer describes how to become a well-informed consumer, including what to do if you have consumer problems. Special chapters explain how a teen can make the best choices in buying a car or a cell phone.

Part III: Understanding Banks explains how to choose between types of banks and the financial services they offer. Various kinds of savings and checking accounts, ATMs, and electronic banking are discussed along with information about bank fees.

Part IV: You And Your Job discusses how teens can gain experience at searching for and applying for jobs, understanding paychecks, and what to do about taxes.

Part V: Understanding Loans And Credit Cards explains the best ways for teens to borrow money for school, cars, and more and, most importantly, how to use credit cards wisely. It outlines the principles of how credit works, the cost of interest, and how to avoid the trap of mounting debt.

Part VI: Avoiding Financial Risks describes how to avoid ID theft, scams and the temptation of illegal activities, such as shoplifting. One chapter is devoted to managing financial risks through insurance.

Part VII: If You Need More Information includes directories of national organizations and websites that provide financial information.

Bibliographic Note

This volume contains documents and excerpts from publications issued by the following government agencies: Bureau of Labor Statistics (BLS); Department of Education; Department of the Treasury, Financial Management Service; Federal Citizen Information Center (FCIC); Federal Communications Commission (FCC); Federal Deposit Insurance Corporation (FDIC); Federal Reserve Board of Governors; Federal Trade Commission (FTC); Food and Drug Administration (FDA); Internal Revenue Service; Minority Business Development Agency; National Women's Health Information Center; Office of the Comptroller of the Currency; Social Security

Administration; Small Business Administration (SBA); United States Secret Service; and the United States State Department.

In addition, this volume contains copyrighted documents and articles produced by the following organizations: Bankrate, Inc.; Better Business Bureau of Oregon and Western Washington; Communities in Schools in Arizona; Consumers Union of U.S., Inc./Consumer Reports®; Credit Union National Association, Inc.; Curators of the University of Missouri; eFunds Corporation; Ellensburg High School, Ellensburg, Washington; Erie County Commission on the Status of Women; Federal Reserve Bank of Atlanta; Federal Reserve Bank of Boston; Federal Reserve Bank of Dallas; Federal Reserve Bank of New York; Federal Reserve Bank of Philadelphia; FrugalShopper.com; Hallman Solutions Group, Ltd. (ChoiceNerd.com); How Stuff Works, Inc.; Idaho Career Information System (CIS); Illinois Department of Financial and Professional Regulation, Division of Insurance; Illinois Division of Banks and Real Estate; InCharge Education Foundation/Young Money Magazine; Junior Achievement; Insurance Information Institute; Maryland Attorney General, Consumer Protection Division; Michigan Office of the Attorney General, Consumer Protection Division; National Association for Shoplifting Prevention; National Consumers League; New York State Attorney General; National Consumers League; Pennsylvania Office of the Attorney General, Bureau of Consumer Protection; Quintessential Careers; State of Michigan Office of Financial and Insurance Services; Visa, U.S.A.; and the West Virginia Office of the Attorney General, Consumer Protection Division.

Full citation information is provided on the first page of each chapter. Every effort has been made to secure all necessary rights to reprint the copyrighted material. If any omissions have been made, please contact Omnigraphics to make corrections for future editions.

Acknowledgements

In addition to the organizations listed above, special thanks are due to research and permissions coordinator Elizabeth Barbour and to managing editor Karen Bellenir.

Part One

You And Your Money

Chapter 1

Take A Look At Your Money

Money, Banking, And Monetary Policy

Money, the banking system, and monetary policy must work together smoothly for the economy to run well. Money makes it possible for people to exchange goods and services without having to rely on a system of bartering. Banking provides a means for savers to lend their money to borrowers and earn interest in the process, and it gives borrowers a place to go for loans. The aim of monetary policy is to ensure that there is sufficient money in the economy to keep it growing, but not so much that the economy overheats. When the economy overheats, the result is inflation. Inflation—too much money chasing too few goods—creates an inefficient price system. It also distorts decision-making, reduces productivity and lowers the economy's long-term rate of growth. This results in lower living standards for everyone.

About This Chapter: This chapter begins with text from "Everyday Economics: Money, Banking and Monetary Policy," August 2003, a publication of the Federal Reserve Bank of Dallas, http://www.dallasfed.org. "Teens Spend Money, Want Credit, Need Education," is from *National Consumers League Bulletin*, Volume 643, Number 2, March/April 2002. © 2002 National Consumers League. All rights reserved. For additional information, visit http://www.nclnet.org. Reprinted with permission.

What Is Money?

We may not think we have enough of it, but in many ways, we tend to take money for granted. When you buy a pair of jeans or a CD, for example, you never wonder whether the merchant will accept the bills and coins in your wallet as payment. But suppose money as we know it didn't exist. How would you pay for the things you want to buy?

That was the situation in the early days of the American colonies. British money was scarce, so colonists substituted basic products of their local economies that were always in demand—things like tobacco, grain and fish. For small change, they often received nails and bullets.

But their system, called barter, had many shortcomings. How many fish would it take to buy a bag of flour or an oil lamp, for example? Suppose the merchant didn't want fish, or they spoiled before he could trade them to someone else. Later, as trade developed with other colonies and countries, colonists used various foreign coins, such as gold Spanish reales. That's when money as we know it finally gained a foothold in the U.S. economy.

Money is a medium of exchange accepted by the community, meaning it's what people buy things with and sell things for. Money provides a standard for measuring value, so that the worth of different goods and services can be compared. And lastly, money is a store of value that can be saved for later purchases.

The young United States experimented with a variety of monetary mechanisms for well over a century before settling on today's system, which is based on coins, paper currency and money in bank checking accounts. The early government tried unsuccessfully several times to make paper money work, but people relied mostly on gold, silver and copper coins because they were made of precious metals that had intrinsic value.

Today, though, our coins don't contain any gold or silver. You can see this for yourself by looking at the edge of a dime or quarter; you'll see a copper core, sandwiched between silvery nickel. The metal value of modern American coins is much less than it's worth as money. American currency no longer is backed by gold or silver either, but it no longer really matters.

That's because what gives money real value is its purchasing power, not what it's made of. In fact, any economy's health can be measured not by how much money people earn, but by how much their money buys. The overall assortment and quantity of goods and services your money lets you buy reflects your standard of living.

The Fed's Role

Keeping prices stable is part of the job of the Federal Reserve, which was created by Congress in 1913. There had been two attempts at establishing a central bank in the United States in the 19th century, but politics killed them even though they were successful. Back then, state-chartered banks issued their own paper money backed only by their individual gold and silver reserves. As a result, there were once more than 10,000 different kinds of bank notes in circulation.

Suppose you owned a store in those days. How would you know which banks had enough gold reserves to make their currency worth its face value? Should you decrease the value of bills from a weaker bank? And how would you keep track of all those bank notes? You can imagine the shopkeeper's dilemma. If a bank went broke, its currency was instantly worthless, and those who held its notes could lose everything.

♣ It's A Fact!!

Like diamonds, money is relatively scarce—on purpose—and that's just what makes it valuable. You as an individual want to earn as much as you can, of course. But the national economy can actually have too much money. When the amount of money circulating grows faster than the rate at which goods and services are produced, the result is inflation. Say you want a new pair of jeans, for example. Last year, they cost $20, but this year an identical pair costs $23. If prices of most other goods have also risen, then you are probably dealing with inflation—too much money chasing too few goods. Prices have inflated and your $20 buys less than it did. You must earn more just to stay even.

Source: From: Everyday Economics: Money, Banking and Monetary Policy," August 2003, a publication of the Federal Reserve Bank of Dallas, http://www.dallasfed.org.

Naturally, people hurried to withdraw their money at the first hint of trouble in the economy. The result was periodic financial panics that could devastate the national economy for years. Finally, after a particularly bad panic in 1907, Congress decided to solve the problem with the creation of the Federal Reserve System. The Fed was established to provide for a safer and more flexible banking and monetary system.

With the Fed as a safeguard, banks can perform their proper role of bringing savers and borrowers together for the benefit of both. For any economy to be successful, a country first needs political stability so its citizens feel safe; then it needs a stable financial system that includes both trustworthy money and reliable financial institutions. Healthy, profitable banks, therefore, are a vital part of the nation's economic welfare.

Banks provide many services, but for most people, banking consists of depositing their salaries into checking accounts and writing checks on that account to buy things that cost more money than they want to carry in their wallets. People also commonly have savings accounts in which they deposit money they don't need right away or they are saving for a particular purpose. The bank pays interest, or a price paid for use of the money, on savings accounts and often on checking accounts, too.

Very little of this money is kept in the bank's vault, however. While the Federal Reserve requires banks to keep a specified percentage of customer deposits on hand to meet routine withdrawals, they lend the excess. Banks, like any other business, must make a profit to stay in business. Their profit comes from interest people pay on the money they borrow.

How Banks Create Money

Banks actually create money when they lend it. Here's how it works: Most of a bank's loans are made to its own customers and are deposited in their checking accounts. Because the loan becomes a new deposit, just like a paycheck does, the bank once again holds a small percentage of that new amount in reserve and again lends the remainder to someone else, repeating the money-creation process many times.

The tricky part of monetary policy is making sure there is enough money in the economy, but not too much. When people have the money to demand more products than the economy can supply, prices go up and the resulting inflation hurts everyone. While in the United States we get concerned when inflation climbs above 3% a year, we've been more fortunate than some other countries. Just imagine trying to survive in post–World War II Hungary, for instance, where inflation for a while averaged nearly 20,000% per month.

Monetary Policy And The Economy

Controlling the money supply to help the economy grow steadily without inflation is the Federal Reserve's job. Called setting "monetary policy," the Fed does this primarily by buying and selling Treasury securities on the open market. Buying securities on the open market can make it easier for banks to loan money and can give the economy a boost, while selling securities can restrict lending and can help cool down an overheated economy. When the Fed buys securities, the Fed pays for them by crediting the reserve accounts of the sellers' banks. With more money in their reserves, banks can lend more. By contrast, when the Fed sells securities, the Fed collects for the sale by debiting the reserve accounts of the buyers' banks. With less money in their reserves, banks can't lend as much.

Conducting monetary policy is a tremendous responsibility, for the nation's economic health is at stake. You can see why politicians might want to control the money supply for short-term interests. For that reason, the Fed, by law, is not government controlled or funded by Congress. While it is a centralized banking system comprised of 12 regional banks, it is independent in operation.

Besides conducting monetary policy, the Fed also acts as the bankers' bank. As people withdraw more currency to buy things when the economy is booming, the banks in turn pull additional currency from their own reserve accounts with the Fed. When the economy slows down and people increase their savings, banks return the surplus to their reserve accounts. The Fed handles check processing for banks as well, to make sure the billions and billions of dollars in checks written each year move smoothly from one bank to another.

The Fed has other functions also. It helps regulate and supervise banks to keep them financially sound, and it serves as the government's banker by maintaining the U.S. Treasury's "checking account."

Teens Spend Money, Want Credit, Need Education

Teens are consumers—big consumers. A Teen Research Unlimited study found that American teens spent an average of $104 per week in 2001, a total of $172 billion. And yet, research shows they are lacking the skills to deal with their finances responsibly.

The National Consumers League (NCL) commissioned a survey by Opinion Research Corporation International that tested teens' knowledge of financial issues and examined their attitudes toward money, work, and savings. It also questioned how they plan to deal with credit cards and other loans. Findings showed that, while teens are thinking about saving, paying for college, and obtaining credit cards, they may not have a grasp of exactly what a credit card is, how much of college expenses their parents can pay, or what they'll make when they get their first job.

☞ Remember!!
The Fight Against Inflation

It's a complex system, but the goal is simple: to keep the economy stable and growing at a pace that can be sustained without inflation. Economic security underlies nearly every hope and dream people have. It enables businesses to know they can afford to hire more workers, and it lets people plan for the future. If you are saving for college now, for instance, you want to know how much you need altogether and how much you must set aside each month. An inflationary economy can wreck your plans—what you've saved isn't nearly enough anymore, and you don't know how much more will be needed.

A healthy monetary policy, sensitive to changing economic conditions, helps prevent such worries, so you can get on with the business of working to turn your dreams into reality.

Source: From: "Everyday Economics: Money, Banking and Monetary Policy," August 2003, a publication of the Federal Reserve Bank of Dallas, http://www.dallasfed.org.

Work, Money, and Savings: It's not news to anyone who has visited a fast food restaurant in the past decade that many teens are working; 62 percent say they get most of their money from part-time employment, summer jobs, or neighborhood jobs such as babysitting or raking leaves. Over half (55 percent) say they work mainly for spending money. Another 35 percent mainly save the money they make.

Saving money is important to American teens; about nine out of ten save money, though 36 percent admit that they're saving for specific items they want to purchase. Almost one quarter (22 percent) are saving for college and 27 percent save for no particular reason. Four out of ten say they save half or more of their money, and three out of four have a savings account. Only about one in five teens report having a checking account, and small percentages say they have ATM (12 percent) and debit cards (8 percent).

Paying for College: Teens are falsely optimistic about their ability to obtain scholarships and grants to pay for college; 38 percent say that's the main way they'll cover the costs. One in four say their parents will carry the burden, 12 percent plan to work through school to pay the costs, and only ten percent believe they'll mainly use student loans to cover the cost. According to a report by The College Board, loans comprise 58 percent of college aid packages, while scholarships and grants make up only 25 percent. Most of NCL's survey respondents (56 percent) believe their parents will pay for 20-50 percent of their college bill, while 12 percent don't expect their parents to make any contribution.

Life After College and Credit Cards: Over one-third (38 percent) of teens believe they will make under $25,000 in their first job out of college. The reality, according to the Collegiate Employment Research Institute, is that the average college graduate with a bachelor's degree makes between $29,300 and $34,600. One in five survey respondents think they'll make more than $36,000 in the first year. Teens are planning to get credit cards; 58 percent plan say they'll get their first card before they graduate from college.

This interest in credit cards is noteworthy since over half (52 percent) wrongly believe that a credit card is an informal agreement to pay money owed. And where are they learning this? Sixty-three percent say they get most of their information about money, credit, and other financial matters from their parents. But parents might not be the best resource. The average American family carries almost $9,000 in credit card debt. And even if their parents are providing sound advice, over half of the teens admitted that, when they do talk to their parents about money, it's to ask for some to spend.

Financial Privacy, Shopping Online

Though thought to be more Internet savvy than their parents, teens have some disturbing misconceptions about shopping online. Sixty-eight percent mistakenly believe it's safer to pay for goods bought online with a check or money order than by giving a credit card number and 55 percent wrongly think that businesses must go through a screening process to make

✤ It's A Fact!!
NCL's Consumer Education Campaign

NCL has launched a new consumer education campaign with an unrestricted educational grant provided by Bank of America. The goal is to help change misconceptions and provide teens with a financial education foundation they can carry with them as they make important financial decisions later in life. The campaign includes new lessons on banking and credit for teachers and LifeSmarts coaches as well as media outreach to promote LifeSmarts, the League's program to bring consumer education to high school students. The lessons are available online at www.lifesmarts.org. Survey results are available at http://nclnet.org/finances/teensurvey1.htm.

Source: From *National Consumers League Bulletin*, Volume 643, Number 2, March/April 2002. © 2002 National Consumers League. All rights reserved. For additional information, visit http://www.nclnet.org. Reprinted with permission.

sure they are legitimate before they can put up a Web site. When asked the same two questions in 2001, adults knew a bit more than the teens, with 41 percent correctly answering the safest way to pay question, and 73 percent knowing that companies are not screened before they put up site. Teen respondents also showed a lack of understanding of important financial privacy issues. A majority (70 percent) wrongly believe that it's illegal for banks to share a person's financial information with other affiliated companies.

Chapter 2

Keeping Track Of Your Money

Why should you keep financial records? There are many reasons to keep track of your money. In addition to tax purposes, you may need to keep records for insurance purposes or for getting a loan. Good records will help you:

- **Identify sources of income:** You may receive money or property from a variety of sources. Your records can identify the sources of your income. You need this information to separate business from nonbusiness income and taxable from nontaxable income.

- **Keep track of expenses:** You may forget an expense unless you record it when it occurs. You can use your records to identify expenses for which you can claim a deduction. This will help you determine if you can itemize deductions on your tax return.

- **Prepare tax returns:** You need records to prepare your tax return. Good records help you to file quickly and accurately.

- **Support items reported on tax returns:** You must keep records in case the IRS has a question about an item on your return. If the IRS examines your tax return, you may be asked to explain the items reported.

About This Chapter: This chapter is excerpted from "Recordkeeping for Individuals," published in October 1999 by the Internal Revenue Service (IRS). For additional information from IRS visit http://www.irs.gov.

Good records will help you explain any item and arrive at the correct tax with a minimum of effort. If you do not have records, you may have to spend time getting statements and receipts from various sources. If you cannot produce the correct documents, you may have to pay additional tax and be subject to penalties.

Kinds Of Records To Keep

You can use your checkbook to keep a record of your income and expenses. In your checkbook you should record amounts, sources of deposits, and types of expenses. You also need to keep documents, such as receipts and sales slips, that can help prove a deduction.

You should keep your records in an orderly fashion and in a safe place. Keep them by year and type of income or expense. One method is to keep all records related to a particular item in a designated envelope.

The IRS does not require you to keep your records in a particular way. Keep them in a manner that allows you and the IRS to determine your correct tax.

Below you will find guidance about basic records that everyone should keep. This list also provides guidance about specific records you should keep for certain items.

Computerized Records: Many retail stores sell computer software packages that you can use for recordkeeping. These packages are relatively easy to use and require little knowledge of bookkeeping and accounting.

If you use a computerized system, you must be able to produce legible records of the information needed to determine your correct tax liability. In addition to your computerized records, you must keep proof of payment, receipts, and other documents to prove the amounts shown on your tax return.

Copies Of Tax Returns: You should keep copies of your tax returns as part of your tax records. They can help you prepare future tax returns, and you will need them if you file an amended return.

If necessary, you can request a copy of a return and all attachments (including Form W-2) from the IRS by using Form 4506, Request for Copy or Transcript of Tax Form. For information on the cost and where to file, see the Form 4506 instructions.

Basic Records

Basic records are documents that everybody should keep. These are the records that prove your income and expenses. [Note for teens: After you are self-supporting, you will also need to keep documents related to home and property ownership and investments.]

Income: Your basic records prove the amounts you report as income on your tax return. Your income may include wages, dividends, interest, and business income. Your records also can prove that certain amounts are not taxable, such as tax-exempt interest.

Note: Keep Copy C of Form W-2 for at least 3 years after the due date for filing your tax return. However, to help protect your Social Security benefits, keep Copy C until you begin receiving Social Security benefits, just in case there is a question about your work record or earnings in a particular year.

Expenses: Your basic records prove the expenses for which you claim a deduction (or credit) on your tax return. [Note: you are unlikely to claim deductions on your tax returns while your financial affairs are relatively straightforward. You will most likely file your taxes using Form 1040 and the IRS will figure your taxes for you.]

☞ **Remember!!**
Basic Records To Keep

For items concerning your income, KEEP as basic records:

- Form(s) W-2
- Form(s) 1099
- Bank statements
- Brokerage statements
- Form(s) K-1

For items concerning your expenses, KEEP as basic records:

- Sales slips
- Invoices
- Receipts
- Canceled checks or other proof of payment

Source: IRS, 1999.

Proof Of Payment

One of your basic records is proof of payment. You should keep these records to support certain amounts shown on your tax return. Proof of payment alone is not proof that the item claimed on your return is allowable. You should also keep other documents that will help prove that the item is allowable. [Note: Another good reason to keep receipts is for proof of purchase for possible returns.]

Generally, you prove payment with a canceled check or cash receipt. If you do not have a canceled check because your bank does not return canceled checks or if you make payments by credit card or electronic funds transfer, you may be able to prove payment with an account statement.

If you make payments in cash, you should get a dated and signed receipt showing the amount and the reason for the payment.

Account Statements: You may be able to prove payment with a legible financial account statement prepared by your bank or other financial institution.

Pay Statements: If you have deductible expenses withheld from your paycheck, such as union dues or medical insurance premiums, keep your pay statements as proof of payment of these expenses.

If payment is by check, then the statement must show the:

• Check number

• Amount

• Payee's name

• Date the check amount was posted to the account by the financial institution

✔ Quick Tip
To obtain publications from the IRS, go to http://www.irs.gov.

If payment is by electronic funds transfer, then the statement must show the:

• Amount transferred

• Payee's name

- Date the transfer was posted to the account by the financial institution

If payment is by credit card, then the statement must show the:

- Amount charged

- Payee's name

- Transaction date

Taxes

Your Form W-2 shows the state income tax withheld from your wages. If you made estimated state income tax payments, you need to keep a copy of the form. You also need to keep copies of your state income tax returns. If you received a refund of state income taxes, the state may send you Form 1099-G, Certain Government and Qualified State Tuition Program Payments.

♣ **It's A Fact!!**
Money Matters

Did you know that in 2003 teens spent $175 billion dollars on clothes, food, and entertainment? Though teens don't have all of the same responsibilities as adults when it comes to money, many teens want to know more about how to manage it. Learning to manage your money now will mean that you won't have to learn as an adult. Whether you get money from allowance, gifts, or a job, it is never too early to learn the basics about spending, saving, and investing.

Source: National Women's Health Information Center, Office of Women's Health, U.S. Department of Health and Human Services, 2004.

Tips

You must keep a daily record to accurately report your tips on your return. You can use Form 4070A, Employee's Daily Record of Tips, which is found in Publication 1244, Employee's Daily Record of Tips and Report to Employer, to record your tips. For information on tips, see Publication 531, Reporting Tip Income.

Chapter 3

How To Create A Personal Budget

Managing Your Budget

What is a budget? It is simply a written plan for spending your money. You will spend your money; a budget just helps you to spend it wisely.

Managing a budget is not as hard as it sounds. Making the initial commitment to live according to your budget is the hardest part. If you have done that, you are well on your way to wise spending and saving.

Step One: Prepare a budget worksheet. You can make one yourself, or use a pre-made form. To make your own, just write down your income in one column and your expenses in another column, then compare the two.

If you would like to use a pre-made budget form, there are many already set up online. Here are a few links to worksheets that you can print out and use:

- http://financialplan.about.com/od/moneyandcollegestudents/l/blcollbudget.htm

About This Chapter: This chapter begins with "Managing Your Budget," excerpted from an article called, "Successful Budgeting for Students" by Sandy Shields, who is a freelance writer and webmaster of TheFrugalShopper.com. She enjoys living the frugal life, saving money, and helping others to do the same. Copyright © TheFrugalShopper .com 1999-2005. Reprinted with permission. "Budgets" is excerpted and reprinted from the Teen Consumer Scrapbook, http://www.atg.wa.gov/teenconsumer/index.htm, a project of Ellensburg High School, Ellensburg, Washington, and sponsored by the Washington State Attorney General. Reprinted with permission.

- http://www.uheaa.org/budget.htm

- http://www.bankrate.com/brm/news/special/20010425b.asp

You will learn a great deal about your financial situation by taking this first step. If you are like most people, you will find that your income is less than your expenses. You are now informed about it though, and can take the necessary action to change your situation.

Step Two: Start tracking your incidental expenses. You know where the bulk of your money is going, but what about all those little extras? This is a very important step if you are serious about finding ways to stretch your money. Find a small notebook, and jot down all money spent each day on meals, snacks, gas, impulse purchases, and entertainment. After you have done this for a few days, you will start noticing how the small things really add up, and where you can start cutting back.

Step Three: Learn all you can about budgeting, spending, and saving your money. The library offers many free resources to help you with this. Talk to your friends, parents, and teachers about what they have learned about budgeting and saving their money.

Step Four: Take advantage of student discounts, and free offers. Here are some helpful student web sites online to help you save:

✔ **Quick Tip: Set Goals**

Most people who have money didn't get it overnight. They set goals and worked hard to reach them.

Write down your short-term and long-term goals. An example of a short-term goal is saving up for holiday gifts; a long-term goal is saving for a home.

- Set due dates for reaching your goals.

- Be realistic.

- Be flexible. (It's OK to adjust your goals and strategies.)

- Go back and look at your goals after six months to check your progress.

Source: Excerpted from "There's a Lot to Learn about Money," Federal Reserve Board of Governors, 2002.

- Student Advantage (https://www.studentadvantage.com/enrollment/ ?promoCode=FRUGALSHOP)

- Student Market (http://www.studentmarket.com/studentmarket/ money.html)

- EDU.com (http://www.makingitcount.com)

- Stubex.com (http://www.stubex.com)

- 1800Student.com (http://www.1800student.com)

Step Five: Live a frugal lifestyle. Shop smart and spend less. [See chapter 5.]

Summary: These are just a few ideas that you can use to start living a more frugal life, and to successfully manage your budget. Learning how to manage your budget in college will help you immensely. The decisions you make early on will affect you later in life. Use your time and money wisely.

Budgets

Whether you're living at home or moving out, budgeting is a learning experience. It is a skill that you will use for the rest of your life. Decisions about money, how much you spend, your standard of living, and balancing your wants and needs all determine how you are going to budget. These factors will affect your budget no matter how much money you make.

✔ Quick Tip
Charitable Giving

You may wish to donate some of your money to worthy causes. Investigate before you donate. Some con artists use names similar to well-known charities or pretend to be raising money for state or local law enforcement agencies.

- Ask for written information, including how much of the money raised is actually used for charitable purposes.

- Ask your Secretary of State if the charity is registered to solicit in your state.

Check the Better Business Bureau and others for information on charities:

- www.give.org
- www.charitywatch.org
- www.guidestar.org.

Source: Excerpted from "Consumer Action Handbook," 2004 edition, a service provided by the Federal Citizen Information Center of the U.S. General Services Administration.

Where To Start

In dealing with personal finances, you need to stop and analyze what your income and expenses are or will be. Record the following information (if you are not attending school there are some items you can disregard):

- Income

    Salary from work (approximately)

    Money from home (approximately)

    Scholarships, grants, student loans (approximately)

    Miscellaneous (approximately)

    Total Income: _____

- Expenses

    Tuition (approximately)

    Books (approximately)

    Food (approximately)

    Utilities (approximately)

    Car expenses (approximately)

    Recreation (approximately)

    Clothing (approximately)

    Insurance (approximately)

    Credit card payments (approximately)

    Personal (approximately)

    Rent (approximately)

    Health care (approximately)

    Savings (approximately)

    Other (approximately)

    Total Expenses: _____

✔ **Quick Tip**

Look for organizations in your community that can help you learn more about setting financial goals, budgeting, saving, using credit wisely and getting the best deal. Here are some possibilities:

- Nonprofit credit counseling service
- Library
- Community college
- Bank or credit union
- Nonprofit community development corporation
- Nonprofit housing organization
- Religious organization
- Employee assistance program
- Cooperative extension service

Source: Excerpted from "There's a Lot to Learn about Money," Federal Reserve Board of Governors, 2002.

This should help you start to break down your income and expenses so that you can estimate on a monthly basis. Can you see some areas where you need to change your spending? Are you saving money?

Savings And Interest

Saving is important because the money in a savings account earns interest. Interest allows you to make money on the money you save. Saving is a habit that you need to start forming when you begin budgeting.

Month-To-Month Budget

After finding out where your money goes each month, use this same format to predict your expenses and income for next month. This is where you can really start budgeting. Figure out what your needs and wants are. Budget first for your needs and necessities, then for your wants with the money left over. Don't forget to put a little money away each month to meet a special goal. It could be a vacation or that spiffy leather jacket, but reward yourself for managing your money effectively.

At the start of the new month, with your income and expenses predicted, you might break your budgeting down to a weekly and daily basis. Record how you spend money daily and weekly. This detailed record will help you find the unneeded expenses and meet the needed expenses.

☞ Remember!!
Develop A Budget

Find out where your money is going. Unless you're tracking your money, it's probably not going where you really want it to.

Write down your total monthly take-home pay. Then list your monthly expenses. At the end of the month, subtract those expenses from your total pay.

- Look for places to save.

- Use this information to set a monthly budget that includes saving.

- Review how things are going each month.

Tip: Carry a small notebook. Write down everything you spend. Include small purchases like candy bars.

Source: Excerpted from "There's a Lot to Learn about Money," Federal Reserve Board of Governors, 2002.

Chapter 4

Twelve Principles Of Personal Financial Literacy For Young Adults

1. **Know your take-home pay**: Before committing to significant expenditures, estimate how much income is likely to be available for you. Net income, after all mandatory deductions, is more important to estimate than gross income before deductions.

2. **Pay yourself first**: Before paying bills and other financial obligations, set aside an affordable amount each month in accounts designated for long-range goals and unexpected emergencies.

3. **Start saving young**: Recognize that your total savings are determined both by the interest you earn on those savings and the time period over which you save. The sooner you start saving, the more funds you'll be able to amass over time.

4. **Compare interest rates**: Obtain rate information from multiple financial services firms to get the best value for your money.

5. **Don't borrow what you can't repay**: Be a responsible borrower who repays as promised, showing you are worthy of getting credit in the future.

About This Chapter: This chapter is reprinted with permission from "Twelve Principles Of Personal Financial Literacy For Young Adults," © 2000 West Virginia Office of the Attorney General, Consumer Protection Division.

Before you borrow, compare your total payment obligations with income that you will have available to make these payments.

6. **Budget your money:** Create an annual budget to identify expected income and expenses, including savings. This will serve as a guide to help you live within your income.

7. **Money doubles by the "Rule of 72":** To determine how long it will take your money to double, divide the interest rate into 72. For example, an account earning 6% interest will double in twelve years (72 divided by 6 equals 12).

8. **High returns equal high risks:** Recognize that no one will pay you high interest rates on a sure thing. In most cases, the higher the interest rate offered to you, the investor, the higher the risk of losing some, or all, of the money you invest. Diversification of assets is the best protection against risk.

9. **Don't expect something for nothing:** Be leery of advertisements, sales people or other sources of financial offers promising anything free. Like non-financial opportunities, if it sounds too good to be true, it probably is.

10. **Make your financial future:** Take time to list your financial goals, along with a realistic plan for achieving them. You can go places you want to go without a roadmap—but seldom on the first try.

11. **Your credit past is your credit future:** Be aware that credit bureaus maintain credit reports, which record borrowers' histories of repaying loans. Negative information in credit reports can affect your ability to borrow at a later point.

12. **Stay insured:** Purchase insurance to avoid being wiped out by a financial loss, such as an illness or accident. An insurance plan should be part of every personal financial plan.

Part Two

You Are A Consumer

Chapter 5

Getting The Most For Your Money (Living Within Your Means)

Even when your income is limited, you can adopt a lifestyle that allows you to live within your means.

Six Money-Saving Tips

The weekend is here and your wallet is empty. There's nothing inside but some pennies and a gum wrapper. Your best friend quoted the evening agenda, "movie, party, club." Guess you're staying home tonight unless you have a secret cash stash hidden somewhere.

The good news is that this doesn't have to happen to you. Learn how to manage your money properly and you'll be surprised at the amount of cash you save.

About This Chapter: This chapter includes text from "Six Money-Saving Tips," by Lauren Berger, reprinted with permission of InCharge Education Foundation, Inc., March/April 2004 issue of YOUNG MONEY, www.youngmoney.com. Text under the heading "Financial Planning Includes Money-Savers," is from "Money Matters: Cost Cutting Considerations," reprinted with permission from http://www.choicenerd.com © 2005 ChoiceNerd.com. All rights reserved. "Are You Bamboozled By Advertising?" is © 2003 Maryland Office of the Attorney General, Consumer Protection Division. Reprinted with permission. "Rules For Evaluating Advertisements" is from *Practical Money Skills for Life*, a financial literacy education program from Visa, http://www.practicalmoneyskills.com © Visa U.S.A. All rights reserved. Reprinted with permission.

Some college advisors say that more students drop out due to financial debt than any other reason. Don't fall into that trap.

Here are six smart tips to better organize your money. Look over these tips, and find ways to make them a part of your daily life. No one wants to be in debt for the rest of his or her life. College can seem like a breeze until your wallet's empty and the bills keep coming. Enjoy yourself but remember to budget your bucks.

1. **Write It Down:** Get a financial record started; any sized notebook will do. Set up the book so that you have a space to write down what you spend and when you spent it. Have another section to keep track of your required expenses for each month (i.e., gas, food). Write down the exact income you expect to have per month whether it be from your parents, financial aid or job. This will enable you to become a better consumer as well as keep track of your funds.

2. **Check Your Options:** Speak with your parents and bank representatives about the different products they offer college students. Most banks and credit card companies have plenty of programs for student use only. Credit cards are convenient but they can also work against you. Try to use cash when making purchases and save credit cards for emergencies. Track all of your transactions in your financial book. [Warning: Transactions are not usually posted on the weekends, so ATMs can give a false account balance. Sometimes your check/debit cards will work even if the funds aren't available. However, banks often charge a big fee for overdrawn accounts.]

3. **Save The Slips:** Keep track of all your receipts—yes, even the ones at the gas station. Place them right into your financial record book. If you are ever charged incorrectly, you'll have proof of what you actually spent.

4. **Don't Overspend:** Only buy what you absolutely need. You can always go back to the store and buy more. You never know when a parking ticket or other surprise expense will come up. Start a savings account. Daily necessities tend to eat away at your wallet so watch what you spend.

5. **Keep It Clean:** Organize your license, cash, coins, Blockbuster card and other items in your wallet or purse. An organized wallet makes it easier to keep track of your expenses. Hold on to coupons and discount cards. They'll come in handy when your budget gets tight.

6. **Pay Up:** Pay your bills in full as they come in. Don't let your credit card balance get out of hand. The interest rates will kick in eventually and you will owe more than you can afford. Paying the full balance each time will force you to stay on top of your expenses.

Financial Planning Includes Money-Savers

Stretching your dollars is not easy, but you can make a difference by being a smart consumer. The following are all cost cutting strategies you can incorporate in your personal budget:

- Write a sensible budget down that is easily accessible and stick with it.

- Buy gas during the middle of the week before the usual weekend price hike.

- When shopping for necessary clothing items, shop at discounted stores that carry name brand clothing. Also try thrift stores, you'll be surprised what you may find.

- Go to the matinee movie instead of paying full price in the evening, or attend the $2.00 movie.

- When grocery shopping, make out a list before you go and stick to it to avoid impulse shopping.

- Use coupons whenever possible.

- Pack your lunches instead of going out every day.

- Try to cook at home instead of eating out.

- Price-shop all major purchases to make sure you are getting the best deal.

- Buy clothing in its off season.

- Pay off your credit cards to avoid interest charges.

- Accept low balance transfer credit card offers and cancel high interest cards.

- Make all credit payments on time to avoid hefty late charges.

- Perform routine maintenance to your car to avoid costly repair.

- Before you go out, place a limit on how much you will spend during a night on the town with your friends.

- Use community or apartment work out facilities instead of joining expensive health clubs.

- Look for airfare deals over the Internet when traveling or purchase tickets far in advance.

- Take designated savings out of your paycheck immediately.

- Get a roommate, if you are renting an apartment, to cut expense.

- Use public transportation to get to work, or car pool.

- Check your bills for overcharges.

- Keep the thermostat around 70 degrees and avoid turning it on and off to stabilize heat bills

- Don't loan money out to people that won't pay you back.

- Groom yourself instead of paying big money to manicurists, beauticians, and barbers.

- Move to a city with a reasonable standard of living.

Are You Bamboozled By Advertising?

Advertisements and commercials are loaded with gimmicks and hype. They want you to buy without thinking. Here's how to look at ads with a critical eye.

Is That Sale Really A Bargain?

"Huge sale! Save up to 60% off!"

60% off sounds good, but it's 60% off what? The most recent price? More likely, it may be off the "regular price" or "manufacturer's suggested retail price," neither of which the store ever charged for the item. It's just a gimmick that sounds good.

✔ Quick Tip
Frugal Living Suggestions For Students

- Define your wants versus your needs. Concentrate on spending money only on your needs.

- Don't drink, smoke, or do drugs. They are bad for you, addictive, and cost money. You don't need them.

- If at all possible, keep a savings account. Pay yourself first.

- Use everything to its full potential. Don't waste anything.

- Recycle and reuse study materials such as pencils, pens, and paper.

- Don't spend money around the plans you make. Make plans around the money you have after all your responsibilities are met.

- Don't be tempted by your friends' spending habits.

- Make things yourself instead of buying them whenever possible.

- Shop smart when buying groceries and household items. Use coupons. Shop the sales.

- Stock up on discounted non-perishable items. Foods like milk, butter, and cheese can be frozen. Don't buy soft drinks, unless they are on sale, or store brand. Drink water. Do not spend money on snack machines.

- Shop smart when buying clothes. Do not pay retail prices. Shop thrift stores, consignment shops, yard sales, clearance racks, and buy during off seasons. Don't buy any item that requires dry cleaning. Consider consigning your own clothes to earn some money.

- Make the most of your college's meal plan, and any college events where there is free food.

- Use your tuition money wisely. Always take the maximum number of credits allowed.

- Get an on-campus job.

- E-mail or write instead of calling home.

Source: Excerpted from "Successful Budgeting for Students," by Sandy Shields. Sandy Shields is a freelance writer and webmaster of TheFrugalShopper.com. She enjoys living the frugal life, saving money, and helping others to do the same. © TheFrugalShopper.com, 1999-2005. Reprinted with permission.

"Get One Free"

Many "get one free" offers require you to buy overpriced items to get your so-called "free" item. To see if an offer is really a good deal, calculate what the per-item price is.

Sparkle Boutique is selling T-shirts: *"Buy 2 at $19 each, get 1 FREE!"*

Do the math:

Pay for 2 shirts x $19 each = $38

$38 ÷ 3 shirts = $12.66 final cost per shirt

Is $12.66 a good price? It might be, if you really want to buy three shirts. But as it turns out, another store is selling similar shirts for just $9.99, with no strings attached. You can buy just one if that's all you want. Even if you wanted three, it would still only cost $29.97 total.

Watch Out For Asterisks

Whenever you see an asterisk in an ad, there's sure to be a catch! Check the asterisks below the claims to see the real deal:

Haircuts only $14!*

Free 8 x 10 Color Portrait!*

Talk Free ALL THE TIME!*

* Long hair extra

* Requires $11.95 sitting fee

* Except weekdays

♣ **It's A Fact!!**

Commonly Used Sales Techniques

• **Guarantees:** Abundant use of statements such as "lifetime guarantee" and "satisfaction guaranteed, or your money back."

• **Scarcity:** Merchant creates a false sense of urgency by claiming that supply or time is limited.

• **Perceptual contrast:** Merchant presents undesirable/inferior option first to make the second option look far superior.

• **Scientific or numerical claims:** "Nine-out-of-ten" may sound good, but many such claims can prove impossible to substantiate.

• **Negative option:** Merchandise arrives automatically unless the consumer takes steps to stop shipment and billing. Often used by book and record clubs.

Source: From *Practical Money Skills for Life*, a financial literacy education program from Visa, http://www.practicalmoneyskills.com © Visa U.S.A. All rights reserved. Reprinted with permission.

Read The Fine Print

If you see fine print at the bottom of an ad, read it! It will list all the terms. After reading it, you may find that the offer isn't so great after all. Like this:

"Wireless for unbelievable $9.99 a month!"

What does the fine print say?: This price does not include calls made on Sunday, Monday, Tuesday, Wednesday, Thursday, or Saturday. Calls made on those days cost $20 per minute. Also, if you sign up with us you can't cancel for seven years.

Recognize The "Image Sell"

Some ads focus on image rather than telling you much about the product itself. Advertisers know that you want to be popular, so they appeal to your vanity. Don't let these emotional appeals blind you to whether the product is really the best value.

Ad's Message: This sporty car is for hip young people—don't you want to be this cool?

... But Your Brain Says: Yeah, but as far as doing what a car is supposed to do—how reliable is it? What gas mileage does it get? Does it have good crash protection?

Ad's Message: If you use this hair color, you'll be as beautiful as this actress.

... But Your Brain Says: Just because they say it's worth $3 more than other brands doesn't mean it is. After all, she's an actress, she gets paid to say that!

Ad's Message: This energy bar will give you the strength of an Olympic cyclist!

... But Your Brain Says: These bars are expensive. What's in them anyway? Is there really anything special about the ingredients? Or could I get the same "energy" from a granola bar or sandwich?

View Scientific And Research Claims Skeptically

"More people prefer...nine out of ten doctors recommend...clinically proven to reduce breakouts...A scientific breakthrough..."

These claims try to make you feel that you should buy the product because other people, or experts, think it's the best. But...who did they survey? What doctors did they ask? Were those doctors paid by the company that makes the product?

"All-Natural Formula"

Just because something is made from plants or minerals doesn't mean it's better or safer. After all, poison ivy is "all-natural."

Rules For Evaluating Advertisements

Ask yourself basic questions:

1. Does the ad appeal to your emotions? Look beyond the appeal to find out what the ad really says (or doesn't say) about the product or service.

2. What are the special features of the product? Are these features necessary?

As you read, listen to, or watch advertisements...

1. Search for fraud and deception in the ad. Be alert to ads that are misleading (those that make unreasonable claims about the product or service).

2. Read the fine print, or listen carefully.

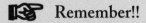 **Remember!!**

Examples Of
Misleading Advertising

- **Health fraud:** Promises of overnight medical cures and treatments. Products developed after "years of research" and "proven to provide immediate positive results." Testimonials from medical experts and satisfied customers.

- **Credit repair:** Offers, for a fee, to fix a bad credit record. (Credit repair is impossible.)

- **"Get rich quick" schemes:** Ads that offer an opportunity to earn a lot of money in a short amount of time with very little effort.

- **Product misrepresentation:** Uses names similar to nationally recognized brand. Merchandise offered at below-market value for a limited time only. Vague descriptions of product.

- **Travel fraud:** Offers accompanied by certificates for free or very low-cost travel. Vague description of services and accommodations.

Source: From *Practical Money Skills for Life*, a financial literacy education program from Visa, http://www.practicalmoneyskills.com © Visa U.S.A. All rights reserved. Reprinted with permission.

Chapter 6

Getting What You Pay For

As a consumer, you need to be informed and alert about a wide variety of marketing techniques.

Trial Offers: The Deal Is In The Details

Chances are you've gotten offers to try a product or service through a "free trial." Companies use these offers to sell a variety of items, from books and CDs to videos, magazines, hosiery and Internet access. But as part of a trial offer, a company also must tell you if any conditions are attached to the deal.

The Federal Trade Commission (FTC) carefully monitors the marketing practices in this area and offers this information to help you make wise purchasing decisions. Be a savvy consumer: read the fine print and ask questions. Trial offers can be a great way to try new products or services without making a long-term commitment to a membership, subscription, or extended service contract. But by accepting the free trial offer, you may be agreeing to buy additional products and services—if you don't cancel.

About This Chapter: This chapter includes text from three documents produced by the U.S. Federal Trade Commission (FTC): "Trial Offers: The Deal Is in the Details," July 2001; "Unordered Merchandise," August 1997; and "Shopping By Phone Or Mail," July 2003.

What Does "No Risks Or Obligations" Really Mean?

A company may claim its free trial offer has no risk or obligation for the consumer. And that may be true, but only if you take timely action to avoid future obligations. For example, you may have to contact the company to cancel during the trial period to avoid receiving additional goods or services or to pay for what you've already received. By not canceling, you may be agreeing to let the company enroll you in a membership, subscription or service contract, and to charge the fees to your credit card.

How Conditional Trial Offers Work

Here are a few examples of conditional free trial offers:

- A company offers you an introductory package of free books, CDs or videos. If you accept the offer, you may be agreeing to enroll in a club that will send you the products and bill you until you cancel.

♣ It's A Fact!! It's The Law

According to the law, companies must clearly and prominently disclose the "material" terms of their trial offers before you give your consent. Material terms may include:

- the fact that by accepting the trial offer, you're actually agreeing to be enrolled in a membership, subscription or service contract or paying for additional products and services if you don't cancel within the trial period;

- how much time you have to cancel before you incur charges;

- the cost or range of costs of goods or services you'll receive if you don't cancel during the trial period;

- how to cancel during the trial period;

- whether you'll be charged a non-refundable membership fee if you don't cancel within the trial period;

- whether fees will be charged automatically to the credit card you used to buy other goods or services.

Source:
FTC, 2001.

- A company offers you the first three issues of a magazine for free. Unless you cancel after receiving the third issue, you may be agreeing to a one-year subscription that is automatically renewed each year.

- A company offers you free Internet service for 30 days or 700 hours, whichever comes first (30 days = 720 hours). Unless you cancel within the 30-day period or after you use the 700 hours, you may be agreeing to pay for continuous Internet service.

- A company offers you a free pair of pantyhose. By accepting the offer, you may be agreeing to receive a second pair as well. You also may be agreeing that, if you keep and pay for the second pair, the company may ship you a third pair. This may continue until you tell the company to cancel your account.

Make Sure You Know Who's Selling What

Sometimes, you call a company for one reason and at the end of the transaction, you may be told about a trial offer that another company is offering. This is called "upselling." If you receive such an offer, pay close attention to the terms and conditions. Make sure you understand who you're dealing with and what you're agreeing to. By accepting the trial offer, you may be agreeing to let the company you called in the first place give your credit card account information to another seller.

If you don't cancel during the trial period, your credit card may be charged by the second seller for the product or service offered for the trial period. If you don't recognize the seller, you may think the charge is an unauthorized transaction. In fact, by accepting the trial offer, you may have agreed to pay if you didn't cancel before the trial period ended.

Protect Yourself

Trial offers are promoted through all kinds of media: newspaper and magazine ads, TV and radio commercials, direct mail, and the phone and Internet. In print ads and offers, the material terms may appear in fine print as a footnote at the bottom of a page, or on the back of the offer. Read the whole offer carefully before you decide whether it's a good deal for you.

When offers are made orally—whether by radio, TV or on the phone—listen carefully to the message. If you don't understand the details, ask the caller to repeat the terms and conditions as many times as it takes until you get it. If you're not satisfied with the responses, consider taking your business elsewhere. Never give in to pressure to agree to a deal.

Here are some questions you may want to ask the seller:

- Is the free trial offer related to a membership, subscription or extended service contract?

- Do I have to contact the company to avoid receiving more merchandise or services? If so, how much time do I have? What is my deadline?

- Whom do I contact to cancel? How do I cancel? By letter? By phone? By e-mail?

- Will I get other products with the free item? If so, will I have to pay for them or send them back if I don't want them? How long do I have to decide before incurring a charge?

- How do I stop getting additional merchandise or services?

- Is there a membership fee? If so, is it refundable?

- Will you automatically bill my credit card for anything?

- Who is offering the trial—you or another company? What is the name and address of the company?

Where To Complain

If you have a problem with a trial offer, try to resolve it with the seller first. If you're dissatisfied with the response, contact your local Better Business Bureau or local consumer protection agency.

You also may file a complaint with the FTC. The FTC works for the consumer to prevent fraudulent, deceptive and unfair business practices in the marketplace and to provide information to help consumers spot, stop, and avoid them. To file a complaint, call toll-free, 1-877-382-4357, or use the complaint form at www.ftc.gov. The FTC enters Internet, telemarketing, identity theft and other fraud-related complaints into Consumer Sentinel, a secure, online database available to hundreds of civil and criminal law enforcement agencies in the U.S. and abroad.

Remember!! Buy Now, Pay Later?

Consumers are hit hard with "buy now, pay later" advertisements of retailers and the direct mail campaigns of credit card companies. One cannot turn on the TV or radio, access the Internet, or take in the mail without viewing or hearing a commercial promising no interest or payments until "2000 whatever." Unfortunately, these tactics often result in an unbearable debt load.

Whether it's a new vehicle, new furniture, or new sound system, people rarely think about it as a financial transaction.

On one hand we know the need for planning and saving. But then businesses appeal to consumer senses with unbelievable offers.

Source: Excerpted from "Your Budget Blueprint," © 2005 Credit Union National Association, Inc. Reprinted with permission. For additional information, visit http://www.cuna.org.

Unordered Merchandise

What do you do when you receive merchandise that you didn't order? According to the Federal Trade Commission, you don't have to pay for it. Federal laws prohibit mailing unordered merchandise to consumers and then demanding payment.

Here are some questions and answers about dealing with unordered merchandise.

Am I obligated to return or pay for merchandise I never ordered?

No. If you receive merchandise that you didn't order, you have a legal right to keep it as a free gift.

Must I notify the seller if I keep unordered merchandise without paying for it?

You have no legal obligation to notify the seller. However, it is a good idea to write a letter to the company stating that you didn't order the item and, therefore, you have a legal right to keep it for free. This may discourage the seller from sending you bills or dunning notices, or it may help clear up an honest error. Send your letter by certified mail. Keep the return receipt and a copy of the letter for your records. You may need it later.

What should I do if the unordered merchandise I received was the result of an honest shipping error?

Write the seller and offer to return the merchandise, provided the seller pays for postage and handling. Give the seller a specific and reasonable amount of time (say 30 days) to pick up the merchandise or arrange to have it returned at no expense to you. Tell the seller that you reserve the right to keep the merchandise or dispose of it after the specified time has passed.

Is there any merchandise that may be sent legally without my consent?

Yes. You may receive samples that are clearly marked free, and merchandise from charitable organizations asking for contributions. You may keep such shipments as free gifts.

Is there any way to protect myself from shippers of unordered merchandise?

When you participate in sweepstakes or order goods advertised as "free," "trial," or "unusually low priced," be cautious. Read all the fine print to determine if you are joining a "club," with regular purchasing or notification obligations. Keep a copy of the advertisement or catalog that led you to place the order, too. This may make it easier to contact the company if a problem arises.

Where can I go for help in dealing with unordered merchandise problems?

Always start by trying to resolve your dispute with the company. If this doesn't work, contact your state or local consumer protection office, local U.S. Postal Inspector, or the Better Business Bureau in your area for help. The Direct Marketing Association, 6 East 43rd Street, New York, New York 10017, also may be able to help you.

Shopping By Phone Or Mail

The Federal Trade Commission's Mail or Telephone Order Rule covers merchandise you order by mail, telephone, computer, and fax machine.

By law, a company should ship your order within the time stated in its ads. If no time is promised, the company should ship your order within thirty days after receiving it.

If the company is unable to ship within the promised time, they must give you an "option notice." This notice gives you the choice of agreeing to the delay or canceling your order and receiving a prompt refund.

There is one exception to the thirty-day rule: if a company doesn't promise a shipping time, and you are applying for credit to pay for your purchase, the company has fifty days to ship after receiving your order.

☞ Remember!!

Tips For Determining Telemarketing Fraud

• High-pressure sales tactics.

• Insistence on an immediate decision.

• The offer sounds too good to be true.

• A request for your credit card number for any purpose other than to make a purchase.

• An offer to send someone to your home or office to pick up the money, or some other method such as overnight mail to get your funds more quickly.

• A statement that something is "free," followed by a requirement that you pay for something.

• An investment that is "without risk."

• Unwillingness to provide written information or references (such as a bank or names of satisfied customers in your area) that you can contact.

• A suggestion that you should make a purchase or investment on the basis of "trust."

Source: Excerpted from "Frequently Asked Questions," United States Secret Service, 2002.

Fair Credit Billing Act (FCBA)

You're protected by the FCBA when you use your credit card to pay for purchases.

Billing Errors. If you find an error on your credit or charge card statement, you may dispute the charge and withhold payment on the disputed amount while the charge is in dispute. The error might be a charge for the wrong amount, for something you did not accept, or for an item that was not delivered as agreed.

Of course, you still must pay any part of the bill that is not in dispute, including finance charges on the undisputed amount. If you decide to dispute a charge:

- Write to the creditor at the address indicated on the monthly statement for "billing inquiries." Include your name, address, credit card number, and a description of the billing error.

✔ Quick Tip

Ways To Avoid Becoming A Victim

- Don't allow yourself to be pushed into a hurried decision.
- Always request written information, by mail, about the product, service, investment or charity and about the organization that's offering it.
- Don't make any investment or purchase you don't fully understand.
- Ask with what state or federal agencies the firm is registered.
- Check out the company or organization.
- If an investment or major purchase is involved, request that information also be sent to your accountant, financial adviser, banker, or attorney for evaluation and an opinion.
- Ask what recourse you would have if you make a purchase and aren't satisfied.
- Beware of testimonials that you may have no way of verifying.
- Don't provide personal financial information over the phone unless you are absolutely certain the caller has a bona fide need to know.
- If necessary, hang up the phone.

Source: Excerpted from "Frequently Asked Questions," United States Secret Service, 2002.

- Send your letter in a timely fashion. It must reach the creditor within sixty days after the first bill containing the error was mailed to you.

The creditor must acknowledge your complaint in writing within thirty days after receiving it, unless the problem has been resolved. The creditor must resolve the dispute within two billing cycles (but not more than ninety days) after receiving your letter.

Unsatisfactory Goods Or Services. You also may dispute charges for unsatisfactory goods or services. To take advantage of this protection regarding the quality of goods or services, you must:

- have made the purchase in your home state or within one hundred miles of your current billing address. The charge must be for more than $50.

- make a good faith effort first to resolve the dispute with the seller. However, you are not required to use any special procedure to do so.

Note: The dollar and distance limitations don't apply if the seller also is the card issuer or if a special business relationship exists between the seller and the card issuer.

Precautions

Before ordering by phone or mail, consider your experience with the company or its general reputation. Determine the company's refund and return policies, the product's availability, and the total cost of your order.

If you have problems with mail or phone order purchases, try to resolve your dispute with the company. If that doesn't work, you may want to contact the state and local consumer protection offices in your home state and where the company is located.

Reducing Direct Marketing Solicitations

You may want to have your name removed from direct marketing lists. Be aware, however, that if you purchase goods by phone or mail after your name is removed, it may be added again. You may want to make a new request to have your name removed every few years. You also may want to ask mail or telephone order companies to retain your name on in-house lists only.

The Federal government has created the National Do Not Call Registry—the free, easy way to reduce the telemarketing calls you get at home. To register, or to get information, visit www.donotcall.gov, or call 1-888-382-1222 from the phone you want to register. You will receive fewer telemarketing calls within three months of registering your number. It will stay in the registry for five years or until the phone is disconnected or you take it off the registry. After five years, you will be able to renew your registration.

The DMA Mail Preference Service lets you opt out of receiving direct mail marketing from many national companies for five years. When you register with this service, your name will be put on a "delete" file and made available to direct-mail marketers. However, your registration will not stop mailings from organizations that are not registered with the DMA's Mail Preference Service. Register online with the DMA at www.the-dma.org/consumers/offmailinglist.html. To register by mail with DMA, send your letter to:

Direct Marketing Association
Mail Preference Service
P.O. Box 643
Carmel, NY 10512

The DMA also has an EMail Preference Service to help you reduce unsolicited commercial e-mails. To "opt-out" of receiving unsolicited commercial e-mail, use DMA's online form at www.dmaconsumers.org/offmaillist.html. Your online request will be effective for one year.

Chapter 7

What If You Don't Like What You Buy?

Every year the Consumer Federation of America and the National Association of Consumer Agency Administrators survey government consumer protection offices to find out what transactions generate the most complaints. Auto sales, auto repair, and auto leasing are usually near the top of the list. Other frequent "winners" include home improvement, retail sales, credit and lending, and mail order. A recent addition to the list is the purchase of household goods such as appliances, computers and furniture.

To avoid problems during these and other consumer transactions, take the steps and heed the warnings set out below.

- Decide in advance exactly what you want and what you can afford. Don't buy on impulse or because a salesperson is pressuring you.

- Ask friends and family for recommendations based on their experience.

- Get advice and price quotes from several sellers. Remember, their goal is to make a sale.

About This Chapter: This chapter begins with text excerpted from "Consumer Action Handbook," 2004 edition, a service provided by the Federal Citizen Information Center (FCIC) of the U.S. General Services Administration. "Avoiding Unhappy Returns—Returning Merchandise Bought On- Or Offline" updated 2/2003, is reprinted with permission from the Michigan Office of the Attorney General, Consumer Protection Division. Copyright © 2003 State of Michigan.

- Review product test results and other information from consumer experts.

- Read and understand any contract you are asked to sign. Make sure there are no blank spaces and that any verbal promises made by the salesperson are in the contract.

- Get a written copy of guarantees and warranties. Compare their features.

- Extended warranties or service contracts are very profitable for business. Decide whether the extra peace of mind is worth the price.

- Get the seller's refund and return policies.

- Consider paying by credit card. If you later have a legitimate dispute with the seller, you do not have to pay a charge made on your credit card.

✔ Quick Tip
After You Buy

Save all contracts, sales receipts, canceled checks, owner's manuals and warranty documents. To avoid problems, read and follow product and service instructions. The way you use or take care of a product might affect your warranty rights.

The first step in resolving a consumer problem is usually to contact the business that sold you the item or performed the service. If you wish to go directly to the headquarters of the company or the manufacturer, ask if they have a consumer affairs office and, if so, report the problem directly to them. Otherwise, communicate with a manager or the president of the business.

To help find the company you are looking for, check the product label, warranty or other papers you received at the time of purchase. These reference books at your public library also have helpful information:

- The Standard & Poor's Register of Corporations, Directors and Executives

- Trade Names Directory

- Standard Directory of Advertisers

- Dun & Bradstreet [now D&B] Directory

- Thomas Register of American Manufacturers

Keep in mind the name of the manufacturer or parent company is often different than the brand name. You may also be able to get a corporation's address from the Attorney General's office in the state where the company is incorporated.

Source: "Consumer Action Handbook," FCIC, 2004.

How To Defend Your Consumer Rights

After you make a purchase, if you think a law has been broken, contact your local or state consumer protection agency right away. Violations of federal law should be reported to the government agency responsible for enforcement.

Don't give up if you are not satisfied. If you believe you have given the company enough time to resolve the problem, file a complaint with one or more of these organizations.

- **State or local consumer protection offices:** These government agencies mediate complaints, conduct investigations, and prosecute offenders of consumer laws.

- **The regulatory agency that has jurisdiction over the business:** For example, some banking and securities, insurance, and utilities are regulated at the state level. State Weights and Measures Offices enforce consumer protections concerning the labeling, weight, and measure or count of packaged goods. They also check the accuracy of weighing and measuring devices such as supermarket scales, gasoline pumps, taximeters and rental car odometers.

- **State and local licensing agencies:** Doctors, lawyers, home improvement contractors, auto repair shops, debt collectors, and childcare providers are required to register or be licensed. The board or agency that oversees this process may handle complaints and have the authority to take disciplinary action.

- **Better Business Bureaus (BBBs):** This network of nonprofit organizations supported by local businesses tries to resolve buyer complaints against sellers. Records are kept on unresolved complaints as a source of information for the seller's future customers. The umbrella organization for the BBBs assists with complaints concerning the truthfulness of national advertising and helps settle disputes with automobile manufacturers through the BBB AUTO LINE program.

- **Trade associations:** Companies selling similar products or services often belong to an industry association that will help resolve problems between their members and consumers.

- **National consumer organizations.**

- **Media programs.** Local newspapers, radio stations, and television stations often have Action Lines or Hotline services that try to resolve consumer complaints they receive. Some handle only the most serious cases or those that occur most frequently. To find these services, check with your local newspapers or broadcast stations.

Dispute Resolution Programs

The auto industry has many of these programs. The National Association of Security Dealers offers a program designed to resolve investment-related disputes. Some small claims courts also offer a dispute resolution program as an alternative to a trial.

Mediation, arbitration, and conciliation are three common types of dispute resolution. During mediation, both sides involved in the dispute meet with a neutral third party and create their own agreement jointly. In contrast, in arbitration the third party decides how to settle the problem. Request a copy of the rules of the program before making a decision to participate in any of them. Because the opposing sides may not be satisfied with the decision, ask in advance:

- Is the decision binding? Some programs do not require both parties to accept the decision.

- Does participation in the program place any restrictions on your ability to take other legal action? The American Bar Association publishes a directory of state and local dispute resolution programs.

Reporting Fraud

People who have no intention of delivering what is sold, who misrepresent items, send counterfeit goods or otherwise try to trick you out of your money are committing fraud. Reporting fraud promptly improves your chances of recovering what you have lost, and helps law enforcement authorities stop scams before others are victimized.

- Start by contacting your state or local consumer agency and local law enforcement officers for advice and assistance.

✔ Quick Tip

Call for Action, Inc. (www.callforaction.org) is a nonprofit network of consumer hotlines that educate and assist consumers with consumer problems. Listed below are hotlines in major markets staffed with trained volunteers who offer advice and mediate complaints at no cost to consumers. Consumers in locations not listed should call the Network Hotline at 301-657-7490.

KPNX-TV, KNAZ-TV Phoenix/Flagstaff, AZ 866-260-1212	WXYZ-TV, WJR Radio Detroit, MI 248-827-3362	WJW-TV Cleveland, OH 216-578-0700
KKTV-TV Colorado Springs, CO 719-457-8211	KCTV-5 Kansas City, MO 913-831-1919	WTOL-TV Toledo, OH 419-255-2255
WTOP AM and FM Washington, DC 301-652-4357	KTVI-TV St. Louis, MO 636-282-2222	WTAJ-TV Altoona, PA 814-944-9336
WINK-TV Fort Myers, FL 941-334-4357	WIVB-TV Buffalo, NY 716-879-4900	WTAE-TV Pittsburgh, PA 412-333-4444
WXIA-TV Atlanta, GA 678-422-8466	WABC Radio New York, NY 212-268-5626	KTVX-TV Salt Lake City, UT 877-908-0444
WBZ Radio Boston, MA 617-787-7070	WFMY-TV Greensboro, NC 336-680-1000	WTMJ-TV Milwaukee, WI 414-967-5495

Source: "Consumer Action Handbook," FCIC, 2004.

- Report suspected violations of Federal Trade Commission rules by contacting the FTC Consumer Response Center, Washington, DC 20580, calling toll-free 1-877-FTC-HELP (1-877-382-4357) or going online to www.ftc.gov.

- Notify the National Fraud Information Center at www.fraud.org.

Remember!!
Beware: Recovery Services

A scam artist has taken your money. Don't be scammed again by a "recovery service" offering to get your money back for you. The service is just trying to take your last dime. There is no charge for filing a complaint with a government agency.

Source: "Consumer Action Handbook," FCIC, 2004.

- Scams that used the mail or interstate delivery service should also be reported to the U.S. Postal Inspection Service. It is illegal to use the mail to misrepresent or steal money.

Product Safety Recalls

If you think you have an item that poses a safety hazard, contact the appropriate federal agency below. Sometimes sale of the item is banned. These agencies also work with manufacturers to reduce product dangers. A manufacturer may establish a recall program that asks consumers to return the defective item for replacement or repair. In some situations, the seller provides a part that reduces the danger of using the product. Ask the agency if your product has been recalled or covered under some other safety program.

- **Automobiles:** National Highway Traffic Safety Administration

- **Drugs, medical devices:** Food and Drug Administration

- **Food:** U.S. Department of Agriculture, Food and Drug Administration

- **Seafood:** Food and Drug Administration, U.S. Department of Commerce

- **Toys, baby and play equipment, household products:** U.S. Consumer Product Safety Commission

Recalls are also posted at www.pueblo.gsa.gov.

Small Claims Court

Small claims courts resolve disputes involving claims for small amounts of money. While the maximum amounts that can be claimed or awarded differ from state to state, court procedures generally are simple, inexpensive, quick, and informal. Court fees are minimal, and you often get your filing fee back if you win your case. Typically, you will not need a lawyer, and some states do not permit them.

If you live in a state that allows lawyers and if the party you are suing brings one, do not be intimidated. Most judges make allowances for consumers who appear without lawyers. Even though the court is informal, the judge's decision is binding and must be followed.

If you file a case and win, the losing party may give you what the court says you are owed without further action on your part. But some losers refuse to follow the court's directions. When this happens, you can go back to court and ask for the order to be enforced. Depending on local laws, the court might order property to be taken by law enforcement officials and sold. You will get the money from the sale, up to the amount owed. Officials may also be directed to take money from a bank account or business cash register. If the person who owes the money receives a salary, the court might order an employer to garnish (deduct money from) each paycheck and give it to you.

Check your local telephone book under the municipal, county or state government headings for small claims court offices. Ask the clerk how to use the small claims court. Before taking your own case to court:

- Request educational material to help you prepare your presentation.

- Observe a small claims court session.

Legal Information And Help

If you need an attorney to advise or represent you, ask friends and family for recommendations. You can also contact the Lawyer Referral Service of your state, county, or city bar association listed in the telephone directory.

Free assistance may be available from a law school program where students, supervised by attorneys, handle a variety of legal matters. Some of these programs are open to all. Others limit their service to distinct groups, such as senior citizens or low-income persons. Contact a law school in your area to find out if such a program is available.

If you cannot afford a lawyer, you may qualify for free legal help from a Legal Aid or Legal Services Corporation (LSC) office. These offices generally offer legal assistance about such things as landlord-tenant relations, credit, utilities, family matters such as divorce and adoption, foreclosure, home equity fraud, social security, welfare, unemployment, and workers' compensation. If the Legal Aid office in your area does not handle your type of case, it should refer you to other local, state or national organizations that can provide help.

To find the Legal Aid office nearest to you, check a local telephone directory or contact:

National Legal Aid and Defender Association
1140 Connecticut Ave. N.W., Suite 900
Washington, DC 20006
Phone: 202-452-0620
Fax: 202-872-1031
Website: http://www.nlada.org
E-mail:info@nlada.org

To find the LSC office nearest you, check a local telephone directory or contact:

LSC Public Affairs
3333 K Street, N.W., 3rd Floor
Washington, DC 20007-3522
Phone: 202-295-1500
Fax: 202-337-6797
Website: http://www.lsc.gov
E-mail: info@lsc.gov

✔ **Quick Tip**

Websites such as:

- www.abalawinfo.org (American Bar Association),
- www.thelaw.com,
- www.freeadvice.com, and
- www.nolo.com

may help you with answers to general legal questions. For information on state-specific legal questions, try the website of the National Association of Consumer Agency Administrators (www.nacaanet.org). Source: "Consumer Action Handbook," FCIC, 2004.

Sample Complaint Letter

When you write a complaint letter, you should:

- describe your purchase
- name the product, with serial number
- include date and place of purchase
- ask for specific action
- enclose copies of documents
- state the problem
- give the history
- allow time for action
- state how you can be reached

Keep all copies of your letter, fax or e-mail, and all related documents.

Your Address
Your City, State, Zip Code
Date

Name of Contact Person, if available
Title, if available
Company Name
Consumer Complaint Division (if you have no specific contact.)
Street Address
City, State, Zip Code

Dear (Contact Person):

Re: (account number, if applicable)

On (date), I (bought, leased, rented, or had repaired) a (name of the product, with serial or model number or service performed) at (location, date and other important details of the transaction).

Unfortunately, your product (or service) has not performed well (or the service was inadequate) because (state the problem). I am disappointed because (explain the problem: for example, the product does not work properly, the service was not performed correctly, I was billed the wrong amount, something was not disclosed clearly or was misrepresented, etc.).

To resolve the problem, I would appreciate your (state the specific action you want—money back, charge card credit, repair, exchange, etc.) Enclosed are copies (do not send originals) of my records (include receipts, guarantees, warranties, canceled checks, contracts, model and serial numbers, and any other documents).

I look forward to your reply and a resolution to my problem, and will wait until (set a time limit) before seeking help from a consumer protection agency or the Better Business Bureau. Please contact me at the above address or by phone at (home and/or office numbers with area code).

Sincerely,
Your name

Enclosure(s)

Avoiding Unhappy Returns—Returning Merchandise Bought On- Or Offline

Consumers wishing to return gifts or purchases to retail stores and online merchants may avoid surprises by taking a little extra time to understand the return process.

If a retailer has a no-return policy, then the law does not require the store to accept returns of items that are as represented and are free of defects. Many businesses, however, have chosen to allow consumers to return unwanted merchandise. And if a store modifies a long-established return policy merchants should clearly, accurately, and completely communicate their return policies to the consumer before the sale takes place.

Even if a merchant clearly discloses its no-return policy, there remain certain situations in which a merchant must allow the consumer to return merchandise.

If the merchandise is defective or not as represented, the consumer may return the item. Other examples include sales solicited at a consumer's home or sales made after a consumer received a gift to attend the company's sales promotion.

With cycles of deep discounting and a sharp increase in online sales, some traditional retail stores have tightened their return policies. Shoppers accustomed to returning items may not only find stricter return policies at the stores but may face unfamiliar obstacles when attempting to return merchandise bought over the Internet. The law that applies to returns generally covers both online and offline sales.

Before You Return An Item

The best way to avoid an unhappy return experience—wherever you shop—is to find out what the merchant's return policy is before you make a purchase. For example, many retailers impose a time limit on returns and require a receipt, or gift receipt even if the item is a store brand. Stores may accept returns for in-store credit but not allow refunds. The tips listed below regarding online sales generally apply to "real world" sales as well.

With regard to returns, online shoppers should scrutinize a merchant's website to determine whether returns are allowed and, if so, what a consumer must do to return an item. If the information is not posted, contact the merchant and ask for the information in writing. In either case, be sure to print and retain the information (along with all receipts, packing slips, and other documentation). In particular, you should find out:

- Does the merchant charge a "restocking fee" to accept returns? Many online merchants charge a substantial percentage of the purchase price to accept a return.

- Are you responsible for paying shipping and handling charges if you return an item? These charges can be quite expensive, particularly if insurance is required.

- Will the merchant charge an "open box" fee or simply refuse to accept items after the package has been opened? Such restrictions are common for purchases of software, videos, and computer equipment.

- Will you receive a refund for the item returned, or will the merchant only give you a credit toward future purchases?

- Will the online business require you to obtain any sort of advance permission before returning an item? Many merchants require consumers to contact the company and obtain a return merchandise authorization (or "RMA") number or other instructions before returning goods. Some merchants may have special shipping instructions.

- Is your right to return an item limited to a very short time period after purchase? Many online merchants have very short return periods—14 days is not unusual.

- If the merchant selling online also operates a retail store in your area, can you simply return an item that you purchased online to the store? Many such retailers, sometimes called "click-and-mortar" merchants, offer consumers this convenience. But be sure to inquire about the details of a particular merchant's policy.

- Does the merchant guarantee satisfaction or your money back? While some online merchants do not offer guarantees or allow returns, many do. Even if such a guarantee is offered, there may be conditions attached, such as time limitations or payment of shipping costs.

Steps You Can Take If You Are Having Trouble Returning Merchandise. If you have received goods that are defective or not as represented, but the merchant refuses to allow you to return the merchandise, or if you discover that the merchant is not honoring its return policy, you have a legitimate complaint. If you paid by credit card, you may wish to contact your credit card company, dispute the charges, and request a "charge back."

Chapter 8

Read The Fine Print

Many purchases involve signing a contract. What do short- or long-term contracts involve?

Music Through The Mail: CD And Tape Clubs

A 14-year-old boy joined a music club. He received as little as two days notice before unsolicited compact disks were mailed to him, giving him too little time to respond that he did not want them. As a result, he frequently received unwanted CDs and returned them at the club's expense. Finally the club canceled his membership, citing the many returned CDs, but billed him for $15.75 to fulfill his purchase agreement.

Another consumer fulfilled his membership requirement with a music club and then requested, in writing, that his membership be canceled. He returned two unopened, unwanted CDs. The club sent a letter asking the consumer why he had returned the CDs, but then billed him repeatedly for one of them.

About This Chapter: This chapter includes "Music Through The Mail," © 1996 and "Paying In Advance For Future Services," © 1995 Maryland Office of the Attorney General, Consumer Protection Division. Reprinted with permission. "Health Club Membership," and "Warranties, Guarantees, And Your Rights," are excerpted from "Warranties...Guarantees...and Your Rights," © 2005 Pennsylvania Office of the Attorney General, Bureau of Consumer Protection. Reprinted with permission. An excerpt from "I Changed My Mind...Can I Cancel This Contract?" updated 2/2003, is reprinted with permission from the Michigan Office of the Attorney General, Consumer Protection division. Copyright © 2003 State of Michigan.

Music clubs have been around for years and are popular with kids and adults. While introductory offers can make the overall cost of buying from clubs lower than stores, you should know what you are getting into before you join. For some consumers, the inconvenience is not worth the savings.

Many music clubs offer great-sounding deals to get you to join: Six CDs for the price of one, or ten CDs free if you buy six more over the next four years. But when you read the fine print, you learn that you also must pay shipping costs. In most cases you also have to fill out cards each month or every other month saying you don't want to receive the offered selection, or you will receive that offering in the mail.

By far the biggest problem is billing. Most consumer complaints deal with billing errors, and most of the errors resulted from what the consumers considered to be unsolicited CDs. The reason, often, is this: Throughout the year most clubs send out catalogs of offerings, usually including current special deals. Some of the clubs also send a card to allow you to choose which selections you want to order. Also listed on the card is the current featured selection. If you do not return the card, you automatically receive the featured selection. If you do not want the selection, you can send it back, but if you do not return it promptly, the company will assume you've kept it and bill you. Often, this can take some time to sort out. During that time, the company might send your account to a collection company. Consumers worry that their credit rating will be damaged if the dispute is not quickly resolved.

According to *Consumer Reports* magazine, some clubs will let you change your status to one that allows you to receive CDs or tapes only if you have ordered them, but they might not agree to this until after you have fulfilled your membership obligation. The companies do not advertise this option.

Some people enjoy the convenience of receiving music at their home, and bargains are possible if you shop carefully and take advantage of sales. If you are thinking of joining a music club, here are some issues to consider before you join:

- Check to see how large of a selection is offered in the category you prefer. Different clubs carry different labels. You can call the toll-free customer service number for more information before joining. You might be able to view catalogs before making a decision and, if you have Internet access, you often can view a list of offerings online.

- Check to see how long it takes for new releases to be offered. If you are a person who likes to purchase a new release as soon as it is available, you might find you still have to buy your music at a music store.

- Be sure you understand the terms of the agreement. Usually, you must buy a certain number of CDs or tapes within a specified time period. Often, items purchased at special 2-for-1 sales or half-price sales do not count toward your required purchases. If you do not fulfill your requirement, you probably will be billed for the amount you would have spent if you had.

- You most likely will be billed for shipping and handling charges on your introductory CDs, tapes or books. Find out in advance how much those charges will be. This will add to the overall cost of joining the club.

♣ It's A Fact!!

Myth: After you sign a contract, you have three days to cancel if you change your mind.

Truth: Most contracts are binding when you sign them. The often-repeated myth that you can cancel a signed contract has given many consumers a false sense of security when making an expensive purchasing decision, like buying a new car. But the cold, hard truth is that you must be sure about your decision before you sign the contract. After you sign, it is usually too late to change your mind.

There are a few exceptions to this rule. Door-to-door sales and health club contracts may give you a three-day right to rescind; timeshares and campgrounds may allow ten days. However, you must carefully follow the rules about how to cancel and even then you might end up in court battling over whether you canceled in time. If you wait until you're sure you want to buy, you won't have to worry about canceling later.

Source: Excerpted from "5 Pesky Consumer Myths," © 1997 Maryland Office of the Attorney General, Consumer Protection Division. Reprinted with permission.

- Ask about the return policy. Can you return a CD or tape if you don't like it after you've played it? Do you have to pay return postage? Do you have to pay return postage if you receive a featured selection because you failed to return a card on time?

As with all consumer transactions, the best time to ask questions is before you agree to make a purchase or sign a contract. Only then do you still have absolute control of the situation.

Health Club Membership

As health and fitness clubs have become popular, some abuses have occurred. State laws regulating health clubs have been passed to provide protections. For example, in Pennsylvania:

- Contracts must be in writing and must contain the date when it was signed and the specific address of the facility. You must be provided a copy of this contract or you can cancel at any time.

- Buyers can cancel a contract within three days of signing and must be refunded all moneys paid, including any initiation fee.

- Club memberships cannot be sold for a period of longer than 36 months. (No "lifetime" memberships at guaranteed rates).

- Health club operators must register with the Bureau of Consumer Protection and post financial security bonds to protect members' fees against potential failure or closing if they write contracts for more than three months. Members have up to six months from a closing to make a claim.

♣ It's A Fact!!

Myth: You actually have won a free prize.

Truth: Think about it. How would a business survive if it were really giving its merchandise away? If it sounds too good to be true, it is. Repeat it to yourself every time you get something in the mail that says you've won a fabulous prize—absolutely free!

Source: Excerpted from "5 Pesky Consumer Myths," © 1997 Maryland Office of the Attorney General, Consumer Protection Division. Reprinted with permission.

- If a club must close for repairs or any other reason for 30 days or less, a member is entitled to an extension of his membership equal to the number of days the facility was closed.

- If a club is closed for more than 30 days, an the operators do not provide an equivalent facility within a 10-mile range, the buyer has a right to cancel her membership and receive a refund.

- If a member becomes temporarily disabled to an extent where he cannot use one-third or more of the health club facilities, he is entitled to an extension of his membership covering the time he is disabled. Members who become permanently disabled can cancel the contract and receive a refund. The health club can request verification of the disability by a physician.

- You have a right to cancel your membership and receive a refund if you move more than 25 additional miles from a health club and the club operator cannot transfer your contract to a comparable facility located within five miles of your new residence.

- Health clubs cannot automatically renew your membership at the end of the term without your permission. That permission must be given at the end of the term, not at the beginning or during the term.

Paying In Advance For Future Services

"We can offer this five-year contract for lawn care services for a special price today only."

"If you buy a two-year membership at our gym, you'll be eligible for our special discount pricing plan."

"Sign our contract today for this special price and if you change your mind, you can always cancel."

These types of sales pitches often encourage consumers to sign long-term contracts for future services, such as memberships in health clubs or vacation clubs, private lessons, lawn or home service contracts, or dating services. However, many consumers who do sign such long-term contracts

♣ **It's A Fact!!**

Myth: Sales offer great deals on quality merchandise at low, low prices.

Truth: Sometimes the prices are low, sometimes they aren't. Just because a store says an item is on sale doesn't mean it really offers the lowest price. You still need to compare prices. If you know how much a particular item usually costs, you can easily determine if it's cheaper at a sale. If you're relying on the "50% Off Everything in the Store" sign on the door, you might be in for a rude awakening. You might even find the prices were marked up before they were marked down. And if the sale is a "going out of business" sale, and you purchase something that does not work, you may not be able to return it if the store that sold it to you doesn't exist anymore.

Source: Excerpted from "5 Pesky Consumer Myths," © 1997 Maryland Office of the Attorney General, Consumer Protection Division. Reprinted with permission.

complain afterwards because the service was unsatisfactory, they really couldn't use the service, or the business closed its doors.

Unless you're totally familiar with the service being sold and the business selling it, it's always best to sign a short-term contract. Then, if you like the service and the company, you can sign a long-term contract. If you don't like it, you're not committed to paying for a contract that extends for a long time into the future.

The Service May Be Unsatisfactory

A couple purchased a 5-year membership in a vacation club for $3,708. When the club arranged air travel and hotel for a trip, the experience was unsatisfactory. Afterwards, the couple was unsuccessful in their effort to obtain a refund.

A consumer paid $1,002 for a one-year contract to eliminate termites. During the year, she continued to notice evidence of termites despite retreatment. The company also said paneling must be removed and reinstalled at her expense in order to treat the problem. She was unable to receive a refund.

Try to find out as much as possible about the service and the company before signing any contract. Check the company's complaint record, and ask the business for names of some customers—and call them.

Make certain you understand exactly what service you'll be receiving under the contract and any additional expenses you may be required to pay. For example, ask an exterminator: Who pays for carpentry work required to treat infested areas? Ask the travel club: Does the package cost include airlines, processing, hotel, taxes, meals, peak season and maintenance? Find out what the company will do if the service doesn't do what it's supposed to do, such as make your lawn grow or get rid of insects. Is the company giving you a warranty and, if so, what relief will it provide you if the warranty is breached?

You May Not Use The Service

A mother contracted with a karate school for classes for her 4-year-old. The agreement obligated her to pay $943 over three years. The mixed-age class was too large and when he lost interest after a few lessons, his mother tried unsuccessfully to cancel her contract.

A man joined a dating service and charged the membership fee of $3,105 on his credit card. The membership representative assured him he'd find many suitable members in their files to contact. But he didn't like the selection and stopped using the service shortly after joining. He requested a refund, but the company refused.

Despite all the best intentions, many consumers find they don't use the services provided under a long-term contract. Such a situation is frustrating because you may be obligated to continue making payments under the contract, despite the fact that you're not utilizing the service. Don't assume you'll use it unless you have used the particular service in the past.

The Business May Close

Arrange to pay dues or other fees monthly or quarterly, so you won't lose as much money if the business closes.

If a company sells its services only through long-term contracts, find a business that uses short-term contracts. Many do.

Beware Of Misleading Statements About Cancellation Rights

Before agreeing to join a health club, a consumer told the club he'd probably move out of state shortly. He was assured that cancellation in that event would be no problem. When he canceled, showing documentation of his move, the club continued to debit his credit card account for the membership fee and late charges. When he complained to the club, he was told his cancellation request hadn't been approved.

Some businesses will try to convince you that you have nothing to lose in signing a long-term contract because if you change your mind, you can cancel. Don't allow this argument to convince you to sign a long-term contract for a service with which you're unfamiliar. Generally, there's no cooling off period after you sign a contract. Most likely, in your state only a few types of transactions allow you to cancel within a few days—but exercising that right is not always easy. You may have the right to cancel a contract within three days to ten days after you sign. But you'll probably not know within three or ten days whether the services will be satisfactory.

In contrast, if you don't sign the contract you'll have an unlimited amount of time to decide if you really want to purchase the service.

You do not have a right to cancel other types of future service contracts unless it is clearly stated in the written

♣ It's A Fact!!

Myth: If you purchase merchandise with a lifetime guarantee, you'll never need to buy another one. Or, if you buy a lifetime membership to anyplace, you can use it until you die.

Truth: From a practical point of view, "lifetime" doesn't mean your lifetime, but the lifetime of the company from which the product is purchased. If you buy a lifetime membership to a timeshare resort and the company goes bankrupt in two years, you're out of luck. The same is true of a product. If you buy a watch with a lifetime guarantee and the company that makes the watch goes out of business, it won't be able to replace your watch.

Source: Excerpted from "5 Pesky Consumer Myths," © 1997 Maryland Office of the Attorney General, Consumer Protection Division. Reprinted with permission.

contract. However, even if you have a right to cancel a long-term contract, don't sign it unless you're 100% certain you want and will use the service, and that the seller will provide you with a service that will satisfy you.

I Changed My Mind... Can I Cancel This Contract?

General Principle: You Have No Right To Cancel Most Contracts. Perhaps because so many large retailers voluntarily allow consumers to return merchandise with no questions asked, many consumers assume that they have a right to cancel a contract or to ask a retailer to take back an item and refund the consumer's money.

As a general matter of contract law, consumers do not have a right to cancel a sale of goods or services. In the case of defective, damaged, or undelivered goods, consumers may be able to demand their money back. And those merchants who choose to offer consumers a "money-back guarantee" must live up to their promises. But where the merchant has provided the goods or services that the consumer agreed to buy, the consumer generally may not insist on canceling a transaction after the fact.

If a seller who is not required by law to allow for cancellation of a contract nevertheless does so, any reasonable seller costs may be passed on to the buyer. The contract may call for a certain agreed-upon amount of damages ("liquidated damages") if the buyer cancels. A term fixing unreasonably large liquidated damages is void as a penalty. If there is no liquidated damages clause and if the purchase primarily involves goods, the maximum amount that can be charged is 20% of the value of the total performance for which the buyer is obligated under the contract, or $500.00, whichever is smaller.

There are special circumstances, however, under which the law gives consumers the right to a "cooling-off period," during which time the consumer may cancel the contract by carefully following the instructions for canceling which must be provided to the consumer in writing. [The law is detailed; you may need to consult an attorney or a state attorney general's office to resolve a situation.]

✔ Quick Tip

Before signing any contract:

- Take time to read and understand what you are signing. Pay attention to the fine print, which may contain important information.

- Do not ever be pressured into signing something you do not understand.

- Know exactly what you are getting, and how much you will have to pay and over what period of time.

- Be sure the contract contains the name, phone number and address of the business and salesperson. Be certain you have a street address (or some other permanent business location) where you can reach the business.

- The contract should be dated.

- Make certain that there are no empty spaces that may be filled in later without your knowledge or approval.

- Be sure that all verbal promises that were made are included in writing in the contract.

- Be certain that the contract contains specifics concerning payment and delivery dates.

- Products with full warranties may cost more than those with limited warranties; however, it may be worthwhile to spend the additional money in order to acquire full protection.

After signing, keep a copy of the contract for your records. Consult your state attorney general's office for specific laws regarding time limits on cancellations of contracts. Keep your sales slip, warranty, owner's manual and, when possible, original box or packing.

Source: Pennsylvania Office of the Attorney General, Bureau of Consumer Protection, 2005.

You have *three* business days to cancel a contract if:

- The sale was solicited in the consumer's home; or

- A gift was offered for attending a sales presentation that led to the contract; or

- A consumer's primary home is used as security and the loan is not used to purchase or construct the home.

You have *one* business day to cancel a contract if:

- The contract is for home improvement and the consumer agrees to make payments over time to the contractor.

Warranties, Guarantees, And Your Rights

Warranties and guarantees are a manufacturer's or seller's promise to stand behind its product or service.

On most major products, warranties must be:

- Easy to read and understand.

- Available for consumers to look at before they buy the products.

- Labeled either "Full" or "Limited."

✎ What's It Mean?

Full Warranty: A defective product will be fixed or replaced free of charge within a reasonable time. Consumers will not have to do anything unreasonable to get warranty service. If the product cannot be fixed, the consumer gets the choice of receiving a new product or a full refund. The warranty is good for anyone who owns the product during the warranty period.

Limited Warranty: Anything that provides less coverage than a full warranty. A limited warranty may cover only parts and not labor, cover only the initial owner, allow charges for handling, require you to return the product to the store.

Source: Pennsylvania Office of the Attorney General, Bureau of Consumer Protection, 2005

Implied Warranties

While a product might not have a written warranty, under state law, consumers are guaranteed certain implied warranties. A "warranty of merchantability" comes automatically with every sale and is the seller's promise that a product is fit for its ordinary use.

A "warranty of fitness for a particular purpose" is created if a consumer buys a product relying on the seller's advice that it can be used for a particular purpose.

Beware of merchandise that is labeled "AS IS" or "NO WARRANTY." This language is used to cancel all warranties and is also intended to apply to implied warranties.

Chapter 9

Before You Buy Your First Car

Buying Or Leasing Car

New Cars

When it's time to look for your first car, you need to decide whether you should buy a new or a used vehicle, or perhaps lease a car. As you consider the cost of the car, you should factor in the expected maintenance and repair costs.

Important advice as you look for a new car:

- Check out different vehicles. Several Internet sites can help you compare features and prices on new motor vehicles. Visit www.where-can-I-buy-a-car-online.com for links to these sites. A scorecard reports on the features of each site including whether quotes are free, the availability of financing, and site security. Two magazines offer information in print and online concerning vehicle performance, service and safety: *Consumer Reports* (www.consumerreports.org) and *Motor Trend* (www.motortrend.com).

About This Chapter: This chapter begins with "Buying Or Leasing A Car," excerpted from the "Consumer Action Handbook," a service provided by the Federal Citizen Information Center of the U.S. General Services Administration, 2004. "Buying A New Car: Know What You're Signing," is © 2000 Maryland Office of the Attorney General, Consumer Protection Division. Reprinted with permission. "The Truth About Used Car Prices," is by Bob Elliston, reprinted with permission of InCharge Education Foundation, Inc., January/February 2004 issue of YOUNG MONEY, www.youngmoney.com.

- Test drive vehicles before you make a final choice.

- Research the dealer's price for the car and options. It's easier to get the best price when you know what the dealer paid for a vehicle. The dealer invoice price is available at a number of websites and in printed pricing guides. *Consumer Reports* offers the wholesale price. Lower than the invoice price, this figure factors in dealer incentives from a manufacturer and is a more accurate estimate of what a dealer is paying for a vehicle.

- Find out if the manufacturer is offering rebates that will lower the cost. Two websites that offer this information are www.carsdirect.com and www.autopedia.com/html/Rebate.html.

- Get price quotes from several dealers. Find out if the amounts quoted are the prices before or after the rebates are deducted.

- Avoid high-profit, low-value extras such as credit insurance, extended service contracts, auto club memberships, rust proofing, and upholstery finishes.

Your Rights: Secret Warranties And Lemon Laws

On occasion, a company makes a mistake in the manufacturing of a motor vehicle. If dealers report a number of complaints about a certain part or vehicle, the maker may allow dealers to repair the problem at no cost to the customer even if the warranty has expired. A service bulletin notifies the dealer of the problem and how to resolve it. Because these free repairs are not publicized, they are called "secret warranties." Some states have passed laws requiring vehicle owners be notified of secret warranties.

Sometimes vehicles have problems that just never seem to get fixed. States with new vehicle "lemon laws" help protect consumers by requiring a refund or replacement if a substantial problem is not fixed within a reasonable number of attempts or if the vehicle has been out of service for a certain number of days. If you believe your car is a lemon:

- give the dealer a list of symptoms every time you bring it in for repairs;

- get and keep copies of the repair orders showing the reported problems, the repairs performed and the dates that the car was in the shop; and

- contact the auto manufacturer, as well as the dealer, to report the problem. Your owner's manual will list an address for the manufacturer.

Service bulletins from many manufacturers are on file with the National Highway Traffic Safety Administration (NHTSA). Visit www.nhtsa.dot.gov to search NHTSA's Service Bulletin database. The Center for Auto Safety (www.autosafety.org) gathers information and complaints concerning safety defects, recalls and service bulletins. It also has a section on state lemon laws. You can reach CAS by phone at 202-328-7700. Help other consumers avoid purchasing your lemon by registering it at www.safetyforum.com.

Contact your state or local consumer protection office for information on protections you have in your state and the steps you must take to resolve a problem.

✔ **Quick Tip**
Make Sure Your First Car Doesn't Turn Out To Be A Lemon

Buying a first car is an important milestone. To help you make a wise purchase, spend some time considering the following:

- Decide how much money you can spend and what type of car best suits your needs.

- Research the various models to determine those that are the safest, most reliable, and otherwise suitable (Resources include *Consumer Reports* and the National Highway Traffic Safety Commission).

- Consider how long you plan to keep the car.

- Consider your budget for operating, maintaining, and repairing a car.

- Check out the dealer with the Better Business Bureau (http://www.bbb.org).

Source: Excerpted from "Make Sure Your First Car Doesn't Turn Out to Be a Lemon," copyright © 2003 Better Business Bureau Serving Oregon & Western Washington.

Your Rights: Vehicle Repossessions

When you borrow money to buy a car, you should know that the lender:

- can repossess the vehicle if you miss a payment or in some other way violate the contract;

- can repossess with cause without advance notice;

- can insist you pay off the entire loan balance in order to get the repossessed vehicle back;

- can sell the vehicle at auction;

- might be able to sue you for the difference between the vehicle's auction price and what you owe; and

- cannot break into your home or physically threaten someone, in the course of repossession. This is called a "breach of peace."

If you know you're going to be late with a payment, talk to the lender to try to work things out. If the lender agrees to a delay or to modify the contract, be sure you get the agreement in writing. Some states have laws that give consumers additional rights. Contact your state or local consumer protection office for more information.

Used Cars

Important advice as you look for a used car:

- Contact your state or local consumer protection office to find out what rights you might have.

- Contact your state's motor vehicle department. Find out in advance what paperwork you will need to register a vehicle.

- Check out the seller. For car dealers, consult your state or local consumer protection office. If it's an individual, check the title to make sure you're dealing with the vehicle owner. Also browse the classifieds for other auto ads with the same phone number—a sign of an unlicensed broker who sells used cars by posing as the owner.

Used Car Sources

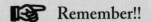 **Remember!!**

Check with the following sources when looking for a used car:

- New car dealers often sell the best of the cars they acquire through trade-in deals. They may cost more, but they're more likely to have undergone necessary repairs in the dealer's service department. They may offer limited warranties.

- Used car dealers generally sell vehicles that have seen a bit more use and abuse than those on the new car dealer's lot. You may pay less, but the car is less likely to have received needed repairs. They may offer limited warranties.

- Car rental agencies may sell used rental cars, however, mileage on rental cars are often high on a per-year basis, and the cars may suffer from wear and tear from other drivers.

- Bank and loan companies sometimes sell repossessed cars to pay off defaulted loans. Quality varies from car to car, but you may get a good price on a good car since it's sold to cover amounts due on loans.

- Private owners usually sell their used cars through newspaper ads. Ask for the car's maintenance and repair records and, if the seller is the first owner, for records of the original purchase. Also, check the title to make sure the person selling the car is the legal owner.

Source: Excerpted from "Make Sure Your First Car Doesn't Turn Out to Be a Lemon," copyright © 2003 Better Business Bureau Serving Oregon & Western Washington.

- Take a test drive. Drive at different speeds and check for smooth right and left turns. On a straight stretch, make sure the wheels are aligned and the car doesn't pull to one side.

- Check prices of similar models using the *NADA Official Used Car Guide* (www.nadaguides.com) published by the National Automobile Dealer Association or the *Kelly Blue Book* (www.kbb.com). These guides are usually available at local libraries.

- Research the vehicle's history. Ask the seller for details concerning past owners, use, and maintenance. Next, find out whether the car has been damaged in a flood, involved in a crash, been labeled a lemon or had its odometer rolled back. The vehicle identification number (VIN) will help you do this.

- Your state motor vehicle department can research the car's title history. Inspect the title for "salvage," "rebuilt," or similar notations. Get the written mileage disclosure statement from the seller that is required by federal law and make sure it matches the odometer reading on the car.

- www.carfax.com and www.autocheck.com sell information on the history of vehicles gathered from state motor vehicle departments and other sources.

- The National Highway Traffic Safety Administration (www.nhtsa.dot.gov) lists VINs of its crash-test vehicles and will let you search an online database of manufacturer service bulletins.

- The Center for Auto Safety (www.autosafety.org) provides information on safety defects, recalls, lemons as well as service bulletins.

- www.safetyforum.com allows a free online search of its database of lemons registered by previous owners. [See chapter 33, Websites About Money, for a list of more websites that can help you compare used cars.]

- Check the warranty. If a manufacturer's warranty is still in effect, contact the manufacturer to make sure you can use the coverage. In every used car and truck offered for sale, dealers are required by the Federal Trade Commission to post a Buyers Guide that specifies whether the vehicle is being sold "as is" or with a warranty, and what percentage of repair costs a dealer will pay under the warranty. Private sellers generally have less responsibility than dealers for defects or other problems. Private sellers generally don't have to post information.

- Ask about the dealer's return policy. Get it in writing and read it carefully.

- Have the car inspected by a qualified mechanic. Agree in advance with the seller that you'll pay for the examination if the car passes muster and the seller will pay if significant problems are discovered. The mechanic should check the vehicle's frame, tire wear, air bags and undercarriage as well as the engine.

- Examine dealer documents carefully to make sure you are buying, not leasing, the vehicle. Dealer finance managers may try to "flip" your purchase to a lease, ignoring the agreed upon sales price and the promised allowance on the trade-in. A balloon payment and "base mileage" disclosures are warning signs you may have a lease.

Leasing A Car

When you lease a car, you pay to drive someone else's vehicle. Monthly payments for a lease may be lower than loan payments, but at the end of the lease you have no ownership or equity in the car.

If you are considering leasing, read these tips:

- Shop for a lease as if you're buying a car. To help you comparison shop, the Consumer Leasing Act requires leasing companies to disclose information concerning monthly payments and other charges.

- Negotiate all the lease terms including the price of the vehicle. Lowering the base price will help reduce your monthly payments.

- Ask for details on wear and tear standards. Dings that you may regard as normal wear and tear may be billed as significant damage at the end of your lease.

✔ **Quick Tip**

To lease a car, a person needs to have a better-than-average credit rating. Since teens rarely have a credit rating, they can rarely qualify to lease a car on their own. However, some parents lease lower-priced new cars for their teens.

To learn more about leasing, here are a few websites to check out:

www.edmunds.com

www.intellichoice.com

www.leaseguide.com

www.leasesource.com

www.leasetips.com

—KRD

✔ Quick Tip
Check Out The Car

Before you sign the contract, have the car inspected by an independent certified auto mechanic.

- Check over the exterior of the car for any damage, such as "dings" or scratches.

- Make sure the spare tire and equipment are where they should be, and that the tire is inflated to manufacturer specifications.

- Make sure all the hubcaps and body moldings are in place.

- Make sure all electrical items function properly.

- Check the Vehicle Identification Number (VIN) on the car to ensure it matches the one on the contract.

- Ask the salesperson to demonstrate each accessory—such as setting the clock or turning on the bright lights. Also ask how to check the oil, coolant, transmission fluid, and battery.

- Test drive the car.

- Make sure you have the owner's manual, warranty forms, and all legal documents. Read these materials carefully before you drive away.

Source: Excerpted from "Make Sure Your First Car Doesn't Turn Out to Be a Lemon," copyright © 2003 Better Business Bureau Serving Oregon & Western Washington.

- Find out how many miles you can drive in a year. Most leases allow 12,000 to 15,000 miles a year. Expect a charge of 10 to 25 cents for each additional mile.

- Make sure the manufacturer's warranty covers the entire lease term and the number of miles you are likely to drive.

- Ask the dealer about early termination charges. Expect to pay a substantial charge if you give the car up before the end of your lease. Ask what happens if the car is totaled six months after the lease is signed.

- Before you sign the deal, take a copy of the contract home and review it carefully away from any dealer pressure. Make sure you are getting credit for any trade-in. Look for any charges that were not disclosed at the dealership, such as conveyance, disposition, and preparation fees.

- Get all the terms in writing. Every item of equipment should be listed on the lease to avoid being charged for "missing" equipment at the end of the lease.

When you finance a car, the finance charge must be stated as an Annual Percentage Rate (APR). There is no similar requirement for disclosing the cost of leases. "Lease rates" or "money factors" do not have standard definitions and are not equivalent to an APR.

Credit And Sublease Brokers

These are con artists who prey on people who have bad credit and who cannot get car loans. "Credit brokers" promise to get a loan for you in exchange for a high fee. In many cases, the "broker" takes the fee and disappears.

"Sublease brokers" charge a fee to arrange for you to "sublease" or "take over" someone else's car lease or loan. Such deals usually violate the original loan or lease agreement. Your car can be repossessed even if you've made all of your payments. You also might have trouble insuring your car.

Auto Service Warranties And Contracts

Dealers may try to sell you an auto service contract or "extended warranty" when you buy a new or used car. A warranty comes with a new car and is included in the original price of the vehicle. A service contract is sold separately and is a promise to pay for certain repairs or services. Service contracts are usually high-profit add-ons, costing hundreds of dollars, to more than $1,000. The service contract may duplicate warranty coverage you get from the manufacturer or dealer. Ask these questions:

- Does the dealer, the manufacturer, or an independent company back the service contract?

- What happens to your coverage if the dealer or administrator goes out of business?

- How are claims handled?

- Can you choose among several service dealers or repair centers or do you have to return to one dealer?

- Is your car covered if it breaks down on a trip or if you move out of town?

- Do you need prior authorization for repair work?

- Are there any exclusions or situations when coverage can be denied? Common repairs for parts like brakes and clutches generally are not included in service contracts. Failure to keep up manufacturer's recommendations for routine maintenance can void the service contract. The contract may also prohibit you from taking your car to an independent station for routine maintenance or performing the work yourself.

Recalls

If your car's problem is a safety hazard, check whether your vehicle has been recalled by the manufacturer. Click on Recalls at www.nhtsa.dot.gov or call the National Highway Traffic Safety Administration at 1-800-424-9393. Hazards that aren't listed should be reported to NHTSA. Use the agency's toll-free Auto Safety Hotline at 1-888-327-4236 or visit the agency's web page for details on other reporting options: the Internet, fax and mail. There is no set number of reports needed before the agency will look into a problem. If a safety-related manufacturing defect exists, the maker must fix it at no cost to you—even if your warranty has expired. The company may also be asked to conduct a product recall. Follow up by contacting the manufacturer's zone representative or the dealer's service department.

Buying A New Car: Know What You're Signing

"The salesman told me that I could bring the car back if I didn't like it, but now he says, 'Sorry, no refunds.'"

"I thought I signed a paper that let them run my credit report. They say I bought the car."

"I didn't realize that I agreed to a 'balloon' loan—the final payment is several thousand dollars!"

"The dealer called and said the loan didn't go through, and they'll repossess the car unless I apply for a new loan at 18% interest."

Every week, new car buyers are unhappy with contracts they have signed. Don't let this happen to you. Before you sign any paper involved in a new car purchase, take your time, read every line, and ask questions about anything that is not clear. Otherwise, you could end up owning a car when you didn't intend to, paying more for a car than you planned, or not getting things you thought you were promised.

There are three important steps you can take to avoid many of these problems:

1. Understand that there is no three-day "cooling-off" period for car sales during which you can change your mind and cancel the contract. Once you have signed a binding contract, you are bound. Understanding that, you should never sign a contract until you are absolutely certain that you want to be bound by its terms.

2. Make sure anything the salesperson promised you is in writing.

3. Tell the dealer you won't take the new car home or deliver your trade-in until the financing has been approved. That way if the financing is not approved or if the dealer tells you the financing will be at a higher rate of interest than originally promised, you can easily walk away from the deal and look elsewhere.

Here are some other tips for avoiding common problems with the two major documents involved in most new car sales: the buyer's order and the retail installment sales contract.

The Buyer's Order: Don't sign a buyer's order until you are ready to buy the car. If a salesperson asks you to sign a buyer's order so you can "try out the car," or so he can run a credit check, don't do it. Tell him to write up a special note that describes those agreements. And never sign a blank buyer's order for any reason.

- Check, line by line, that every item on the order is accurate and reflects what you negotiated. Is the selling price, the value of your trade-in and the down payment what you agreed to?

- Make sure that any "accessory purchases" or "dealer-installed items" listed on the contract, such as service contracts or paint sealants, are items you agreed to buy. Consumers are often given a hard sell for these items, many of which are unnecessary. Even if the consumer declined, sometimes they still appear on the contract.

♣ **It's A Fact!!**

Common Customer Complaints And How To Avoid Them

1. "I've had to fix the car several times since I bought it." (Fact: Most used cars are sold "as is." "As is" means just that-any repairs are your responsibility. Have the car checked out by an independent auto mechanic before buying it.)

2. "I thought I had 72 hours to return the car." (Fact: You do not have a 72-hour return period unless specifically stated in your contract. Make sure you're comfortable with the purchase *before* you sign any paperwork.)

3. "The salesman promised this" or "The salesman promised that." (Fact: Your contract generally has a clause which releases the dealership from any verbal promises made by the salesman or other employees. Get it in writing or the dealership will not consider it a part of the agreement.)

4. "The price or finance rate on the contract wasn't what was verbally agreed upon." (Fact: Make sure to read over the contract before you sign to ensure it's what you verbally agreed upon. Never sign a contract with blank spaces.)

5. "They pressured me into signing the contract." (Fact: You have the right to choose where you do business and if you're uncomfortable with the dealership, *leave*.)

6. "I found the same car at another dealership for a lot less." (Fact: Businesses have the right to charge whatever they choose. Do your shopping around *before* you sign a contract. Contact the Better Business Bureau [http://www.bbb.org/] for reliability reports on used car dealers.)

Source: Excerpted from "Make Sure Your First Car Doesn't Turn Out to Be a Lemon," copyright © 2003 Better Business Bureau Serving Oregon & Western Washington.

- Read both sides of every paper. Make sure there are no blank spaces in the contract before you sign it. Draw a line through or write "N.A." on items that don't apply.

- Make sure the sales manager signs the order. This will protect you from a dealer saying the salesperson made a mistake and they can't sell you the car on those terms.

- Get a copy of the fully completed and signed buyer's order, along with loan papers and other documents, before you leave the dealership. Even if the dealership says they will mail you your copies or you can drop by in a day or two to get them, don't take the new car until you have the copies.

The Retail Installment Sales Contract: This is the contract used if you are buying your new car on credit arranged by the dealer. You don't have to finance your car through the dealer. Before you begin shopping for a car you should see what loan terms a bank or credit union would give you and, if possible, get pre-approved. Then you'll have something to compare to what the dealership offers.

- Check the loan terms (the interest rate, number of payments, and amount of monthly payment) carefully. Don't just focus on the monthly payment. Look at all the numbers to understand how your loan is structured. Is there a high final payment? When is the first payment due?

- Know that credit life insurance or credit disability insurance is almost always an option, not a requirement. If you do not wish to buy this insurance, make sure that you correctly indicate that—some forms ask you whether you accept, others ask whether you decline.

- Be sure you are signing a retail installment sales contract and not a lease agreement. These two contracts can look similar.

- Read the contract to find out what will happen if the dealer is not able to arrange credit on the promised terms. This often happens to buyers with weak credit. Don't sign a contract that attempts to obligate you to accept a different loan, which may have a higher interest rate or other terms not favorable to you. Don't leave your trade-in with the dealer or you may be left without a car if the deal falls through. To avoid these problems, tell the dealer you won't take the new car or deliver your trade-in until the loan is approved.

Remember, it's your money. Insist on taking the time to read all documents before you sign them. Don't rely on a salesperson's statement that you can "bring the car back if you are unhappy for any reason" unless that statement is written into the contract. Make sure all the terms of the deal have been finalized and you are happy with them before you take the car.

Negotiating A Deal 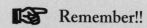 Remember!!

Don't sign any papers until you've negotiated the details of a deal. Shop around at several dealerships, and narrow your choices to several cars. Don't make the mistake of having your heart set on one car—it may reduce your bargaining power.

- Reviewing a *Kelly Blue Book* or *NADA Guide* to compare dealer costs with prices listed on the window sticker will tell you how much bargaining room you have on the basic car and individual options. You can also call the bank for a *Blue Book* quote.

- Consider taking along an experienced car shopper to help you negotiate.

- Get a firm quote, in writing, from the dealer.

- Keep negotiations separate. Consider questions about financing, service contracts, trade-ins, or other extras after you have settled on a price.

- Shop around for financing and service contracts, and compare the terms carefully.

- Read and understand the contract thoroughly before signing it.

Source: Excerpted from "Make Sure Your First Car Doesn't Turn Out to Be a Lemon," copyright © 2003 Better Business Bureau Serving Oregon & Western Washington.

The Truth About Used Car Prices

Before you buy a used car from a car dealer, you should understand a little about pricing. A franchise dealer with a used car operation will usually price his cars at a certain percentage more than what the car is deemed to be worth on the wholesale market.

The wholesale value of a car is usually determined by factors such as the demand for the car coupled with the age, make, model, options, mileage and general condition. The dealer's markup on a used car, van or pickup is frequently determined by any or all of several factors:

- The price the dealer paid to acquire the car. He might have taken it in trade against a new car—which means that he accepted the car in lieu of cash or he might have purchased it from a private seller, a wholesaler or bought it at auction.

- The dealer adds what it has cost him to repair and recondition the car.

- The dealer adds a markup to cover his profit objectives and to pay for his overhead.

The markup will also reflect such things as the condition of the car, the mileage, the make, model, options and most important, the market demand. The point, simply, is that used car markups will vary greatly for any number of factors. Your objective is to discover what has it cost him to buy and recondition the car and put it on his lot. That will give you the basis for planning your negotiation.

Negotiating Tricks

Many dealers will also include a "negotiation pad" in their markups. They recognize that most people won't buy a car—new or used—unless they feel they're buying it for less than the advertised price. So a dealer will build in a large enough cushion to give the buyer a discount and still end up with whatever he considers to be a reasonable, or maybe even a more than reasonable, profit.

The key to a dealer's survival and profitability in the used car business is to buy used cars at or below what the industry calls the "wholesale price" and then to sell them at a retail price that, in the final analysis, is whatever a buyer will pay. Here is an actual example:

- Let's track a GM car that was purchased by a dealer for $9,500. After spending $400 for repairs and reconditioning, he put it on the lot at $13,800. That's a markup over his purchase cost of more than 45%.

- The used car sales manager confides that this markup gives him built-in room for negotiation. A buyer finally appears, and after a negotiated agreement, buys the car for $12,450. The customer felt he'd gotten a deal and the seller said nothing to disabuse him of that notion.

Determining The "Wholesale" Price

Whether you buy from a private owner or a dealer, one of the most important pieces of information you can have is the current "wholesale" price of the car in your area of the country. One source of auto price information is the car loan department of your bank. They will usually have all the latest price books and possibly even auction reports that show what various makes are bringing on the auction market.

The industry uses any of several books as price guides: The *NADA Official Used Car Guide*, *National Auto Research Black Book*, *Kelley Blue Book Auto Market Report* and *Galves Auto Price List*. These books—also available online—purport to reflect the average wholesale prices that various cars are bringing across the country. The only problem is that they usually don't agree on a set price.

Compare the suggested wholesale prices for a 2000 Chevrolet four-door Lumina from the same month:

- *Kelley Blue Book*: $7,875 (Tends to reflect West Coast prices)

- *NADA*: $6,875 (Combination of auction and dealer reports)

- *Black Book*: $5,650 to $8,850 (Dealer auction sales reports)

You can find used car price books on your newsstand or on various Internet sites, e.g., Edmunds.com. For example, Edmund's wholesale price for a 2000 Lumina is $7,387. Their figures provide a general range, but they may not present a true picture of any given car's "real" price because they cannot account for the myriad factors that impact the dealer's costs.

Chapter 10

Car Ownership Costs: Insurance And Maintenance

Real Car Costs

Can't wait to get a car? It's tempting to look at car ads and think, "Monthly payment $199 ... I could handle that!" But you might not realize that the loan payment is only part of the cost of owning a car. You also have to pay for insurance, registration, gas, maintenance, and repairs.

Some Cars Cost Less To Own

Just as different cars have different price tags, they cost different amounts to keep after you buy them. The cost of insurance, gas, and repairs can be very different. Here are some things you can find out ahead of time about any car you are considering buying:

- How much will it cost to insure? Call an insurance agent to ask.

- What gas mileage does it get? Look up the "mpg" at www.fueleconomy.gov.

About This Chapter: This chapter begins with "Real Car Costs," from "Dude, What about Cars?" © 2003 Maryland Office of the Attorney General, Consumer Protection Division. Reprinted with permission. "Don't Overpay For Car Insurance," is reprinted with permission of InCharge Education Foundation, Inc., Spring 2003 issue of YOUNG MONEY, www.youngmoney.com. "Common Repair Questions," "Heading Off Problems," and "Trouble Shooting," are excerpted from "Auto Repair Tips," January 24, 2003; reprinted with permission from the Office of the New York Attorney General.

Table 10.1. Typical Monthly Expense

Loan payment: depends on price of car and down payment	$200-$400
Insurance: depends on your age, gender, type of car, coverage wanted, and where you live	$120-$200
Gas: depends on price of gas, miles driven, and car's mpg	$30-$100
Maintenance/Repairs: includes regular maintenance like oil changes, tire rotation. Older cars may need major repairs. New cards have major repairs under warranty, but they can get a nail in a tire or lose a hubcap.	$20-$70
Other: car washes, parking tickets, etc.	$20
Total	$390-$790

As you can see, the actual cost of owning a car may be twice as much as the loan payment.

Source: © 2003 Maryland Office of the Attorney General, Consumer Protection Division. Reprinted with permission.

- What is its reputation for reliability? Look it up in consumer magazines like *Consumer Reports*.

- If a used car, what repairs is it likely to need soon? Ask a mechanic.

This information can help you compare choices. Let's say you can spend $10,000 on your first car. Two choices interest you: a 3-year-old compact car and a 6-year-old SUV. After doing your research, you could compare what you found out (see Table 10.2).

Why Is Car Insurance For Teens So Expensive?

Car insurance for teen drivers is very expensive, and it's more expensive for male teens than for female teens. That may not seem fair, but it is based on statistics. Teen drivers are four times as likely to get in an accident as older drivers are, and male teen drivers are involved in more accidents than female teen drivers.

Don't Overpay For Car Insurance

After getting the big lecture warning against driving without insurance, how can you lower the price tag for such a basic necessity? Thankfully, there are several ways to cut costs. While the methods below are not going to prevent you from paying through the roof, they are proven cost-saving methods that could cut hundreds of dollars off your premiums:

Table 10.2. Total Operating Costs		
	3-year-old compact car	**6-year-old SUV**
Insurance for 1 year	$2,300	$2,000
Oil changes for 1 year	4 @ $20 each = $80	4 @ $20 each = $80
Gas to drive 10,000 miles	Car gets 28 mpg. (357 gal. @ $2/gal = $714)	SUV gets 15 mpg. (667 gal. @ $2/gal = $1,334)
Repairs likely needed soon?	Still under warranty for 1 more year; cost = $0	Replace muffler, water pump and/or timing belt likely; cost = $600
Total operating cost, 1 year	**$3,094**	**$4,014**
Comparison points	This car gets good gas mileage. The car is still pretty "young" so won't need a lot of repairs in the next few years, and it's still under warranty for 1 more year. Also, this model is rated high by consumer magazines	This vehicle costs a little less to insure. But it doesn't get as good gas mileage. Also, at six years old it will probably need some major repairs soon, which won't be covered under warranty. This model is rated poor by consumer magazines.

Source: © 2003 Maryland Office of the Attorney General, Consumer Protection Division. Reprinted with permission.

- Drive an older, "everyday" car. You likely won't turn heads driving an older Ford Escort, as opposed to a newer Corvette, but you will save a ton of cash on your auto insurance policy. Cars that are made out of steel are far cheaper to fix than sports cars made out of fiberglass. The rate of injury and theft is also lower in an Escort than a hot rod. Plus, if your car is worth $3,000 or less, you can choose to eliminate collision insurance from your policy.

- Good grades, better rates. If you make good grades in school, let your insurance company know. Students with a "B" average or higher (3.0 on a 4.0 scale) are considered lower risk drivers. Earn a substantial discount just by presenting a copy of your report card.

- Maintain good credit. Pay all of your bills on time so that your credit score is strong. Automobile companies look at your credit history because they believe there is a significant correlation between good credit and good driving habits—and vice versa.

- Strive for a good driving record. As tempting as it is to drive your Maserati 185 miles per hour, obey speed and traffic laws. The money

---

✎ What's It Mean?

Insurance Terms You Should Know

Bodily Injury Liability: Insurance that pays for another person's bodily injury or death in an automobile accident that you caused.

Property Damage Liability: Insurance that pays for damage you cause to someone else's property in an automobile accident.

Medical Payments: Insurance that pays the medical and funeral expenses, up to the limits purchased, for you or any passengers riding in your car at the time of an accident. Medical payments will provide coverage whether you or someone else caused the accident.

Collision: Insurance that pays for damages to your own car if it is involved in a collision, regardless of who is at fault. Collision coverage may carry a deductible—a stated amount that you must first pay out of your own pocket.

Car Ownership Costs: Insurance And Maintenance 91

you save from fines and higher insurance rates is worth the "slowpoke" label you may get from fool-hearted friends. Also, if you can find a driver's education course, take the class, and let your insurance company know about it. It can save you bucks on your insurance premiums.

- Membership has its privileges. Let your insurance company know about any memberships in clubs or organizations. For example, GEICO offers significant discounts for fraternity membership, Golden Key National Honor Society membership, and scores of other student and alumni organizations. AAA members can get discounted rates by purchasing auto insurance through AAA's insurance partnership with American Insurance Group (AIG).

- Drive on Mom and Dad's policy for as long possible. Students who get their own policy pay more because they are listed as a "primary" driver, placing them in a higher risk pool. But, if you stay on your family's policy and list yourself as a "secondary" driver on a car, you get the price break of your parent's age as the primary vehicle operator and can get another cost savings from having a multi-car discount on the policy.

Comprehensive: Insurance that pays for non-collision losses to your car such as fire, theft, flood, hail, vandalism, glass breakage, and falling objects. Comprehensive coverage may also carry a deductible. (Note: if your car hits an animal, some insurance companies will treat it as a collision claim, while others will treat it as a comprehensive claim.)

Uninsured Motorist Bodily Injury: Insurance that pays for bodily injury or death to you and your passengers if an uninsured driver strikes your car. This coverage does not pay for damages to your car. If you do not have collision insurance, you may purchase uninsured motorist property damage coverage. This coverage offers very limited protection and should be discussed with your insurance producer/agent.

Source: Excerpted from "Illinois Insurance Facts: Auto Insurance Facts for Teen Drivers," © 2002 Illinois Department of Financial and Professional Regulation, Division of Insurance. Reprinted with permission.

• Higher deductibles, lower premiums. By raising your deductible, say from $250 to $500 for liability insurance (covers medical costs caused by you in an accident), you can save several hundreds of dollars in premiums. Also, you can save by lowering the limits of coverage. So, instead of carrying 100/300 ($100,000 of coverage per person/ $300,000 per accident) of liability insurance, you can decrease this coverage to 50/100 ($50,000 per person/

> **✔ Quick Tip**
> **Emergency Information**
>
> Keep the following information in a safe place in your vehicle for ready reference in the event of an emergency:
>
> Insurance Company: _____
>
> Policy #: _____
>
> Agent's Name: _____
>
> Agent's Phone #: _____
>
> Police Dept. Phone #: _____
>
> Towing Company: _____
>
> Towing Co. Phone #: _____
>
> Source: Excerpted from "Illinois Insurance Facts: Auto Insurance Facts for Teen Drivers," © 2002 Illinois Department of Financial and Professional Regulation, Division of Insurance. Reprinted with permission.

$100,000 maximum. But make sure you carry the state-required minimums for legal operation of your car and that you carry enough insurance to adequately protect you if the worst-case scenario happens.

• If you work while going to school, let them know if it is close to home. You can save money on car insurance if you work within three miles of home and primarily use your car to go to and from the workplace.

Common Repair Questions

Look for shops that display various certifications like an Automotive Service Excellence seal. Certifications indicate that some or all of the technicians have met basic standards of knowledge and competence in specific technical areas. Make sure the certifications were recently obtained. Remember, however, that certification alone is not an absolute guarantee of good or honest work.

Repair Charges: Unlocking The Mystery

What should be included in an estimate?

- Always get and keep a signed written cost estimate for the work to be performed. Make sure the estimate specifically identifies the condition to be repaired, the parts needed and the anticipated labor charge.

- Make sure the estimate states that the shop will contact you for approval before performing any work exceeding a specified amount of time and money. Your state may require this; check with your state attorney general's office to determine your rights.

- Some shops charge a flat rate for labor on auto repairs. This published rate is based on an independent or manufacturer's estimate of the time required to complete repairs. Other shops charge on the basis of the actual time the technician worked on the repair. Before having any work performed, ask which cost method the shop uses.

Remember!!
What You Should Do If You Have An Accident

- Get medical help for anyone who may be injured.

- Call the police and follow their instruction. If you are in an unsafe area, you may relocate to the nearest police station or public place and then call the police.

- Get names, addresses, telephone numbers, and insurance information of anyone involved in or witnessing the accident.

- Call your parents or guardian and tell them what has happened and where you are located.

- Notify your insurance producer/agent or insurance company.

Source: Excerpted from "Illinois Insurance Facts: Auto Insurance Facts for Teen Drivers," © 2002 Illinois Department of Financial and Professional Regulation, Division of Insurance. Reprinted with permission.

When should you get a second opinion?

- Even though you bring in your car with a specific problem, additional repairs may be recommended. If you are uncertain whether the work needs to be done, you may want to consult your owner's manual or get a second opinion.

- On expensive or complicated repairs, or if you have questions about suggested repair work, get a second opinion or estimate.

- Ask if there will be a diagnostic charge if you decide to have the work performed elsewhere. Many repair shops charge for diagnostic time.

- Shops that do only diagnostic work and do not sell parts or repairs may be able to give you an objective opinion about which repairs are necessary.

After your repair is done, what do you need?

- After repairs are finished, get a completed repair order describing the work done. This should list each repair, all parts supplied, the cost of each part, labor charges and the vehicle's odometer reading when the vehicle entered the shop and when the repair order was prepared. Your state may require that the shop provide this; check with your state attorney general's office or local consumer protection agency.

- Get back all replaced parts. Your state may require this; check with your state attorney general's office or local consumer protection agency.

What should you know about the parts to be repaired or replaced on your vehicle? Parts are classified as:

✔ **Quick Tip**
If You're In An Accident

If you're in an accident with another driver, don't forget to ask:

- Driver's Name
- Driver's Address
- Driver's Phone #
- Insurance Card Information
- Witness's Name
- Witness's Address
- Witness's Phone #

Source: Excerpted from "Illinois Insurance Facts: Auto Insurance Facts for Teen Drivers," © 2002 Illinois Department of Financial and Professional Regulation, Division of Insurance. Reprinted with permission.

- **New auto parts:** These parts are generally made to original manufacturer's specifications, either by the vehicle manufacturer or an independent company. Your state may require repair shops to tell you if non-original equipment will be used in the repair. Prices and quality of these parts can vary widely.

- **Remanufactured, rebuilt and reconditioned parts:** These terms generally mean the same thing: parts have been restored to a sound working condition. Many manufacturers offer a warranty covering replacement parts, but not the labor to install them.

- **Salvage parts:** These are used parts taken from another vehicle without alteration. Salvage parts may be the only source for certain items, though their reliability is seldom guaranteed.

Preventive Maintenance

What are the consequences of postponing maintenance? Since many parts of your vehicle are interrelated, ignoring maintenance can lead to failure of other parts or an entire system. Neglecting even simple preventive maintenance, such as changing the oil or checking the coolant, can lead to poor fuel economy, unreliability, or costly breakdowns, and could invalidate your warranty.

What maintenance guidelines should you follow to avoid costly repairs?

- The best way to keep a vehicle in good condition is to follow the manufacturer's maintenance schedule in your owner's manual for your type of driving. If you do not have an owner's manual, contact the manufacturer to obtain one or to get a recommended maintenance schedule.

- Some repair shops create their own maintenance schedules, which call for more frequent servicing than the manufacturer's recommendations. Compare shop maintenance schedules with those recommended in your owner's manual. Ask the repair shop to explain—and make sure you understand—why it recommends service beyond the recommended schedule.

Protecting Your Auto Repair Investment

What warranties and service contracts apply to vehicle repairs?

- There is no such thing as a "standard warranty" on repairs. Make sure you understand what is covered under your warranty and get it in writing.

- Check with the Federal Trade Commission or your state or local consumer protection agency for information about your warranty rights.

- Warranties may be subject to limitations, including time, mileage, deductibles, businesses authorized to perform warranty work or special procedures required to obtain reimbursement. Make sure you understand these limitations.

- Compare warranty policies when selecting a repair shop.

- Many vehicle dealers and others sell optional contracts, called service contracts, issued by vehicle manufacturers or independent companies. Not all service contracts are the same; prices vary and are usually negotiable. To help decide whether to purchase a service contract, consider the following:

  1. The cost of the service contract.

  2. The repairs to be covered.

  3. Coverage of the service contract and whether it overlaps that provided by any other warranty.

  4. The deductible.

  5. Where the repairs are to be performed.

  6. Procedures required to file a claim, such as getting prior authorization for specific repairs or meeting required vehicle maintenance schedules.

  7. Whether repair costs are paid directly by the company to the repair shop or whether you will have to pay first and get reimbursed.

  8. The reputation of the service contract company, which can be checked with your state attorney general's office or the local consumer protection agency.

How do you resolve a dispute regarding billing, quality of repairs or warranties?

- Be prepared to take action if something goes wrong. Keep records of all transactions. Write down your experiences, dates, times, expenses and the names of people you dealt with. Keep copies of all written materials you receive, such as bills and estimates.

- If there is a dispute over a repair or charge, first try to settle the problem with the shop manager or owner. Some businesses have programs for handling disputes. You may then want to seek help from your state attorney general's office or local consumer protection agency. These groups also can tell you if low-cost alternative dispute resolution programs are available in your community. In addition, you may want to consider filing a claim with a local small claims court, where you do not need a lawyer to represent you.

- Many states have laws regulating how a repair shop operates, spelling out each party's obligations. You

✔ **Quick Tip**
Finding The
Right Repair Shop

- Look for an auto repair shop before you need one. Avoid being rushed into last-minute decisions.

- Ask for recommendations. Word-of-mouth often is the best advertising for a good technician. Ask friends, family members and others for recommendations of repair shops or technicians they trust.

- State or local law may require the repair shop to be licensed or registered, and you should ask to see current licenses. Also, ask your state attorney general's office or local consumer protection agency about the repair shop's complaint record.

- Be sure the repair shop is capable of performing the repairs needed.

- Find a repair shop that honors your vehicle's warranty.

- Shop around among comparable shops for the best deal.

Source: New York State Attorney General, 2003.

may wish to contact your state attorney general's office or consumer protection agency for specific information about your rights and options for recourse.

Heading Off Problems

The more you know about your vehicle, the more likely it is you can head off problems. Many common vehicle problems can be spotted by using your senses. You may learn a lot by inspecting the area around your vehicle, listening for strange noises, sensing a difference in the way your vehicle handles, or even noting unusual odors.

Looks Like Trouble

Identifying the cause of a puddle of fluid under your vehicle may save you serious trouble down the road. Small stains or an occasional drop may be of little concern. But wet spots deserve attention and bigger puddles should be checked immediately by the nearest service station.

Fluids can be identified by their color and consistency:

- Yellowish green, pastel blue or florescent orange colors indicate an overheated engine or an antifreeze leak caused by a bad hose, water pump or leaking radiator.

- Dark brown or black oily fluid means the engine is leaking oil. The leak could be caused by a bad seal or gasket.

- A red oily spot indicates a transmission or power-steering fluid leak.

- A puddle of clear water is usually no problem. It may be normal condensation from your vehicle air conditioner.

Smells Like Trouble

Some problems can be detected simply by following your nose. Consider these causes if you smell something unusual about your vehicle:

- Burned toast or a light, sharp odor often signals an electrical short and burning insulation. To be safe, try not to drive the vehicle until the problem is diagnosed.

- Rotten eggs or a continuous burning-sulfur smell usually indicates a problem in the catalytic converter or other emission control devices. Do not delay diagnosis and repair.

- A thick acrid odor usually means burning oil. Look for signs of a leak.

- If you smell gasoline vapors after a failed start, you may have flooded the engine. Wait a few minutes before trying again. If you constantly smell gas, you probably have a leak in the fuel system. This is a potentially dangerous problem that should be repaired immediately.

- Burning resin or an acrid chemical odor may signal overheated brakes or clutch. Check the parking brake. Stop and allow the brakes to cool after repeated hard braking on mountain roads. Light smoke coming from a wheel indicates a stuck brake. The vehicle should be towed for repair.

- A sweet, steamy odor indicates a coolant leak. If the temperature gauge or warning light does not indicate overheating, drive carefully to the nearest service station, keeping an eye on your gauge. If the odor is accompanied by a hot, metallic scent and steam from under the hood, your engine has overheated. Pull over immediately. Continued driving could cause severe engine damage. The vehicle should be towed for repair.

Sounds Like Trouble

Squeaks, squeals, rattles, rumbles and other sounds can provide valuable clues about problems and maintenance needs. Here are a number of the more common noises and what they may mean:

1. Squeal—A shrill, sharp noise, usually related to engine speed.
   - Loose or worn power steering, fan or air conditioning belt.
2. Click—A slight sharp noise, related to either engine speed or vehicle speed.
   - Loose wheel cover.
   - Loose or bent fan blade.
   - Stuck valve lifter or low engine oil.

✔ Quick Tip

Troubleshooting

Sometimes problems may require a simple repair, not a major overhaul. Here are a few common repair tips:

- **Alternator:** Loose wiring can make your alternator appear defective. Make sure the technician checks for loose connections and performs an output test before replacing it.

- **Battery:** Corroded or loose battery terminals can make the battery appear dead or defective. Make sure the technician cleans the terminals and tests battery function before replacing it.

- **Starter:** What appears to be a defective starter may actually be a dead battery or poor connection. Ask your technician to check all connections and test the battery before repairing the starter.

- **Muffler:** A loud rumbling noise under your vehicle indicates the need for a new muffler or exhaust pipe. Quality replacement parts obviously cost more. Low-priced parts are seldom a good buy unless you keep the vehicle less than a year. Make sure you understand exactly what the warranty covers, because many exhaust system warranties have serious exceptions and limitations.

- **Tune-up:** The old-fashioned "tune-up" may not apply to your vehicle. Fewer parts need to be replaced on newer vehicles other than belts, spark plugs, hoses and filters. Follow recommendations in your owner's manual.

Source: Excerpted from "Auto Repair Tips," Reprinted with permission from the Office of the New York State Attorney General, 2003.

3. Screech—A high-pitched, piercing metallic sound, usually occurs while the vehicle is in motion.

    • It is caused by brake wear indicators to alert the driver that brake maintenance is needed.

4. Rumble—A low-pitched rhythmic sound.

    • Defective exhaust pipe, converter or muffler.

    • Worn universal joint or other drive-line component.

5. Ping—A high-pitched metallic tapping sound, related to engine speed.

    • Usually caused by fuel with a lower octane rating than recommended. Check your owner's manual for the proper octane rating. You may want to switch to a different gas octane or gas station. If the problem persists, engine ignition timing could be the culprit.

6. Heavy Knock—A rhythmic pounding sound.

    • Worn crankshaft or connecting rod bearings.

    • Loose transmission torque converter.

7. Clunk—A random thumping sound.

    • Loose shock absorber or other suspension component.

    • Loose exhaust pipe or muffler.

Feels Like Trouble

Difficult handling, a rough ride, vibration and poor performance are the kinds of symptoms you can feel. When the driving experience doesn't feel quite right, look for:

1. Steering.

    • Wandering of difficulty steering in a straight line can be caused by misaligned front wheels and/or worn steering components such as the idler arm or ball joints.

    • Pulling, the vehicle's tendency to steer to the left or right, can be caused by something as simple as under-inflated tires, or as serious as a damaged or misaligned front end.

2. Ride and Handling.

    -   Worn shock absorbers or other suspension components can con-
        tribute to poor cornering characteristics. Also check for proper
        tire inflation.

    -   While there is no hard and fast rule about when to replace shock
        absorbers or struts, try this test: bounce the vehicle up and down
        hard at each wheel and then let go. See how many times the
        vehicle bounces. Weak shocks will allow the vehicle to bounce
        twice or more.

    -   Springs do not normally wear out and do not need replacement
        unless one corner of the vehicle is lower than the others. Over-
        loading your vehicle can damage your springs.

    -   Tires always should be balanced properly. An unbalanced or
        improperly balanced tire will cause the vehicle to vibrate and
        may prematurely wear steering and suspension components.

3. Brakes. The following symptoms indicate problems with your brakes.
    Diagnosis and repair should be scheduled.

    -   The vehicle pulls to the left or right when the brakes are ap-
        plied.

    -   The brake pedal sinks to the floor when braking pressure is main-
        tained.

    -   Scraping or grinding is heard or felt during braking.

    -   The "brake" light on the instrument panel is lit.

4. Engine. All of the following symptoms indicate problems with your en-
    gine. Diagnosis and repair are needed.

    -   Difficulty starting the engine.

    -   Rough idling or stalling.

    -   Poor acceleration.

    -   Poor fuel economy.

- Excessive oil use (more than one quart between changes).

- The "check engine" light on the instrument panel is lit.

5. Transmission. Poor transmission performance may come from actual component failure or a simple disconnected hose or plugged filter. Make sure the technician checks the simple items first; transmission repairs are normally expensive. Some of the most common symptoms of transmission problems are:

  - Abrupt or hard shifts between gears.

  - Delayed or no response when shifting from neutral to drive or reverse.

  - Failure to shift during normal acceleration.

  - Slippage during acceleration. The engine speeds up, but the vehicle does not respond.

Chapter 11

What You Should Know About Cell Phones And Cell Phone Contracts

Wireless telephones are hand-held phones with built-in antennas, often called cell, mobile, or PCS phones. These phones are two-way radios. When you talk into a cell phone, it picks up your voice and converts the sound to radiofrequency energy (or radio waves). The radio waves travel through the air until they reach a receiver at a nearby base station. The base station then sends your call through the telephone network until it reaches the person you are calling.

When you receive a call on your wireless telephone, the message travels through the telephone network until it reaches a base station close to your wireless phone. Then the base station sends out radio waves that are detected by a receiver in your telephone, where the signals are changed back into the sound of a voice.

About This Chapter: This chapter begins with text excerpted from "Cell Phone Facts," U.S. Food and Drug Administration, July 16, 2003. "Choosing a Cell Phone Plan," is by Cassandra Heckman, © 2005 Credit Union National Association, Inc. Reprinted with permission. (For additional information, visit http://www.cuna.org). "How To Get A Good Deal On A Cell Phone," is by Lucy Lazarony, Bankrate, Inc., North Palm Beach, FL, © 2005.

Choosing A Cell Phone Plan

By June 30, 2002, there were 134.5 million cell phone subscribers, up 14% from the previous year. Two of the fastest growing markets for wireless companies are teenagers and young adults. Parents find cell phones are a convenient way to keep track of their kids, and busy kids can use them to stay in touch with friends.

But for many youths, buying a cell phone can be a daunting task with seemingly endless options. And while options and competition help keep prices down, any cell phone owner will tell you it's easy to end up paying more than you should for wireless service simply because you have so many confusing choices to make.

Which companies provide service in my area?

Letstalk.com or GetConnected.com can tell you which phone carriers provide service in your area. It's also important to find out how reliable this coverage is. Wireless companies include on their maps all areas where you can get service, but reception may be low quality or spotty in some places. Web sites like Cellmania.com or Decide.com have "call quality maps" that show you exactly where your reception will be best and worst. You also can ask your friends and relatives how they feel about their service.

✔ Quick Tip

The easiest way to ensure your wireless solution fits your needs and budget is to research before you buy. In many cases, the best resource is the Internet, where you can easily compare plans, features, and prices. Even then, it's sometimes hard to know what to look for. Before you pick a wireless plan, ask yourself these questions:

- Which companies provide service in my area?
- Do I expect to make mostly local, regional, or nationwide calls?
- How often do I plan on using my cell phone?
- At what time of day will I make most of my calls?
- How much am I willing to spend?
- How long am I willing to stay with the service provider?
- Which features like voice mail, caller ID, call waiting, or text messaging are most important?

Answering these questions first will make it much easier to wade through all the options as you find a plan that fits your budget.

Source: Cassandra Heckman, © 2005 Credit Union National Association, Inc.

Who will I call on my cell phone?

Do you expect to make calls mostly from your local area to other people in your local area? Will you be calling mostly to and from only a few surrounding states? Do you plan to travel and call people all over the country?

The three main types of monthly cell phone plans are local, regional, and national. Cell phone carriers define your "home service area" or "local coverage area" as a metropolitan area, a region of states, or the entire nation.

- Local plans usually encompass a metropolitan area and are the cheapest. However, long distance charges may apply when you call people who live outside your area.

- Regional plans encompass about two to five states and are a good choice if you will be mainly making calls to and from one specific region of the country such as the Midwest. They can be a good choice for college students who are going to school in another state that's close to home. Again, long distance may apply if you call outside your region.

- National plans are a little trickier. While they are great for people who travel or have friends all over the country, you have to be careful to read the fine print. While all major carriers offer nationwide plans, some only offer service on their "nationwide network," while others offer service anywhere in the U.S. While most of the major carriers have huge "nationwide networks," you have to be careful because if you make a call in a rural area that's not on their coverage maps, you can incur heavy roaming and long distance charges which are sometimes upwards of 50 cents a minute.

How often and when will I use my cell phone?

These questions may be the most important to answer so that you find a plan that fits your budget and doesn't overcharge. Many people don't know their calling habits and end up paying for minutes that they don't even use.

First, you can keep track of your "land line" home phone use. This can give you a good general idea of who and when you call. However, since people's calling habits often change when they get a cell phone, another solution, instead of signing up for monthly service right away, is to start with a pre-paid cell phone for a month or two so you can see how much time you're on the phone and when.

Most monthly plans offer combinations of "peak" and "off-peak" minutes and each minute you are on the phone is deducted from your allotted monthly amount. Peak minutes are commonly referred to as "daytime" or "anytime" minutes and generally count as any calls initiated between 9:00 a.m. and 9:00 p.m. However, these times differ for some carriers, so be sure to check. In any case, be careful because if you start your call at 8:59 p.m. you will be using your "daytime" minutes since providers usually define the call by when it started.

While the amount of peak or anytime minutes allotted in most plans is limited, it is becoming increasingly common to find plans with unlimited "off-peak" minutes. Off-peak minutes or "nights and weekends" generally include weekdays after 9:00 p.m. and all day Saturday and Sunday.

The distinction between peak and off-peak is why it is so important to know your calling habits before you buy. If you go over your allotted monthly minutes, you'll get charged extra per minute, which adds up quickly. Since the cost of a monthly plan mainly depends on the number of peak minutes you get each month, you don't want to pay for more than you will use. Plans with fewer peak minutes are cheaper than those that have more.

How much can I spend?

Once you've determined your needs, it's time to figure out how much you are willing to spend. It can be helpful to figure out a budget and add up how much money you make from jobs or allowances and compare that with how much you already spend each month. How does a cell phone fit in?

You may want to consider a family plan if your parents will be paying your phone bill. Most major carriers have plans in which family members each have their own phones but share minutes each month. In some cases, calls among family members are free.

If you decide to sign up for monthly service, it's important to look around for the best deal for you. This is where the real research comes in. Weigh the cost of the plan against the coverage area, features, monthly allotment of minutes, and your budget. You can find monthly plan information on wireless providers' Web sites or go to sites like About.com to compare plans from the major providers. Call the company directly if you have specific questions.

How long can I commit?

You'll also want to know how long you are willing to commit yourself to one service provider. Some companies offer month-to-month service that doesn't require a contract, but it's usually more expensive.

The alternative is a one- or two-year contract. If you sign a contract, you enter into an agreement to stay with that provider for one or two years. And while most providers will let you switch from one of their plans to another for free, if you want to switch providers you can face contract termination fees of up to $200.

Do research to ensure your wireless solution fits your needs and budget. The advantage is that in order to entice you to sign up with them, most providers will provide great discounts on the cellular phone itself.

What extra features are most important to me?

Today most companies include standard features like voice mail and caller ID free with monthly plans. However, there is a dizzying array of other features to choose from. Many, like text messaging or wireless Internet access, will have a monthly or per use charge. So once you've figured out how much you can afford to spend, see if these extras fit your budget. If you don't really need wireless Internet or text messaging, eliminating them from your plan can be a good way to save money.

You also have to make sure that the phone you choose is compatible with the features that you want. For example, older phones may not even have the ability to transfer data on the wireless Internet, so be sure to check with your provider.

What else do I need to know?

There a few other tips for saving money and things you need to know when you sign up for a cellular phone plan:

- Your first bill will be more than you expect. Don't be upset if you receive your first bill and it's higher than the cost of the plan you chose. There will be one-time charges for activation and/or security deposits, accessories, and taxes.

- You will be charged for both outgoing and incoming calls. Your provider will deduct the minutes of both the calls you make and the calls you receive from your monthly allotment.

- Use your caller ID. Avoid wasting minutes on incoming calls by using caller ID to skip calls from blocked or unfamiliar numbers.

- Don't count on your phone's call timer. Newer phones often include a call timer that keeps track of how many minutes you have talked on the phone per month. However, these timers will not differentiate between calls made during peak and off-peak times. In addition, almost all providers will count a fraction of a minute that you're on the phone as a full minute. For example, if you make a call that's three minutes and 30 seconds long, your call timer probably will record it as such, but your provider will round it up to four minutes. Over the month, these fractions of minutes will add up to be a big difference between what your call timer and your provider says you've used. Luckily, most providers allow you to check your minutes used online or over the phone.

- Know your coverage area. One of the easiest ways to save is to be familiar with your plan and coverage area. That way you can avoid costly roaming and long distance charges.

- Read the fine print. Be familiar with the terms of your contract. It is essential to know what is included and for what you'll have to pay extra. It's also helpful to know exactly when you have to pay extra for long distance. Knowing what you're agreeing to is the best way to save money and know if there is a problem with your bill.

- Re-evaluate. It's a good idea to re-evaluate your plan periodically. That way if your use, needs, or budget changes you won't be spending more than you need to. While it can be expensive to switch providers because of termination fees and new equipment, most providers will let you switch from one of their plans to another for free.

Overall, the best advice is to know what you're buying before you buy. The telecommunications industry is infamous for having tons of competition and lots of options, but that also makes things more confusing. Before you buy, be sure to understand your needs, your budget, and the terms of your contract, and you'll be sure to find a cell phone plan that works for you.

♣ It's A Fact!!

How does prepaid work?

While prepaid cell phones can be a good way to gauge your calling habits, they are becoming more popular as an alternative to monthly plans.

According to an article in *Credit Card Management,* more and more cellular companies are beginning to emphasize prepaid plans to young adults. While about 66% of Western European cell phone users have prepaid plans, in the U.S. only about 13% do. However, providers expect this number to rise rapidly and they hope to position programs like Verizon's Free-up or AT&T's Free2Go Wireless as a more flexible and hassle-free alternative to monthly plans for their younger customers.

Currently, with most prepaid plans, you buy a plastic card to activate minutes to use on your cell phone. It works just like a prepaid calling card. Credit Card Management explains that most companies also hope to make prepaid minutes available through toll-free numbers, automatic billing, websites, and even ATMs (automated teller machines).

The advantages to prepaid service are that it does not require a credit check, there are no monthly fees or bills, no contracts, and your minutes do not expire after only one month.

There are disadvantages too. In general, you will pay more per minute with a prepaid plan than with a monthly one. Some features like wireless Internet access may not be available, and you may have to pay more than monthly customers do for extras like long distance.

Source: Cassandra Heckman, © 2005 Credit Union National Association, Inc.

What are roaming and long distance charges?

Roaming charges occur when you make or receive calls outside the border of your "home service area" or "local coverage area."

Depending on your type of plan, this can mean that you're outside the physical borders of your local area, your regional area, or you're somewhere in the country where your provider doesn't offer service. While your phone will still work, your provider might charge you as much as 69 cents per minute! Luckily, you can set most new phones to display when you're in a roaming area and avoid making calls there.

Long distance charges also can apply to each of the three types of plans. You are charged for long distance when you make a call from inside your "local calling area" to someone outside of it. A "local calling area" is a lot like an area code. Unfortunately, to make things even more confusing, your "local calling area" is not always the same as your "local coverage area." While the "local coverage area" is the area where you can make and receive calls without being charged for roaming, a "local calling area" works like an area code and is the area that you can make calls to without it being considered long distance.

Many people don't know their calling habits and end up paying for minutes that they don't even use. Before you choose a plan, make sure to check with your provider about exactly what they consider long distance as it can vary between companies.

Are free cell phones really free?

There are three main ways to buy a cell phone: third party Web stores, directly from the service provider, or directly from the manufacturer.

While it's good to shop around and compare prices, it's important that you make sure you know which phones are compatible with the provider that you've chosen. For example, Sprint PCS service only works with certain models and brands, while Verizon or AT&T only work with others.

Web stores and manufacturers can offer great limited-time discounts, but it seems that in most cases the biggest discounts and "free" phones are available from the service providers themselves. These offers help save you money, but you have to be careful about offers that seem too good to be true; there's usually a catch.

Service providers offer great discounts on phones as a way to cash in on your monthly subscription. In fact, usually you can't even get the discount unless you sign a contract. In some cases, the discount is smaller if you only want a one-year agreement instead of two.

The other catch is that while Web stores and manufacturers simply discount their phones, service providers usually provide the discount in the form of a mail-in rebate. So that low or "free" price is usually the price after rebate. During my research, I found that up to 95% of people never complete mail-in rebates. And even if you do, the rebates are complicated and take at least 6 to 8 weeks.

Providers use this marketing ploy to lure you in and make you think you're getting a great deal when really the company is counting on your laziness, confusion, or forgetfulness about the rebate to make a huge profit. Some experts even suggest that some companies make rebate forms complicated on purpose so that people will get confused, fill them out incorrectly, and forget to find out why their rebate never came.

The only way to deal with this practice is to remember to send in your mail-in rebate. Read all instructions, double check, and make copies of everything you send. In addition, make a note on your calendar or use an online reminder service to note when your rebate should arrive so that if it doesn't, you can contact the company and see what the problem is.

—Above section by Cassandra Heckman

How To Get A Good Deal On A Cell Phone

Source: Bankrate, Inc., North Palm Beach, FL, © 2005

Cell phone users, listen up. Hear that loud noise coming from your phone? That's the sound of your hard-earned money being sucked away by a calling plan that doesn't fit your needs.

It happens all the time. Lots of folks walk into a shop, find a cell phone they like and sign a contract on the spot.

"They're more concerned about the color of the phone than the contract they're signing," says Rosemary Kimball, a spokeswoman for the Federal Communications Commission. "And then they get a lot of surprises."

The biggest surprise is just how much a cell phone is costing them each month. The most expensive mistake you can make is signing up for a calling plan with a rock-bottom rate and exceeding your allotted airtime each month.

"We have clients that have cell phone charges well over $300 a month," says Steve Rhode, president of Myvesta.org, a financial crisis and treatment center. "They're really charged the maximum amount for every call."

One client signed on for a calling plan with a basic monthly fee of $29.99 and wound up with bills of almost $500 a month. The reason? He was way over his allotment of free minutes each month and had to pay heavy long-distance and roaming charges on a ton of calls.

Rhode advised him to switch to a calling plan costing $99.95 a month with free long-distance and roaming. You pay roaming charges when you make and receive calls outside your home calling area. "We changed his plan so it included everything and he didn't have any extra charges," Rhode says.

Of course, signing up for a plan with too many minutes isn't ideal either.

"If you have minutes left over, you might want to consider reducing your plan to a less expensive one because you're just wasting those minutes," Rhode says.

Getting The Best Deal

How do you go about scoring a super deal on a cell phone plan that's right for you? Zero in on your calling needs, brush up on your cell phone terminology and then research, research, research.

"Figure out what your calling pattern is," Kimball says. "When you call and where you call are crucial. Those are two things to ask yourself and work into your plan."

Having trouble getting a handle on your calling habits? Answering these questions will help:

- What time of day do you make most of your calls? Do you make a bunch of calls on weekends or weekdays or both? Do you make a lot of long-distance calls?

- How long does a typical call last?

- Who has your cell phone number? Everyone you know? A few close friends and family? Keep in mind that with a cell phone you're paying for calls that you receive as well as calls that you make.

- Do you travel a lot? How often do you use your phone outside your home calling area? Someone who travels a lot should consider a plan with no roaming or long-distance charges.

Once you assess your calling needs, take a closer look at your calling plan. Get out your bills, get out your contract and start reading.

Here are some important terms to look for:

Basic Monthly Fee: This fee, which some providers call a service charge, is the monthly amount you pay to receive cellular phone service. This fee is fixed. You pay the same amount each month, regardless of how much or how little you use your phone.

Airtime: These are the charges you pay for time spent talking on a cell phone. If you exceed the monthly allotment of minutes included in your calling plan, a higher per-minute fee may kick in. Are you talking well beyond or well below your minutes each month? If so, it might be time for a new calling plan.

Long-Distance Rate: This is the rate you pay per minute for calls outside of your local area. If you make a lot of long-distance calls each month, you may want to consider a plan that includes long-distance calling in the cost of your airtime.

"In this day and age, you shouldn't be paying extra for long-distance," says Joni Blecher, who writes the "Ask the Cell Phone Diva" column for CNET.com.

Roaming Charge: This is the cost you pay for the ability to make and receive calls outside your home calling area. Roaming charges can get really expensive. If you travel a lot outside your home calling area, you may want to opt for a plan without an additional per-minute fee for roaming.

Peak: Peak hours are the times, typically on weekdays, when a cell phone user pays the maximum rate for calls.

Off Peak: Off-peak hours are the times, typically weekday evenings and weekends, when a cell phone user pays a discounted rate for calls. Off-peak hours used to begin as early as 6 p.m. on weeknights. But these days you'll be hard-pressed to find off-peak hours beginning before 8 p.m. or 9 p.m. on a weeknight. Be sure to check for any changes in off-peak hours when you renew a cell phone contract.

Cancellation Charge: This is a charge, ranging from $100 to $200, that you pay for canceling a cell phone contract. If you cancel your cell phone contract and sign up for a plan with another company, you'll probably pay a hefty cancellation fee. But the fee may be worth it, if the new calling plan will save you a ton of money.

Home Calling Area: This area is defined by your service plan. If you make or receive calls outside your home calling area, you may have to pay long-distance or roaming charges. Home calling areas vary by calling plan and service provider. If you're being zapped with a bunch of roaming charges, consider a plan with a larger home calling area.

For more tips on deciphering your cell phone bill, check out this consumer brochure from the FCC at http://ftp.fcc.gov/cgb/phonebills/WirelessPhonebill.html.

Now that you've taken a good, hard look at your cell phone bills and contract, is your calling plan up to snuff? Are you paying absurd charges every month? Why not ask for a better deal?

You may be able to switch to another calling plan within the same company or make changes to your plan without penalty during the length of your contract. Be sure to ask.

Comparison Shop

Do plenty of homework before you start negotiating. Take a close look at several other plans offered by your service provider. Is another plan better suited to your calling needs?

Be sure to check out calling plans from other service providers as well. Having information handy on a calling plan from another service provider may prompt your company to sweeten your service deal.

"The best way to negotiate is not to demand a cheaper plan but to go in with information," Rhode says. "Cell phone companies have all kinds of different promotional plans that they never tell people about."

Checking out special offers and calling plans from other service providers in your area may take some time. With half a dozen service providers in your area all offering a range of calling plans, there's a lot of information to sift through.

"You really have to dissect," Blecher says.

Not sure what companies provide cell phone service in your area? Flip open your phone book and find out. Next hop online, visit the company websites and find out what types of calling plans are available in your area.

A list of cellular service comparison sites is available on CallSense.com.

Knowing precisely what you're looking for in a calling plan will help speed along your search.

"Good data leads to good solutions," Rhode says.

For more tips on comparing cell phone plans, check out the consumer brochure by the FCC at http://www.fcc.gov/cgb/cell_phones.html.

The more information you have when you contact a cell phone company, the better your chance of landing a good deal.

If you're unhappy with the quality of your calls or service, it may be time for a new provider.

Ask Friends And Family

Not sure what service provider to choose? Ask family, friends, co-workers, and neighbors about their cell phone service. Do they have service troubles? Do all their calls come in crystal-clear all the time? How big is their home calling area? Do they get zapped with roaming charges?

When it comes to choosing a service provider, word of mouth in your local area rules.

Once you've settled on a service provider and a calling plan, it's time to pick out a phone.

 Remember!!
Do you really need a cell phone?

Cell phones are becoming expensive status symbols rather than being used practically by most consumers.

There are still plenty of pay phones around and friends with cell phones in a real emergency. Remember also, in an emergency, a charged cell phone is supposed to connect to 911 whether the caller has a cellular service agreement or not. If you do feel you need to have a phone, be sure to sign the shortest contract you can possibly sign and never go into debt for cellular service.

It is important to try to determine what type of cell phone user you will be. We all start with good intentions of only using the phone in emergencies or just calling to check in at home once in a while, but it seems difficult to avoid using the phone more than we originally plan. Even with the best intentions, it is hard to avoid others calling you with the latest gossip once you start to give out your new number.

But, as a new user, unless you have specific business uses for your phone, you should start with a modest service plan and sign no more than a one-year commitment. After the first year, you will be able to review your phone use habits and needs, and can then enroll in a cellular plan that is more suited to your usage patterns.

Some service providers allow you to change calling plans before your initial commitment is up. There might be a fee charged to change service plans, so be sure to clarify any costs prior to making changes before a contract ends.

And again, the best deals go to people that ask for them. Be sure to ask the manufacturer and service provider about rebates on the phone you want. Manufacturer rebates change weekly.

"There are always rebates," Blecher says. "Ask the carrier first because you're very much tied to your service provider."

Unless you're madly in love with your service provider, it's a good idea to steer clear of super-cool and super-pricey phones. The reason? If you decide to switch service providers, you'll have to ditch the phone.

Once you decide on a phone, calling plan and service provider, you're ready to make a deal.

Competition in the industry has helped keep costs fairly stable. On average, a cellular user with basic needs should be able to find a good plan that offers 400 to 600 anytime minutes per month, unlimited free weekends and night minutes, free long distance calling and free roaming for about $39.95 per month.

The monthly price may include many features such as Voice Mail, Caller ID, Call Waiting, Call Forwarding, 411 Information service, etc. Options like text messaging, e-mail, picture messaging and Internet access are generally available at extra per minute and per message costs that will vary between service providers.

If you mainly use your cell phone during the free call periods at night and on weekends, then try signing up for a plan with less "anytime" minutes included, which should reduce your monthly base price.

Your knowledge of what is included and what is an extra charge will go a long way toward helping you find the best deal for the money.

—by Mike Schiano

Mike "The DebtBuster" Schiano is a nationally syndicated radio talk show host and book author. His show can be heard via the Web at www.inchargeradio.com.

Source: Reprinted with permission of InCharge Education Foundation, Inc., July/August 2004 issue of YOUNG MONEY, www.youngmoney.com

Before signing on the dotted line, ask about taking your phone out for a test drive. Many companies will allow you to try out the phone for a couple of days or a couple of weeks before holding you to the terms of the contract.

Make the most of your testing time. Try out your phone at your home, at your office, at your friend's apartment. How's the service? Will you have to pay roaming charges to make a call from your office? It's best to find out before your contract kicks in.

"Really work that phone," Blecher says. "They need to find out if the service works for them because service varies from area to area."

If you decide the phone is not for you, be sure to return it on time.

Part Three

Understanding Banks

Chapter 12

Why Are There So Many Banks?

Making Sense Of Savings

What do you do with your money? You have many choices concerning what you do with your money—spend it, invest it, or hide it under your mattress. If you invest or save your money, you have many alternatives. For example, you can buy U.S. savings bonds or Treasury bills; purchase stocks or bonds; invest in a mutual fund; or open a savings or other deposit account with a bank, savings and loan association, savings bank, or credit union.

Opening an account is like buying a car. Many products are available—some plain, some fancy, and some less and some more expensive than others. Because features of accounts and costs can vary greatly, it is important to shop around to make sure the account you choose is the best one for you.

Determining The Right Type Of Account For You

What type of account should you open? The answer depends on how you plan to use the account. If you want to build up your savings and you think that you will not need your money soon, a certificate of deposit may be right for you.

About This Chapter: This chapter begins with text excerpted from "Making Sense of Savings," Federal Reserve Board of Governors, 2000. Text under the heading "So, Why Are There So Many Different Types Of Banks?" is excerpted from "Banking Basics," a publication of the Federal Reserve Bank of Boston, revised 1999. The complete text of this publication is available on the Federal Reserve Bank of Boston website, http://www.bos.frb.org.

If you need to reach your money, however, a savings or checking account may be a better choice. You will probably find that a checking account is best for you if you plan to write several checks each month (for example, to pay bills). But if you usually write only two or three checks each month, then a money market deposit account (MMDA) might be a better deal. MMDAs usually pay a higher rate of interest than do checking accounts, but minimum balance requirements are often higher as well.

Remember, account features and fees vary from one institution to the next. If you have questions, you should ask a representative of the institution about any account features and fees *before* you open an account.

♣ **It's A Fact!!**
Do You Need
A Bank Account?

There are many reasons for opening a bank account. (1) an account may help you save money—since it is often easier not to touch your savings if you keep them in a bank or other institution. (2) an account may bee less expensive way to manage your than are alternatives. Buying money orders to pay your bills or paying a business to cash your paycheck may end up costing you a lot more than keeping an account would. (3) having your money in an account is safer than holding cash. Finally, keeping track of your money and how you spend it may be easier.

Source: Federal Reserve Board of Governors, 2000.

Account Features To Compare

In shopping for an account, it is important to look closely and compare features. Here are some of the most common features to compare:

Interest Rates. What is the interest rate? Can the institution change the rate after you open the account? Does the institution pay different levels of interest depending on the amount of your account balance, and, if so, in what way is interest calculated?

Interest Compounding. How often is interest compounded? In other words, when does the institution start paying interest on the interest you've already earned in the account?

The Annual Percentage Yield (APY). (The APY is a rate that reflects the amount of interest you will earn on a deposit.) What is the minimum balance required before you begin earning interest?

When You Start Earning Interest. Do you begin earning interest on the day you deposit a check into your account—called earning on your ledger balance; or Do you begin earning interest later, when the institution receives credit for the check—known as earning on your collected balance?

Table 12.1 Comparison Of Types Of Accounts

Type of account	Will I earn interest?	May I write checks?	Are there withdrawal limitations?	Are fees likely?
Regular checking	No	Yes	No	Yes
Interest checking (NOW)	Yes	Yes	No	Yes
Money Market Deposit Account (MMDA)	Yes, usually higher than NOW or savings	Yes, only 3 per month	Yes, 6 transfers per month	Yes
Savings	Yes	No	Same as MMDA	Yes
Certificate of Deposit (CD)	Yes, usually higher than MMDA	No	Yes, usually no withdrawals of principals until the date of maturity	Yes, if you withdraw principal funds before the date of maturity

Source: Federal Reserve Board of Governors, 2000.

Fees. Pay special attention to fees:

- Will you pay a flat monthly fee?

- Will you pay a fee if the balance in your account drops below a specified amount?

- Is there a charge for each deposit and withdrawal you make?

- If you can use ATMs to make deposits and withdrawals on your account, is there a charge for this service? Does it matter whether the transaction takes place at an ATM owned by the institution?

- If you have a checking account or an MMDA, how much will ordering checks cost? Will you be charged for each check you write?

- Are fees reduced if you have other accounts at the institution?

- Are fees reduced or waived if you agree to directly deposit your paycheck or government payments, like a social security check?

- What is the fee if you request the institution to stop payment on a check you have written?

- Is there a charge for asking how much money you have in your account (a balance inquiry)?

- Does the institution charge a fee for closing an account soon after it is opened? If it does, when will the fee be imposed?

- What is the charge for writing a check that bounces (a check returned for insufficient funds)?

- What happens if you deposit a check written by another person, and it bounces? Are you charged a fee?

Other Features. Does the institution limit the number or the dollar amount of withdrawals or deposits you make? If you close the account before interest is credited to your account, will the institution pay you the interest that has been earned until that time? How soon does the institution allow you to withdraw funds that you have deposited to your account?

Time Deposits. Ask these questions:

- What is the term of the account? In other words, how long is it until the maturity date?

- Will the account roll over automatically? In other words, does the account renew unless you withdraw your money at maturity or during any grace period provided after maturity? A grace period is the time after maturity when you can withdraw your money without penalty. If there is a grace period, how long is it?

- If you are allowed to withdraw your money before maturity, will the institution impose a penalty? If so, how much?

- Will the institution regularly send you the amount of interest you are earning on your account—or regularly credit it to another account of yours, like a savings account?

> ✤ **It's A Fact!!**
> **Tiered Rates**
>
> Institutions may pay different tiered rates that are tied to different balance amounts. For example, an institution may pay a 5% interest rate on balances up to $5,000 and 5.5% on balances above $5,000. If you deposit $8,000, the institution that pays interest on the entire balance pays you 5.5% on the entire $8,000. Other institutions may pay you 5% on the first $5,000 and 5.5% only on the remaining $3,000.
>
> To tell which method an institution uses, check the annual percentage yield (APY) disclosure. If it is a single figure for a balance level, you will be paid the stated interest rate for the entire balance. Getting paid the stated interest rate on the entire balance is a better deal than if the APY is stated as a range for each balance level.
>
> Source: Federal Reserve Board of Governors, 2000.

The Truth In Savings Act

The Truth in Savings Act, a federal law, requires depository institutions to provide you with—or disclose to you—the important terms of their consumer deposit accounts. Institutions must tell you:

- The annual percentage yield and interest rate;

- Cost information, such as fees that may be charged; and

- Information about other features such as any minimum balance amount required to earn interest or to avoid fees.

To help you shop for the best accounts, an institution must give you information about any consumer deposit account the institution offers, if you ask for it. You also will usually get disclosures before you actually open an account. In addition, the Truth in Savings Act generally requires that interest and fee information be provided on any periodic statements sent to you. And if you have a roll-over CD that is longer than one month, the law requires also that you get a renewal notice before the CD matures.

✎ What's It Mean?

Annual Percentage Yield (APY): The amount of interest you will earn on a deposit on a yearly basis expressed as a percentage.

Compounding Interest: Earned interest is added to the principal so that you begin to earn interest on that amount as well as on the principal. Often referred to as interest on interest. The more often interest is compounded, the greater the annual percentage yield.

Crediting Interest: When you have access to the interest. Usually, posting the interest you have earned to your account.

Grace Period: The period after an automatically renewing time deposit, such as a certificate of deposit, matures. During this time you may withdraw funds without being charged a penalty.

Interest: Money an institution pays you for its use of your funds.

Interest Rate: The rate of interest, expressed as a percentage, that an account will earn if funds are kept on deposit for a full year. It does not reflect the effect of compounding interest.

Tiered Rates: An interest-rate structure by which the rate paid on an account is tied to a specified balance level.

Time Deposit: An account, such as a certificate of deposit, with a maturity of at least seven days, from which you are not generally allowed to withdraw funds unless you pay a penalty.

Source: Federal Reserve Board of Governors, 2000.

Federal Deposit Insurance

Federal deposit insurance sets apart deposit accounts from other savings choices. Only deposit accounts at federally insured depository institutions are protected by federal deposit insurance. Generally, the government protects the money you have on deposit to a limit of $100,000. Accounts for special relationships, such as trusts or co-owners, may also have some effect on the amount of insurance coverage you have. Asking how the deposit insurance rules will apply to your deposit accounts is always a good idea.

Federally insured depository institutions also offer products that are not protected by insurance. For example, you may purchase shares in a mutual fund or an annuity. These investments are not protected by the federal government.

So, Why Are There So Many Different Types Of Banks?

Not all banks are exactly the same. There are commercial banks, savings banks, savings and loan associations (S&Ls), cooperative banks, and credit unions. They now offer many of the same services, but once they were very different from one another.

Commercial Banks. Commercial banks originally concentrated on meeting the needs of businesses. They served as places where a business could safely deposit its funds or borrow money when necessary. Many commercial banks also made loans and offered accounts to individual customers, but they put most of their effort into serving business (commercial) customers.

Savings banks, S&Ls, cooperative banks, and credit unions are classified as thrift institutions or "thrifts" rather than banks. Originally, they concentrated on serving people whose banking needs were ignored or unmet by commercial banks.

Savings Banks. The first savings banks were founded in the early 1800s to give blue-collar workers, clerks, and domestic workers a secure place to save for a "rainy day." They were started by public spirited citizens who wanted to encourage efforts at saving among people who did not earn much money.

Savings And Loan Associations (S&Ls), Cooperative Banks. Savings and loan associations and cooperative banks were established during the 1800s to help factory workers and other wage earners become homeowners. S&Ls accepted savings deposits and used the money to make loans to home buyers. Most of these loans went to people who did not make enough money to be welcome at traditional banks.

Credit Unions. Credit unions began as a 19th century solution to the emergency needs of people who were unable to borrow money from traditional lenders. Before the opening of credit unions, ordinary citizens had no place to turn when they faced unexpected home repairs, medical expenses, or other emergencies. Credit unions were started by people who shared a common bond such as working in the same factory, belonging to the same house of worship, or farming in the same community. Members pooled their savings and used the money to make small loans to one another.

Although there are still differences between banks and thrifts, they now offer many of the same banking services to their customers. Most commercial banks now compete to make car loans. Many thrift institutions have begun to make commercial loans, and some credit unions make loans to home buyers.

What types of accounts do banks offer?

People use banks for different purposes. Some have extra money to save; others need to borrow. Some need to keep their household finances in order; others need to meet a business payroll. Banks help their customers meet those needs by offering a variety of accounts.

Savings Accounts. Savings accounts are for people who want to keep their money in a safe place and earn interest at the same time. You do not need a lot of money to open a savings account, and you can withdraw your money at any time.

Checking Accounts. Checking accounts offer safety and convenience. You keep your money in a checking account and write a check when you want to pay a bill or transfer some of your money to someone else. If your checkbook is lost or stolen, all you need to do is close your account and open a new one so that nobody can use your old checks. When cash is lost or stolen, you rarely see it again. (It is likely gone forever.)

♣ It's A Fact!!
What is a credit union?

A credit union is a not-for-profit financial institution owned and operated by its members. Credit unions provide their members with a safe and sound institution to save and borrow at reasonable and affordable rates. A volunteer board elected by members manages each credit union. Credit unions exist to serve their member-owners and are often able to offer favorable rates on savings and loans.

To join a credit union, you must be eligible for membership. Usually, members of each credit union share a "common bond" such as being employed by the same employer, belonging to an organization or church, or living in the same community. Each credit union serves the specific field of membership it decides upon.

Credit unions offer a variety of financial services and products, including savings, loans, check cashing, wire transfers, financial counseling and more. Each credit union offers its own line of products and services.

Approximately 10,000 credit unions serve more than 80 million people in the United States. Federal credit unions are chartered, regulated and insured by the National Credit Union Administration (NCUA). Through NCUA's National Credit Union Share Insurance Fund (NCUSIF), federal credit union member accounts are insured up to $100,000. NCUA also insures most state-chartered credit union accounts.

To learn more about credit unions in your area, or to inquire about the insurance status of a specific credit union, contact the National Credit Union Administration at www.ncua.gov.

Source: From "Is a Credit Union Right for Me," National Credit Union Administration, © 2002; reprinted with permission.

An attractive feature of a checking account is that every month your bank sends you a record of all the checks you have written, which you can use as a receipt if a disagreement arises over whether or not you paid a bill. Businesses use checking accounts to hold the money they receive and to transfer money to other people or other businesses. Checking accounts do not earn interest. These are the types of accounts on which banks generally charge fees because banks incur significant costs to process the checks drawn on checking accounts.

NOW Accounts. NOW accounts are checking accounts that pay interest. (NOW stands for Negotiable Order of Withdrawal.) Sometimes banks require you to keep a certain minimum amount of money (a minimum balance) in your NOW account in order to keep earning interest. Only non-business customers may open NOW accounts; businesses must use regular checking accounts that do not pay interest.

> **♣ It's A Fact!!**
> **Credit Union Accounts**
>
> Credit unions offer accounts that are similar to accounts at other depository institutions, but have different names. Credit union members have share draft (rather than checking) accounts, share (rather than savings) accounts, and share certificate (rather than certificate of deposit) accounts.
>
> Source: Federal Reserve Board of Governors, 2000.

Money Market Deposit Accounts. Money market deposit accounts are similar to NOW accounts except that they usually pay a higher rate of interest and require a higher minimum balance (often $2,500 or more), and limit the number of checks you may write per month.

Certificates Of Deposit (CDs) Certificates of deposit (CDs) are savings deposits that require customers to keep a certain amount of money in a bank for a fixed period of time (example: $1,000 for two years). As a rule, the rate of interest your money earns is higher if you agree to keep your money on deposit for a longer period of time, so the bank can plan on using your money for a longer period of time. Banks do not offer check-writing privileges on certificates of deposit.

Individual Retirement Accounts. Individual retirement accounts are savings deposits that require customers to keep their money in the bank until they reach a certain age. Generally, these accounts offer excellent rewards to customers who make these long-term deposits. However, one must be careful because banks can charge a significant penalty to individuals who withdraw their funds from these accounts before they reach a specified age (usually age 60 or older).

Other Names. Banks do not always call their accounts by the same names. Often, they choose distinctive names in hopes of attracting customers. But sometimes there can be a real difference between one bank's accounts and another's, so shop around.

What happens to your money after you deposit it in your bank account?

What happens to a ten-dollar bill after you deposit it in your savings account? Does the bank teller take it to a vault and put it into a separate compartment or cubbyhole marked with your name and account number? No.

The bank begins by adding ten dollars to the amount that is already in your account (your existing balance). Your ten dollar deposit and your new balance are then recorded in your bank book and in the bank's computer system. The ten dollar bill you deposited is mixed in with all the other cash your bank receives that day.

When you and other customers deposit money in a bank, the bank "puts most of it to work." Part of the money is set aside and held in reserve, but much of the rest is loaned to people who need to borrow money in order to buy houses and cars, start or expand businesses, buy farm equipment or plant crops, or do any of the other things that require people to borrow money.

Of course, banks do not lend money just to provide a service. They do it to make money.

When you keep your savings in a bank, the bank pays you extra money, which is called interest. The interest is added to your account on a regular basis, usually once a month or once every three months.

Let's say a bank pays its depositors interest of 3% a year on their savings. In simple terms, that means if you keep $100 in your savings account, the bank will add three dollars to your account balance during the course of a year.

But, there is another side to interest. When someone borrows money from a bank, the bank charges interest, and it charges borrowers a higher rate than it pays savers. For example, it might pay savers 3% and charge borrowers 8%. The difference, 8% minus 3%, goes to the bank. Charging interest on loans is one of the main ways for a bank to make money.

The rate of interest a bank charges borrowers largely depends on two things:

1. how many people want to borrow money, and

2. how much money banks have available to lend.

If a bank has plenty of money to lend and the demand to borrow money is not particularly strong, interest rates will tend to be low in order to attract customers. But when banks have a smaller amount of money to lend and the demand to borrow is fairly strong, interest rates will rise. As a depositor, you want interest rates to be high, but as a borrower, you want them to be low.

When it comes to paying interest on savings deposits, one bank usually pays much the same rate as another. The rate that one bank pays needs to be competitive with the rate that other banks pay, and it needs to be just high enough to attract deposits. If a bank is offering a much better (higher) rate than most other banks, try to find out why. And remember the old adage: If something sounds too good to be true, it probably is.

What happens when someone applies for a loan?

Your old car has carried you faithfully over many miles of highway, but last week your mechanic advised you not to spend any more money on it. The time has come to shop around for a new one.

But cars were a lot cheaper when you last bought one. This time you will have to borrow most of the money from a bank.

Your first step is to decide on a bank. You do not necessarily have to take out a loan from the bank where you have an account. In fact, you should around for a bank that offers the best deal, including the best (lowest) interest rate.

In addition to seeking out local banks you can also use the Internet if you have access. There is a wealth of resources available her that you can research from the comfort of your home or office.

You will not know if you can afford the loan, or if the bank will be willing to lend you the amount you are seeking, until after you complete the bank's loan application. In addition to routine personal information such as your name, address, telephone number, and social security number, a loan application also asks for information on how much money you earn, how long you have worked at your current job, and how much money you already owe on credit card bills and other debts.

♣ It's A Fact!! Basic Or No Frill Banking Accounts

Many institutions offer accounts (often referred to as basic or no frill accounts) that provide you with a limited set of services for a low price. Basic accounts give you a convenient way to pay bills and cash checks for less than you might pay without an account. They are usually checking accounts, but they may limit the number of checks you can write and the number of deposits and withdrawals you can make. Interest generally is not paid on basic accounts. Compare basic and regular checking accounts for the best deal in low fees or low minimum: balance requirements.

Source: Federal Reserve Board of Governors, 2000.

People in the bank's loan department then evaluate your application and try to decide if you are a "good risk." Before they lend you money, they want to be as certain as possible that you will be able to pay them back. Do you make enough money to keep up with your loan payments? Have you always paid your debts on time, or do you have a history of falling behind on your bills? To answer these questions, lenders rely heavily on credit bureaus and credit reports.

There are approximately 1200 local and regional credit bureaus in the United States. All are private companies (not government agencies), and

☞ Remember!!
Federal Deposit Insurance

In most cases, the insurer for commercial banks, savings banks, and savings and loan associations is the Federal Deposit Insurance Corporation (FDIC). The FDIC administers two insurance funds: the Bank Insurance Fund (BIF) and the Savings Association Insurance Fund (SAIF). Generally, though not always, BIF is the fund for commercial banks and state savings banks originally chartered as such. SAIF insures federal savings banks, some state savings banks, and most S&Ls.

Credit unions, meanwhile, are insured either by the National Credit Union Administration or through state-authorized programs.

Keep in mind that not all accounts offered by depository institutions are covered by federal deposit insurance. If you are unsure about the insurance arrangements at your institution, ask someone there to explain them to you.

Source: Excerpted from "Know Your Depository Institution," and reprinted with permission from the Federal Reserve Bank of Philadelphia, 1993, http://www.philadelphiafed.org,

most are linked by computer to three nationwide credit bureaus. They provide lenders with much of the information needed to evaluate loan applications.

When you apply for a loan, your bank contacts a credit bureau and asks for a copy of your credit report, which is basically a summary of your payment habits. Most credit reports contain information about loans, charge accounts, credit card accounts, bankruptcies, and court judgments that might require the potential borrower to pay a large sum of money as a settlement.

How the information gets into your credit report is no mystery. When you apply for a new charge account or credit card, clerks transfer information from your application to computer tapes that are forwarded to one or more of the nationwide credit bureaus. The information is updated every month. If you are late in paying your bills or if you miss a payment, the information goes into your credit report. Lenders then evaluate your report and try to decide if you are a "good risk."

After weighing all the information, your bank will either approve or deny your loan request. If your request is denied, the bank must notify you in writing within 30 days. The letter must state the reason for denying your loan. If your loan is approved, the bank will give you a check made out to your auto dealer. To protect itself in case you fail to repay the loan, your bank will hold the legal title (ownership papers) to your purchase until you pay off the loan.

Before you apply for a loan, you should request a copy of your credit report. If you have any questions beforehand, you may be able to address them before processing a loan application. Generally, you can do this rather quickly either over the Internet or by a telephone call for a very small fee.

Do banks keep large amounts of gold and silver in their vaults?

Banks rarely keep gold or silver in their vaults anymore. That is because our paper money is no longer backed by gold or silver, and our coins do not contain precious metal.

The U.S. government still holds millions of ounces of gold and silver, but citizens and foreign governments can no longer exchange their U.S. paper money for the precious metals. The government's gold and silver are considered valuable assets and precious metals rather than forms of money. Today's coins and paper money (currency) are backed by the "full faith and credit" of the United States government—the promise of the U.S. government.

Of course, coins and currency are not the only forms of money. You do not have to keep your money in the form of cash. Money held in a savings account or a checking account is still money; it just is not cash.

Contrary to popular belief, credit cards are not a form of money even though people often refer to them as "plastic money." Credit card users are actually taking out a loan, and sooner or later they will have to pay the bill for all those things they have charged. They are buying something now and agreeing to pay for it at a later date with money. Credit card finance charges, annual fees, and merchant fees have become an important source of income for banks.

Finally, there's another plastic card that resembles a credit card in appearance but is actually very different in function—the debit card. A debit card is more like an ATM card than a credit card. When someone uses a debit card at the gas pump or at a store, the amount of the purchase is electronically deducted from the user's bank balance. There is no monthly bill because the amount of each purchase is deducted almost immediately from the user's account. With this card, many merchants will offer you the opportunity to get cash back, too, when you pay for your purchase using your debit card.

Chapter 13

What Do Banks Do With My Money?

Banking Basics

A bank is a business. But unlike some businesses, banks do not manufacture products or extract natural resources from the earth. Banks sell services—financial services such as car loans, home mortgage loans, business loans, checking accounts, credit card services, certificates of deposit, and individual retirement accounts.

Some people go to banks in search of a safe place to keep their money. Others go to the bank seeking money for loans to buy houses and cars, start businesses, expand farms, or do other things that require borrowing money.

Where do banks get the money to lend? They get it from people who open accounts. Banks act as mediators between people who save and people who want to borrow. If savers do not put their money in banks, the banks have little or no money to lend. Your savings are combined with others' savings

About This Chapter: This chapter includes text excerpted from "Banking Basics," a publication of the Federal Reserve Bank of Boston, revised 1999. The complete text of this publication is available on the Federal Reserve Bank of Boston website, http://www.bos.frb.org. "Special Types Of Checks" is excerpted from "Checkbooklet," a financial education publication of the Federal Reserve Bank of Atlanta, 2001. To view the most current information, visit the Federal Reserve Bank of Atlanta website at http://www.frbatlanta.org, or the website of the Federal Reserve Board of Governors, http://www.federalreserve.gov.

to form a big pool of money. The bank uses that pool of money to make loans. The money does not belong to the bank's president, board of directors, or stockholders. It belongs to you and the other depositors. Because bankers are lending out others' money, they have a special obligation not to take uncalculated risks when they make loans.

How do people start banks?

The process of starting a bank varies from state to state, but here's a simple version of what it takes to start a bank in Massachusetts:

1. At least fifteen individuals get together and decide to start a bank.

2. They file an application with the Commonwealth's Board of Bank Incorporation (BBI), which consists of the Commissioner of Banks, the Commissioner of Revenue, and the Treasurer.

3. If the application is deemed complete, a hearing before the BBI is held.

4. The BBI, by law, must look closely at the financial condition and the character of the applicants as well as the capital structure for the proposed bank. In addition, the BBI will consider whether the public convenience and advantage will be promoted by the establishment of the new bank. The BBI will also look at the adequacy of the banks in the area to be served.

5. The BBI will then either grant a Certificate of Public Convenience and Advantage or deny the application.

6. The group that applied to start the bank will then have one year to raise necessary capital, secure a full management team, and obtain federal deposit insurance. The BBI currently requires at least $8 million in capital to start a bank.

7. The group will give notice to the BBI upon successfully raising the minimum capital. The BBI will review the list of proposed investors. If the BBI has no objection to such a list, if the bank is insured, and if an acceptable management team is in place, it will issue a Certificate to Transact Business and the bank may open for business.

How did banking begin?

No one knows who started the world's first bank, but it's safe to say that banking has its roots in the early trading civilizations of the Mediterranean. Without trade there would have been little need to establish banks, and without banks there would have been far less money to finance trading ventures.

Imagine for a moment that you are a merchant in ancient Greece or Phoenicia. You make your living by sailing to distant ports with boatloads of olive oil and spices. You don't grow the olives and spices yourself; you buy them from growers or other merchants. If all goes well, you will be paid for your cargo when you reach your destination, but before you set sail you must have money to outfit your ship.

> ☞ **Remember!!**
>
> Under federal law, you could lose all the money in your bank account and the unused portion of your line of credit established for overdrafts if you fail to report an unauthorized transfer or withdrawal within 60 days after your bank statement is mailed to you.
>
> Source: Excerpted from the "Consumer Action Handbook," a service provided by the Federal Citizen Information Center of the U.S. General Services Administration, 2004.

You find it by seeking out people who have money sitting idle. They agree to put up the money for your cargo and supplies in exchange for a share of you profits when you return from you voyage … if you return.

The people with the idle money are among the world's first lenders and you are among the world's first borrowers. You complain that they're demanding too large a share of your profits. They reply that your voyage is perilous and they run a risk of losing their entire investment. Lenders and borrowers have carried on this debate ever since.

Today, most people who want to borrow money go to banks rather than to wealthy individuals. But the basic concepts of borrowing and lending have not really changed. People do not let you have their money for nothing.

It is risky to lend money. The lender has no guarantee that he or she will get the money back, even if the borrower is an old friend. So why lend money?

♣ It's A Fact!!
The Federal Deposit
Insurance Corporation

Regardless of whether your money is in a savings or checking account, certificate of deposit, money market, IRA or Keogh account, the FDIC protects up to $100,000 of your funds.

The FDIC also is the federal bank regulator responsible for supervising certain savings banks and state-chartered banks that are not members of the Federal Reserve System. As a regulator, the FDIC strives to prevent bank failures by monitoring the industry's performance and enforcing regulations intended to make sure financial institutions operate in a safe and sound manner.

When a bank fails, the FDIC staff is on location at the failed institution, using money from the FDIC insurance fund to promptly reimburse insured depositors. Later, the FDIC staff will recover a portion of this money by selling the failed financial institution's loans and other assets.

Source: Excerpted from "What Is the FDIC?" Federal Deposit Insurance Corporation (FDIC), 2004

Why take the risk? Because lending presents an opportunity to make even more money. People will often take a financial risk if they believe there is a good chance of making more money.

For example, if a bank lends $50,000 to a borrower, the bank is not satisfied just to get its $50,000 back. In order to make a profit, the bank charges interest on the loan.

Interest is the price borrowers pay for using someone else's money. If a loan seems risky, the lender will charge more interest to offset the risk. (If you take a bigger chance, you want a bigger payoff.)

Of course, the opportunity to earn lots of interest will not mean much if a borrower fails to repay a loan. Because of this risk, banks often refuse to make loans that seem too risky. In deciding whether or not to give an individual a loan, they generally consider his or her credit rating or ability to pay their bills. They consider:

- how much and what types of credit you use, such as credit cards, auto loans, or other consumer loans;

- how long you have had and used credit; and

- how promptly you pay your bills.

Banks also use interest to attract savers. After all, people who have extra money do not have to put it in the bank. They have lots of choices:

1. They can bury it in the backyard or stuff it in a mattress. But if they do that, the money will just sit there. It will not increase in value. It will not earn interest.

2. They can buy land or invest in real estate. But real estate can tie up an investor's money because buildings and land can take a long time to sell if the market is weak. And there is always the risk the real estate will drop in value.

3. They can invest in the stock market. But if the stock market drops, investors can lose their money.

4. They can buy gold or invest in collectibles such as baseball cards, but gold and collectibles fluctuate in value. Who knows what the value will be when it is time to sell? (In 1980, gold sold for $800 an ounce. By 1983, the price had sunk below $400.)

✔ **Quick Tip**
To find out if your bank account is protected by the FDIC, go to www.fdic.gov. Credit union accounts have similar protection from the NCUA (The National Credit Union Association, www.ncua.gov).

Source: Excerpted from the "Consumer Action Handbook," a service provided by the Federal Citizen Information Center of the U.S. General Services Administration, 2004.

Or they can put their money in a bank. Not only will the money be safe, but it may also earn interest, depending on the type of account selected. Additionally, many types of bank accounts offer depositors the added advantage of being able to get at their money quickly.

Why do banks fail, and what happens when they do?

A bank is a business, and like other businesses, banks sometimes fail. But why should banks go out of business? Don't they have lots of money?

Sometimes banks fail because the people who run them make poor business decisions such as expanding too quickly or putting too much money into one type of loan.

Sometimes banks fall because of fraud. Maybe the president makes questionable loans to friends or hires unqualified relatives and pays them huge salaries.

Things like that happen, and they sometimes lead to bank failures. But in most cases, banks go out of business because changing economic conditions make it difficult or impossible for borrowers to repay their loans.

Do depositors lose their money when a bank fails?

The Federal Deposit Insurance Corporation (FDIC) has protected bank deposits since 1934. In all that time, no one has lost money in an FDIC-insured account.

Federal deposit insurance covers most types of deposits, including savings deposits, checking deposits, and certificates of deposit. The basic insured amount is $100,000 per depositor.

In the days before federal deposit insurance, the U.S. banking system was plagued by bank "runs" or "panics." At the slightest hint of trouble, depositors would run to the bank and line up to withdraw their money. All too often, only the first few people in line had any hope of ever seeing their money again; others lost everything. Even healthy banks sometimes failed after rumors caused depositors to panic and withdraw their money.

For many years, the public seemed willing to accept the tragic losses that resulted from bank failures. But then came the Great Depression of the 1930s. Hard times and financial pressures forced thousands of banks to close their doors forever. Financial losses ran into the hundreds of millions of dollars. The human suffering was impossible to calculate.

The wave of bank failures had shattered public confidence in the banking system, and Americans looked to the federal government for help. Congress responded by establishing the FDIC, which provided deposit insurance coverage of up to $2,500 per depositor. Public confidence rebounded, and bank failures declined from approximately 4,000 in 1933 to 62 in 1934.

Over the years, federal deposit insurance has helped to maintain public confidence in the U.S. banking system. Bank failures have not been eliminated, but long lines of panic stricken depositors have become an uncommon sight. When people are confident that their money is safe, they do not panic and rush to withdraw it.

Do depositors lose money if their bank is robbed?

No. Nearly all banks have private insurance that covers them if they are robbed. (It is not the same as federal deposit insurance.)

In addition, most banks take elaborate measures to safeguard the cash and other valuable items left in their care.

☞ **Remember!!**
Look For The
Sticker On The Door

You can tell if a bank or savings institution is insured because it must have a special sticker on its door that reads "FDIC: Federal Deposit Insurance Corporation. Each depositor insured to $100,000."

There is one important thing to remember about the FDIC. The FDIC does not protect banks and savings institutions from failing. These are businesses and their owners must make sure they are earning money. If they aren't earning money, they fail and go out of business. But if they fail, the FDIC is there to insure you and all of the other depositors.

Source: Excerpted from "What Is the FDIC?", Federal Deposit Insurance Corporation (FDIC), 2004.

Bank vaults have long been protected by reinforced concrete walls, time locks, and metal alloy doors that resist drilling and explosions.

At one time, armed security guards stood watch over banks, but today most banks seem to have decided (wisely) that they would rather not expose their customers and employees to gunplay. Shotguns and revolvers have been replaced largely by closed circuit television cameras that maintain a constant watch over everyone who enters or exits the bank.

Another fairly recent innovation is the exploding dye pack. In certain cases, bank employees are able to place a package of red dye in with the robber's stash of stolen cash. Later, when the crook opens the stash, the concealed dye pack explodes, covering the robber and the ill-gotten money with dye that will not wash off.

♣ It's A Fact!! Teens And Money Orders

Teens may, under most circumstances, purchase a money order at a U.S. Post Office. (The U.S. Postal Service has no restrictions for minors purchasing postal money orders; however the Clerk of a particular station can have particular policies concerning minors.) The Post Office charges 85 cents for a money order, payable only in cash.

Banks typically charge $2.00–$4.00 for a personal money order, although if you have an account, you can purchase the money order with a check that will debit your account. Convenience stores often charge less than $1.00 for a personal money order, and it is generally a cash-only purchase.

Remember with either type of money order, if the "payable to" line is left blank, the money order is like cash—someone can write in his or her own name and cash it.

—KRD

Special Types Of Checks

For most personal financial transactions, a check drawn on a personal checking account is acceptable. In certain situations, though, a special type of check that carries a greater guarantee of payment may be needed.

Certified Checks: Certified checks are usually used when called for by legal contract, such as real estate or automobile sale agreements. Certified checks are considered less risky than personal checks because the bank on which they are drawn has certified that the funds are available to the payee.

To certify a check, a bank takes the following steps:

- A bank officer or other authorized employee verifies the check writer's signature and determines that there is enough money in the checking account to pay the check.

- The authorized employee signs the check and certifies it by marking, stamping, or perforating it so that it will be less likely to be altered. By certifying the check, the bank guarantees payment and becomes liable for the amount certified, and the check writer no longer has access to the funds.

Cashier's Checks: A less expensive alternative to a certified check is a cashier's check, sometimes called a bank money order or a treasurer's check. A person who buys a cashier's check does not need to have a checking account. He or she merely goes to the bank, requests a cashier's check for a certain amount, and pays the bank that amount plus a service charge.

In some financial transactions, the payee may prefer a cashier's check to a personal check. A cashier's check has a better guarantee of payment because it is drawn by a bank against itself.

Personal And Postal Money Orders: For people who don't maintain a checking account or who prefer not to make payments with cash, money orders often serve the same function as personal checks.

Personal money orders, sometimes called register checks, can be purchased at banks and some retail stores. Personal money orders are usually issued in smaller amounts and are cheaper than cashier's checks. Often, only the amount is filled in at the time the money order is issued. Until the blanks are filled in for the payee's name, the date, and the purchaser's signature, the money order is as risky as cash to the buyer. For this reason, some banks require that the blank spaces be filled in when the money order is issued.

Postal money orders, issued by the U.S. Postal Service, are similar to those issued by banks, but there are some differences. A postal money order will not be paid if it has more than one endorsement, so it must be cashed or deposited by the payee.

There is no provision for stop-payment orders on postal money orders. If the money order is lost or stolen, though, the purchaser may file a form with the Postal Service, which will replace the money order if it has not been cashed within 60 days. If it has been cashed by someone other than the original payee, the purchaser can file an affidavit and receive a replacement.

Government Checks: Almost everyone has received a government check of one type or another, such as a tax refund. Federal government checks are usually drawn on the U.S. Treasury, and state or local government checks may be drawn on commercial banks or on the government treasury.

Sometimes people are surprised that a bank may be unwilling to cash a government check. A bank faces the risk that the person cashing the check may provide fraudulent identification, and it has no recourse to recover the funds.

Traveler's Checks: Traveler's checks are sold through banks and travel companies, usually in $20, $50, $100, and $500 denominations. The usual cost is the check's face value plus a small percentage. Widely accepted both in the United States and abroad, traveler's checks are nearly as convenient to use as cash.

The purchaser of traveler's checks signs them at the time of purchase and again when they are cashed. This practice protects both the user and the cashing party. Lost or stolen traveler's checks will be replaced by the issuing company.

Chapter 14

How To Choose A Bank

Shopping for a Bank

In the 1950s and 1960s, banks used to give away toasters to new depositors. Choosing a bank was easy. You went to the one that gave away the best toaster.

Banks generally do not give away toasters anymore, and choosing a bank is a little more complicated than it used to be. For starters you should shop around to find out which banks offer the most competitive services. Some banks charge a monthly fee if your account falls below a certain level, and that fee can be higher than the interest your account earns. Other banks may charge a fee for every transaction you make, especially withdrawals of any sort. You do not want that.

In certain states, the law prohibits banks from charging fees on savings accounts held by people under the age of 18 or over the age of 65. Find out if your state has such a law.

About This Chapter: This chapter begins with "Shopping for a Bank," excerpted from "Banking Basics," a publication of the Federal Reserve Bank of Boston, revised 1999. The complete text of this publication is available on the Federal Reserve Bank of Boston website, http://www.bos.frb.org. "Your First Account" is a summary of information provided by the editor. "Your Rights And Responsibilities" is from "Correcting Bank Account Errors," a consumer information document provided by the Federal Deposit Insurance Corporation (FDIC), August 22, 2003.

Before you open an account, ask a few people if they are happy with their bank. All banks are not the same. You have to do some comparison shopping before you open an account.

Is It Difficult To Open An Account?

You have finally decided to take the plunge. With your cash tucked deep in your pocket, you walk into the bank and ask to open a savings account.

The bank's receptionist directs you to a desk where a customer service representative will help you with the paperwork. To your surprise, the only form you need to fill out is a signature card, which requires you to sign your name and then print your name, ad-

✔ **Quick Tip**

Other things you might want to consider:

1. Does your bank pay its depositors a competitive interest rate?

2. Is the bank in a convenient location and are its business hours convenient for you?

3. Is your deposit insured by the FDIC (Federal Deposit Insurance Corporation)?

4. Is the bank a good corporate citizen? Does it invest in your neighborhood?

5. And last, but certainly not least, does your bank provide courteous and efficient services?

Source: Federal Reserve Bank of Boston, 1999

dress, telephone number, date of birth, social security number, and your mother's maiden name (as a means of further identification). After you complete the signature card, you receive a bank book (sometimes called a passbook) that lists your account balance (the total amount of money in your account).

Whenever you make a deposit (put money in) or a withdrawal (take money out), the transaction should be recorded in your bank book. It is especially important for you to keep track of your transactions in your bank book.

You do not need lots of money to start a savings account. Some banks let you open one with as little as twenty dollars. Nor do you need to wait until you are eighteen. In most cases, you can open a savings account as soon as you are old enough to sign your name, or even earlier than that if you open the account with a parent or guardian.

Your First Account

Some banks (and many credit unions) offer special accounts for youth under the age of 18. Often, the account documentation must be co-signed by a parent or guardian. Features of youth accounts often include incentives such as gifts or scholarship contests, reduced fees, very low minimum balances, and, of course, an opportunity to "learn the ropes" at an early age. After a few months, some youth checking accounts offer ATM and debit cards. Most youth savings accounts require co-signers for withdrawals.

Call your local bank or credit union to see if they offer accounts for young people. You can compare checking and savings accounts by ZIP code or city by visiting Bankrate.com (www.bankrate.com). Go to the Credit Union National Association website (www.cuna.org) to find local credit unions that you might be eligible to join.

As with any type of financial service, avoid accounts with fees, service charges, or minimum balance requirements that will eat up deposits.

☞ **Remember!!**
Comparing Banks

With the Internet, you can now compare local bank services and credit offers with those from financial institutions around the nation.

- www.bankrate.com provides up-to-date interest rate reports on mortgages, auto loans, credit cards, home equity loans, savings and other banking products.

- www.gomez.com rates banks, credit cards, investment brokers, insurance, mortgages, real estate brokers in the U.S. and Canada.

Source: Excerpted from the "Consumer Action Handbook," a service provided by the Federal Citizen Information Center of the U.S. General Services Administration, 2004.

Your Rights And Responsibilities

It is important to check your credit account and bank account statements regularly. The Fair Credit Billing Act and Electronic Fund Transfers Act establish procedures for resolving mistakes on credit account and bank account statements.

When many customers find a mistake on their bill, they pick up the telephone and call the company to correct the problem. You may do this if you wish, but telephoning does not trigger the legal safeguards under the Fair Credit Billing Act. To be protected under the law, you must send a separate written billing error notice to the creditor. Your notice must reach the creditor within 60 days after the first bill containing the error was mailed to you. The written notice must be sent to the address provided on the bill for billing error notices (and not, for example, directly to the store, unless the bill says that is

✔ **Quick Tip**
When choosing a savings or checking account, you will want to:

• consider the rate of interest the account will earn (if any)

• look for a checking account that has a low (or no) minimum balance requirement that you can, and do, meet.

To compare checking accounts, request a list of fees that are charged on each. Some institutions will drop or lower checking fees if you have paychecks directly deposited by your employer. Direct deposit offers the additional advantages of convenience, security, and immediate access to your money.

Source: "Consumer Action Handbook," 2004 edition, a service provided by the Federal Citizen Information Center of the U.S. General Services Administration.

where it should be sent). In your letter, you must include the following information:

- Your name and account number;

- A statement that you believe the bill contains a billing error and the dollar amount involved, and;

- The reason you believe there is a mistake.

The Fair Credit Billing Act generally applies to "open end" credit accounts, such as credit cards or revolving charge accounts (such as department store accounts). The Electronic Fund Transfers Act applies to electronic fund transfers transactions involving automated teller machines (ATMs), debit cards, other point-of-sale debit transactions, and other electronic banking transactions that can result in the withdrawal of cash from your bank account.

Under the EFTA, if there is a mistake or unauthorized withdrawal from your bank account through the use of a debit card, you must notify your financial institution of the problem or error within 60 days after the statement containing the problem or error was sent. For retail purchases, your financial institution has up to 20 business days to investigate after receiving notice of the error.

You must notify your institution immediately upon learning that your debit card or credit card has been misplaced or lost. If you do not report the loss within two business days after you realize the card is missing, and if someone uses the card without your permission, you may lose from $50 to $500. If you do not report an unauthorized transfer or withdrawal within 60 days after your statement is sent to you, you risk unlimited loss.

Chapter 15

How To Open And Use
Your Checking Account

Introduction To Checking Accounts

There are many different types of checking accounts—all with various benefits and rules attached. Some are perfect for paying bills and expenses. Some pay interest, some do not. Some give you an unlimited number of checks while others charge you for each check you write. Some require that you maintain a minimum balance each month.

The key to smart banking is to find the checking account that works for you. Start by answering the following three questions:

1. For what purposes will you use a checking account?

2. How much money will you be able to keep in your account each month?

3. How often are you going to write checks?

About This Chapter: This chapter includes "Introduction to Checking Account" and "Which Type of Account Is Best for You?," both reprinted with permission from The Consumer Debit Resource site, http://www.consumerdebit.com © 2004 eFunds Corporation. All rights reserved. "What Are Checks And How Do They Work?" is from "Banking Basics," a publication of the Federal Reserve Bank of Boston, revised 1999. The complete text of this publication is available on the Federal Reserve Bank of Boston website, http://www.bos.frb.org; "Checking Accounts Have Changed" is excerpted from "What You Should Know about Your Checks," produced by the Federal Reserve Board of Governors, February 16, 2005.

Your answers will help you select the right checking account. In addition, you will need to compare financial institutions to understand what products and services they offer. It'll take a little effort, but by doing your homework, you'll be well on your way to getting a checking account that's ideally suited to your needs.

Which Type Of Account Is Best For You?

Basic Checking: Basic checking accounts let you deposit and withdraw money and write checks to pay bills and daily expenses. They are perfect if you don't plan to keep a high account balance.

The details of basic checking accounts are different for each financial institution. Before opening an account get the answers to the following questions. Does the financial institution:

✎ What's It Mean?

Automated Teller Machine (ATM): Also known as the money machine or cash machine.

Bad Check: A check that is written when there is not enough money in the account. Also known as a bounced check.

Balance: The amount of money you have in your account.

Cash: Money in the form of bills or coins.

Check Register: A form to keep track of your checking account transactions.

Check: A document used for payment.

Cleared Check: A check that has gone through the financial institution's processing center and is listed on your monthly statement.

Deposit Ticket: The form you use to put money into your account.

Endorse: To sign your name on the back of a check in order to cash it or deposit it.

Memo: The area on a check that notes what the check was written to pay for.

- Pay interest on a basic checking account? (Note: Most basic checking accounts do not pay interest.)

- Require direct deposit or a minimum balance?

- Charge a monthly fee for services?

- Charge a fee for each check you write over a certain limit?

"Free Checking": "Free Checking" accounts typically require you to maintain a minimum balance in your account, but certain fees, like ATM and per-check fees, are eliminated. This reduced fee structure can be an attractive checking alternative for some people. However, it is important that you maintain the minimum balance or your account will no longer be "free" and you will be charged fees.

Outstanding Check: A check that is still going through financial institution processing.

Overdraft: When your account goes below zero-there is not enough money to cover the withdrawal.

Reconcile: A process to make sure your checkbook balance matches your financial institution's balance for your account.

Statement: The papers you get every month from your financial institution that list all of the activities in your account for the month.

Transaction: When money goes into, or out of, your account. Can include deposits, withdrawals, payments, fees, ATM transactions or transfers.

Void: This means that a check is not good or not usable. You would write "VOID" across a check that has a mistake written on it, tear it up, and throw it away.

Withdrawal: When you take money out of your account. This can be by check, ATM, automatic payment or other methods.

Source: Excerpted from "Glossary of Checking Terms," and reprinted with permission from The Consumer Debit Resource site, http://www.consumerdebit.com. © 2004 eFunds Corporation. All rights reserved.

Interest-Bearing Accounts: An interest-bearing checking account pays interest on the money you have in your account. However, most banks require:

- More money to open an interest-bearing account than other accounts.

- A high minimum balance in the account or you will be charged fees.

Interest is paid monthly, at the end of your statement cycle. The higher your balance, the more interest the bank pays. Be aware, however, the fees for falling below the minimum balance may be more than any interest you might earn.

NOW Accounts: A NOW account (Negotiable Order of Withdrawal) is a "Free Checking" and an interest-bearing account offered by a savings and loan or "thrift" institution. Typically the minimum balance on a NOW account exceeds that of a "Free Checking" account and if your balance falls below the minimum, you could pay a high fee. However, if you maintain the minimum balance, you can earn interest income every year.

Super NOW Accounts: A Super NOW Account has a higher interest rate and a higher minimum balance than the NOW Account.

Express Checking: Express checking accounts are designed for people who are on the move and who don't go inside the bank often. These people prefer to bank by ATM, telephone, or computer. Because you don't spend much time working with bank employees, express accounts usually offer the following features:

- Unlimited check writing

- Low minimum balance requirements

- Low or no monthly fees

Note: There is a catch. When you do visit a bank branch, you can expect to pay a fee to talk to a teller on either a per-visit or a monthly basis.

Lifeline Checking: Lifeline checking accounts are meant for low-income bank customers. Lifeline accounts have low:

- Minimum deposit and balance requirements.

- Monthly fees, ranging from zero to $3 depending on the bank.

- Limits on the number of checks per month that you can write.

Certain states have laws requiring banks to offer lifeline accounts. In these states, laws set the rules for Lifeline accounts.

"No-Frills" Checking: Many banks offer special checking deals if you are age 55 or over or if you are a student. The following are some of the benefits that may be included:

- Free personal checks

- Free cashiers or traveler's checks

- Wider ATM use

- Better rates on loans and credit cards

- Discounts on a variety of items including travel or prescriptions

Credit Union Share Drafts: Most credit unions offer checking accounts, called Share Drafts, often with no service charges or reduced fees.

Advanced Types Of Checking Accounts

Money Market: If you can afford to maintain a high account balance and do *not* plan to write more than three to five checks each month, a money market account is a great way to put your money to work for you.

Money market accounts normally put your money in short-term investments such as commercial paper, Certificates of Deposit, or Treasury bills. These accounts combine checking with savings or investment opportunities. They require a high minimum deposit to open. This is usually between $1,000 and $10,000. You must also keep a higher balance to avoid fees. In addition, most banks set strict limits on the number of checks you can write.

On the up side, a money market account can pay more than double the interest rate of a basic checking or savings accounts. Actual interest rates will vary based on the current market conditions. (Note: Don't confuse a money market account with a money market fund. They are very different. Money market accounts offered by banks are insured by the FDIC and are not charged the normal management fee that funds incur.)

Asset Management Accounts: Asset management accounts are a type of checking account offered by many brokerage houses and banks. They offer the convenience of one account to take care of all your banking and investments.

Asset management accounts normally provide unlimited check-writing privileges and a comprehensive end-of-year statement that documents all of your transactions. However, many financial institutions require a higher minimum balance to open an asset management account and charge an annual fee.

> ✔ **Quick Tip**
> Visit www.consumerdebit.com and click on "Checkbook Basics" to get interactive training for how to write a check, use a check register, deposit money in your account, review your statement, and balance your account.
>
> —KRD

What Are Checks And How Do They Work?

Checks have become a safe and convenient method of paying for things or transferring money. But what exactly is a check?

In simple terms, a check is a written set of instructions to your bank. When you write a check, you are instructing your bank to transfer a specific amount of money from your checking account to another person or an organization. You can even write a check just to convert some of the money on deposit in your checking account into cash.

When you fill in the blank spaces on one of your checks, you are telling your bank how much of your money you want to transfer, when you want to transfer it, and to whom you want it to go. You authorize the transfer by signing the bottom of the check.

One reason why checks are so popular is that people can use a canceled check [or a bank-supplied substitute check] to prove they have paid a bill. In most cases, a canceled check is as good as a receipt because it bears the endorsements of all the persons, banks, companies, or other organizations that have handled it. For example, if the landlord claims you did not pay your rent, all you need to do is find your canceled check and point out that it was endorsed by your landlord and your landlord's bank.

If you lose your checkbook: All you do in that case is close your checking account and open a new one. After that, your lost or stolen checks are worthless to anyone who might try to use them.

Checking Accounts Have Changed

Checks are being processed more quickly these days. Faster processing means that when you write a check, the money may be deducted from your account sooner. Be sure you have enough money in your account at the time you write a check.

The items listed on your checking account statement may look different from one another. Some items may be listed by check number, and others may be listed by the name of the company you paid. Always review all of the charges listed on your account statement to make sure they match your receipts or records.

Some banks do not return checks at all. Consumers who need a canceled check to prove that they made a payment can ask for copies of their checks. Some banks charge a fee for these copies.

If you have questions about your checking account or how your checks are processed, contact your bank, savings and loan, or credit union.

Chapter 16

Understanding How Your Checking Account Works

New Rules, New Strategies

Changes to the way banks manage checks make it more important than ever to actively manage your checking account to avoid costly mistakes. This is not your father's checking account.

How often do you visit or have some contact with your bank? Chances are you'd say it's only once in a while and certainly not every day. But if you think about it, you probably do have dealings with your bank almost every day through your checking account.

Consider how often you write checks, make deposits (including direct deposits), use your ATM or debit card or make automated payments from your checking account, and you'll be reminded about how much you depend on these services from your bank. According to the Federal Reserve System,

About This Chapter: "New Rules, New Strategies" and "Using A Checking Account: What To Know" are excerpted from "Checks and Balances: New Rules, New Strategies for Bank Customers in the 21st Century," *FDIC Consumer News*, Summer 2004, an online publication of the Federal Deposit Insurance Corporation; and "Check 21: What the New World of Substitute Checks Means to You," *Financial Connection*, April/May 2004, an online publication of Financial Management Service, U.S. Department of the Treasury. Table 16.1 is reprinted from *Consumer Reports*, August 2004; a complete citation accompanies the table.

Americans write about 40 billion checks a year. In addition, electronic payments from checking accounts—using a debit card (to deduct payments directly from your bank account), online banking (to pay bills, move money or conduct other transactions using your computer), or other automated services—already outnumber paper checks as a payment of choice.

And while consumers access their checking accounts all the time, people often have questions or concerns about their checking accounts, including how to resolve errors, avoid bouncing checks, keep fees low and protect against fraud.

Table 16.1. Your Rights Will Depend On How You Pay

Different forms of payment are governed by different federal and state laws and by industry practices. Below are listed various methods of payment and the protections that are associated with each.

Payment type	Protections
Credit card	Discover, MasterCard, and Visa policy: $0 liability for unauthorized charges, subject to some limitations. Legal rights: $50 maximum liability for fraudulent charges; right to dispute charges for merchandise not delivered as agreed; right to get clerical and other billing errors fixed.
Debit card with Visa or MasterCard logo (with either pin or signature)	MasterCard and Visa policy: $0 liability for unauthorized debits, subject to some limitations. Legal rights: Same as for debit card, below.
Debit card without	$50 maximum liability for unauthorized debits

Especially important: More changes will be coming as a result of "Check 21," short for the Check Clearing for the 21st Century Act. This law, which took effect in October, 2004, allows financial institutions to process "substitute checks," high-quality paper reproductions of both sides of original checks. Each substitute check will be created from an electronic image of an original paper check. This will make check processing faster, and that has real implications for check writers and check depositors. Example: If you currently get your original canceled checks back with your monthly statement, in the future you may get substitute checks instead.

Visa or MasterCard logo (with pin only)	reported within 48 hours of discovery; $500 liability limit if you notify bank more than 2 business days after discovering the card lost or stolen; no limit if you give such notice more than 60 days after postmark on an account statement containing unauthorized debits; legal right to get unauthorized or erroneous debits re-credited to your account within 10 days if issue is not resolved immediately.
Check	Errors covered by state law. With substitute check, right to get erroneous amounts and double-debits fixed; if such errors can't be resolved immediately, right to get first $2,500 of disputed amount and unauthorized debits re-credited to your account within 10 days, remainder within 45 days; serves as legal proof of payment. Check images usually voluntarily accepted as proof of payment.

The New World Of Substitute Checks

A substitute check is a paper reproduction of the original, and must meet specific standards including an image of the front and back of the original; a statement that the check can be used in the same way as the original; and an MICR line containing all the information on the original check's MICR line. [Note: The MICR line is the magnetic ink character recognition Line, the string of digits at the bottom of the front of a paper check that provides bank, account, and check number identifiers. It is printed with a special character font in magnetic ink.]

A substitute check is legally enforceable, just like the original check.

Checks: Declining, But Still King

While more and more business is transacted electronically, the number of checks processed in the United States remains staggering.

While some speculate that financial institutions will pursue electronic image exchange even more aggressively in the future, Check 21 does not require that they do so. It does require that all financial institutions accept substitute checks for presentment. Financial institutions also may agree to accept electronic check presentments without the substitute checks.

Using A Checking Account: What To Know

Given these changes, it's important to know what to look for—and what to look out for—when choosing and using a checking account.

1. It's more important than ever to avoid bouncing checks.

A check deposited in a bank generally travels by airplane and truck until it reaches the paying bank, typically about one or two days later. As a result of Check 21, more checks will be processed electronically—and faster. That means you need to have enough money in your account when you write a check or run the risk of having checks bounce. While it's always good advice to have enough money in your account before you write a check, of course people don't always do that—they'll write a check on the 28th of the month expecting their paycheck to be deposited on the 30th of the month, just in time to cover that check. Now that strategy will not work. And a bounced check can be costly, with fees typically in the range of $30 per check.

What can you do to avoid bounced checks? The first step is to keep your checkbook up to date. Be sure to deduct ATM withdrawals, bank fees, and debit card purchases. Compare your checkbook with your monthly statement. Do not rely on your ATM receipt for balance information because it may not reflect outstanding checks or debit card transactions.

Also, carefully consider the pros and cons of signing up for an overdraft line of credit, which means the bank will automatically cover checks you write (up to an agreed amount) even if you don't have enough funds in the account. You should be aware that some banks, at their discretion and usually for a fee, may pay overdrafts under certain conditions even if the customer hasn't signed up for a particular program. Overdraft services—and their costs—can vary significantly from bank to bank. This service is essentially a loan, so there can be interest charges or other fees. Also, if you do not pay the overdraft and the bank closes the account, you most likely will have difficulty opening a bank account elsewhere.

♣ It's A Fact!! Why Check Users Prefer Checks

There appear to be four basic reasons why some people stick with checks instead of switching to direct deposit: inertia or lack of motivation to switch; the need for more information about the benefits of electronic transfers; a strong emotional preference for checks; and mechanical reasons—the lack of a bank account in which to receive electronic transfers, for example. Checks give recipients a sense of control. Check users appear to like the "tangibility" of checks.

—Marshall Kofler

From a study by Wirthlin Worldwide as reported in, "Treasury Department Brings New Focus to Boosting Direct Deposit," by Marshall Kofler, *Financial Connection*, the online publication of Financial Management Service, United States Department of the Treasury, April/May 2004.

The potential for faster check processing has other implications for check writers. One is that you may have less time to place a "stop payment" on a check you've written.

2. Expect to get substitute checks from your bank as proof of payment instead of original canceled checks.

For many years, banking institutions have "truncated" checks for some customers. This means the institutions do not return canceled checks in monthly statements. Instead, they keep original checks for a short period and send statements showing images of canceled checks. Or, some banks only list check transactions on monthly statements and don't routinely send canceled checks or images. Now, original checks will be returned with statements in even fewer instances.

As before, if you write a check to someone who is not an account holder at your bank, your original check will be deposited at another institution. The check then travels to your bank for payment. But now the bank where the check is deposited has two choices. Option one is to return the original check to your bank, as was done in the past. The second option is to create an electronic image of the check, produce a substitute check and send it to your bank. This second option means your original canceled check is no longer available to you.

What if you must prove a disputed payment and your bank has given you a substitute canceled check, not your original canceled check? As long as the substitute check meets Check 21's standards, legally it would serve as proof of payment. And if a bank's substitute check falls short of those standards, the law provides warranties and remedies to protect parties to the transaction. Banks have been providing images of checks for decades to millions of customers who do not receive original checks. These images often are accepted as proof of payment by the IRS, courts, and other parties, provided they meet certain requirements.

3. Protect against check fraud, which is getting increasingly sophisticated.

Bank security procedures cannot stop all frauds, which may involve printing or altering checks or obtaining account numbers used to arrange for "payments" from accounts. You can help by promptly reviewing your bank statement each month and immediately reporting any unauthorized transactions. Or, better yet, monitor your account more regularly online or through telephone banking programs at your bank. Timely notification of a problem can limit your potential liability, stop a fraud, or assist in an investigation.

Also protect your account information. For example, only give your checking account number, including the routing numbers at the bottom of your check, to businesses you know are reputable. Never provide checking or credit card information, Social Security numbers, or other personal information in response to an unsolicited call or e-mail, which could be fraudulent.

☞ Remember!!
How can you protect
yourself against check fraud?

- Don't give your checking account number to people you don't know, even if they claim they are from your bank.

- Reveal checking account information only to businesses you know to be reputable.

- Report lost or stolen checks immediately.

- Properly store or dispose of canceled checks, and guard new checks.

- Report any inquiries or suspicious behavior to your banker who will take measures to protect your account and notify proper authorities.

- Do not leave your automated teller machine receipt at the ATM; it contains account information.

- Check your bank statements carefully and often.

- Use direct deposit.

Source: Excerpted from "Frequently Asked Questions," United States Secret Service, 2002.

Be wary of offers to send money—perhaps to buy something you're selling or forward lottery winnings you've supposedly won—and you're asked to accept a cashier's check for more than the amount due and wire the "excess" money back. The cashier's check often will be counterfeit and you will be responsible for the money you wired to the con artist.

Take safety precautions with your checks, too. Don't carry more checks than you expect to use, keep extra checks in a secure place, and contact your bank immediately if any of your checks are lost or stolen.

Consider direct deposit of your paycheck and other checks you may receive, such as Social Security payments, as a way to prevent them from being lost, misplaced or stolen out of mailboxes. Some banks will reduce their checking account fees if you use direct deposit."

4. Periodically ask yourself, and your bank, if you're getting the best deal.

If you think all checking accounts are pretty much alike, think again.

Your bank probably has several types of checking accounts with different features, fees, yields, minimum amounts to open an account, and other characteristics tailored to certain kinds of customers. And different banks offer different checking products. Checking accounts from the bank down the street or even on the Internet may be more to your liking.

How can you take advantage of this freedom of choice? First, ask yourself, "How many checks do I write each month?" "Do I plan to pay most of my bills without checks, perhaps by phone or over the Internet?" "Do I use an ATM or a debit card regularly?" "How much of a balance do I plan to routinely keep in the account?"

Perform this kind of review every year or two. Perhaps you'll discover that your existing checking account is still right for you or that switching to a different account (at your bank or elsewhere) could save you money or bring you a better value.

Chapter 17

Debit Cards And Automated Teller Machines (ATMs)

Automated Teller Machines (ATM) are bank machines that offer round-the-clock access to a bank account. With an ATM card and a personal identification number (PIN), cash can be withdrawn, money can be deposited or transferred, and even bills can be paid, depending on the machine.

Debit cards have also steadily gained in popularity over the last several years. They look the same as credit cards, but they provide instant access to checking and/or savings accounts. There are two kinds of debit cards: online and offline. Online debit cards use a PIN to make debit card transaction. The money is instantly subtracted from an account. With offline debit cards a transaction is completed when a slip of paper is signed. The money will take one (1) to three (3) days to be subtracted.

About This Chapter: This chapter beings with text excerpted from "ATM/Debit Card," © 2002 Illinois Division of Banks and Real Estate. (Neither the State of Illinois, nor any of its agencies, is liable for any improper or incorrect use of the information contained herein and assumes no responsibility for anyone's use of the information.) This chapter also includes text from *Debit Cards: Beyond Cash and Checks*, © 2005 National Consumers League. All rights reserved. For additional information, visit http://www.nclnet.org. Reprinted with permission. "Limiting Your Losses If Your Cards Are Lost Or Stolen," is excerpted from "Credit, ATM and Debit Cards: What to Do If They're Lost or Stolen," Federal Trade Commission, June 2002. "Review: A Primer on Debit and ATM Cards" is from *Practical Money Skills for Life*, a financial literacy education program from Visa, http://www.practicalmoneyskills.com © Visa U.S.A. All rights reserved. Reprinted with permission.

In most cases, an ATM card and a debit card are offered in one card by the financial institution.

When it comes to safety, common sense is key when using a debit or ATM card. If your card is lost or stolen, the most important thing to remember is to report it immediately. Cards should not be left unattended. Do not tell anyone your PIN. Do not use ATMs that are poorly lit late at night, and always be observant of your surroundings before beginning your transactions.

Debit Cards: Beyond Cash And Checks

Debit cards are also known as check cards. Debit cards look like credit cards or ATM (automated teller machine) cards,

> ### ☞ Remember!!
>
> Advantages to using an ATM/Debit card:
>
> • Easily obtained
>
> • Easy to use
>
> • No need to carry a checkbook
>
> • Debit cards are more readily accepted than checks
>
> • Can be used anywhere credit cards are accepted
>
> • ATM machines are available 24 hours a day, seven days a week
>
> Disadvantages to using an ATM/Debit card:
>
> • Unlike credit cards, immediately after a transaction money is taken out of an account: no grace period
>
> • Numerous receipts makes recordkeeping more difficult
>
> • Debit cards have limited protection once the transaction occurs
>
> • Fees for using ATMs owned by other financial institutions
>
> Source: © 2002 Illinois Division of Banks and Real Estate.

but operate like cash or a personal check. Debit cards are different from credit cards. While a credit card is a way to "pay later," a debit card is a way to "pay now." When you use a debit card, your money is quickly deducted from your checking or savings account.

Debit cards are accepted at many locations, including grocery stores, retails stores, gasoline stations, and restaurants. You can use your card anywhere merchants display your card's brand name or logo, even on the Internet. They offer an alternative to carrying a checkbook or cash.

Do You Have A Debit Card?

You may not realize that you have a debit card. Many banks are replacing their standard ATM cards with upgraded ATM cards that have a debit feature. You may also receive in the mail what looks like a credit card when in fact it is a debit card.

What Is The Difference Between A Debit Card And A Credit Card?

It's the difference between "debit" and "credit." Debit means "subtract." When you use a debit card, you are subtracting your money from your own bank account. Debit cards allow you to spend only what is in your bank account. It is a quick transaction between the merchant and your personal bank account.

Credit is money made available to you by the bank or other financial institution, like a loan. The amount the issuer allows you to use is determined by your credit history, income, debts, and ability to pay. You may use the credit with the understanding that you must repay the charges, plus interest, if you do not pay the account in full each month. You will receive a monthly statement detailing your charges and payment requirements.

Two Ways Debit Cards Work

- **With a PIN:** You provide your personal identification number, or PIN, at the time of sale.

- **Without a PIN, or PIN-less:** You sign a receipt for the purchase, as you would with a credit card.

Some debit cards are designed to work only with a PIN, others can be used with either a PIN or a signature. PIN-only debit cards offer greater security because it's more difficult for unauthorized people to use them. Cards that can work both in the PIN and PIN-less methods offer more flexibility, especially when dealing with merchants who do not have the equipment needed to process PIN transactions.

In either case, the funds are automatically deducted from your account within a short time.

What You Should Know About Debit Cards

- Obtaining a debit card is often easier than obtaining a credit card.

- Using a debit card instead of writing checks saves you from showing identification or giving out personal information at the time of the transaction.

- Using a debit card frees you from carrying cash or a checkbook.

- Using a debit card means you may no longer have to stock up on traveler's checks or cash when you travel.

- Debit cards may be more readily accepted by merchants than checks, even when you travel.

- The debit card is a quick, "pay now" product, giving you no grace period.

- As with credit cards, you may dispute unauthorized charges or other mistakes within 60 days. You should contact the card issuer if a problem cannot be resolved with the merchant. However, using a debit card may mean you have less protection than with credit card purchase for items which are never delivered, are defective, or were misrepresented.

- Returning goods or canceling services purchased with a debit card is treated as if the purchases were made with cash or a check.

Be Aware

If your debit card works with either a PIN or a signature and the store accepts both, you choose which way to use it at the point of sale.

If you choose "debit" on the merchant's terminal and "swipe" your card through, you will be asked for your PIN. If you choose "credit" on the terminal and swipe your card through, you will be asked to sign a receipt. "Credit" does not mean that you will be billed, as with a credit card. The money will be debited from your account automatically.

What You Should Know Before You Use a Debit Card

1. Know if it is a credit card or a debit card. Also, decide whether you want a PIN-only debit card or one that can be used with either a PIN or a signature. Ask the card issuer about your options.

2. Know if there are fees applied to using the card. Some financial institutions charge a monthly fee or a per-transaction fee, others do not. These fees are set by the card issuer and must be disclosed to consumers.

3. Know about your liability for the unauthorized use, theft, or loss of your debit card. Ask if the issuer has any special liability policies and how they work.

✔ Quick Tip
Seven Tips for Using Debit Cards Responsibly

1. If your card is lost or stolen, report the loss immediately to your financial institution.

2. If you suspect your card is being fraudulently used, report this immediately to your financial institution.

3. Take your receipts. Don't leave them for others to see. Your account number may be all someone needs to order merchandise through the mail or over the phone at your expense, especially if the card can be used without a PIN.

4. If you have a PIN, memorize it. Do not keep your PIN with your card. Also, don't choose a PIN that a smart thief could figure out, such as your phone number or birthday.

5. Never give your PIN to anyone. Keep your PIN private.

6. Always know how much money you have available in your account. Don't forget to consider money that you have set aside to cover a check that has not yet cleared your bank.

7. Deduct debits and any transaction fees from the balance in your check register immediately. Keep the receipts in one place in case you need them later.

4. Know how problems with nondelivery, defective merchandise or misrepresentation will be handled. This is especially important when you use a debit card to purchase goods or services for future delivery, rather than on a "cash and carry" basis. Ask the issuer about its policies for these types of disputes.

What If My Card Is Lost Or Stolen?

In the event that your card is lost or stolen, you need to know the extent of your protection. Government regulations require debit card issuers to set a maximum liability of $50 if the debit card is reported lost or stolen within two days of discovery. Liability increases to $500 if the lost or stolen debit card is reported within 60 days. Neglect to notify the bank of the theft within 60 days after a bank statement is sent, and you could lose everything in your checking and overdraft accounts.

☞ Remember!!

With a debit card and personal identification number (PIN), you can use an Automated Teller Machine (ATM), to withdraw cash, make deposits, or transfer funds between accounts. Some ATMs charge a fee if you are not a member of the ATM network or are making a transaction at a remote location. ATMs must disclose the fee on the terminal screen or on a sign next to the screen.

Retail purchases can also be made with a debit card. During the transaction you will have to enter your PIN or sign for the purchase. Although a debit card looks like a credit card, the money for the purchase is transferred immediately from your bank account to the store's account. The purchase will be shown on your bank account statement.

When you use a debit card, federal law does not give you the right to stop payment. You must resolve the problem with the seller.

Source: Excerpted from "Consumer Action Handbook," 2004 edition, a service provided by the Federal Citizen Information Center (FCIC) of the U.S. General Services Administration.

Check with your financial institution about your liability. Many debit card issuers offer consumers better protection than the government regulations require. Some even offer consumers "zero liability" in cases of fraud, theft, or other unauthorized card use if the cardholder reports the problem within a certain time.

If a problem arises, remember that it is your money that is at stake.

- Under government regulations, financial institutions may have up to 20 days to provide provisional credit to consumers for losses due to debit card theft or unauthorized use of the card.

- In cases where a cardholder's debit card has been used fraudulently, some issuers promise even faster provisional credit for lost funds, in as few as five business days after notification.

- You may not know that your debit card or its number has been stolen until checks you have written have bounced. Be aware that the issuer is not required to waive bounced check charges or cover any fees that may be imposed by the recipients of checks that unintentionally bounced because a debit card was stolen. Many banks do, however, refund these fees as a measure of good customer service.

Debit cards offer the consumer many conveniences. They are more readily accepted by merchants than checks, especially when you are out of your own state or in other countries. You are not required to provide identification or give personal information when using a debit card. This makes the transaction quicker and allows you to keep personal information to yourself.

However, because the money spent using a debit card comes directly from your bank account, you need to be careful in order to prevent fraudulent use of your card number.

Limiting Your Losses If Your Cards Are Lost Or Stolen

Report the loss or theft of your ATM or debit cards to the card issuers as quickly as possible. Many companies have toll-free numbers and 24-hour service to deal with such emergencies. It's a good idea to follow up your phone calls with a letter. Include your account number, when you noticed your card was missing, and the date you first reported the loss.

Your liability under federal law for unauthorized use of your ATM or debit card depends on how quickly you report the loss. If you report an ATM or debit card missing before it's used without your permission, the card issuer cannot hold you responsible for any unauthorized transfers. If unauthorized use occurs before you report it, your liability under federal law depends on how quickly you report the loss.

You risk unlimited loss if you fail to report an unauthorized transfer within 60 days after your bank statement containing unauthorized use is mailed to you. That means you could lose all the money in your bank account and the unused portion of your line of credit established for overdrafts. However, for unauthorized transfers involving only your debit card number (not the loss of the card), you are liable only for transfers that occur after 60 days following the mailing of your bank statement containing the unauthorized use and before you report the loss.

If unauthorized transfers show up on your bank statement, report them to the card issuer as quickly as possible. Once you've reported the loss of your ATM or debit card, you cannot be held liable for additional unauthorized transfers that occur after that time.

The best protections against card fraud are to know where your cards are at all times and to keep them secure. Also:

- Don't carry your PIN in your wallet or purse or write it on your ATM or debit card.

- Never write your PIN on the outside of a deposit slip, an envelope, or other papers that could be easily lost or seen.

- Carefully check ATM or debit card transactions before you enter the PIN or before you sign the receipt; the funds for this item will be fairly quickly transferred out of your checking or other deposit account.

- Periodically check your account activity. This is particularly important if you bank online. Compare the current balance and recent withdrawals or transfers to those you've recorded, including your current ATM and debit card withdrawals and purchases and your recent checks. If you notice transactions you didn't make, or if your balance has dropped suddenly without activity by you, immediately report the problem to your card issuer. Someone may have co-opted your account information to commit fraud.

Buying A Registration Service

For an annual fee, companies will notify the issuers of your credit card and your ATM or debit card accounts if your card is lost or stolen. This service allows you to make only one phone call to report all card losses rather than calling individual issuers. Most services also will request replacement cards on your behalf.

Purchasing a card registration service may be convenient, but it's not required. If you decide to buy a registration service, compare offers. Carefully read the contract to determine the company's obligations and your liability. For example, will the company reimburse you if it fails to notify card issuers promptly once you've called in the loss to the service? If not, you could be liable for unauthorized charges or transfers.

Review: A Primer on Debit and ATM Cards

What is a debit card?

A debit card is a banking card enhanced with automated teller machine (ATM) and point-of-sale (POS) features so that it can be used at merchant locations. A debit card is linked to an individual's checking account, allowing funds to be withdrawn at the ATM and point-of-sale without writing a check. Each financial institution creates an identity for its debit card to customize the product and differentiate it in the market. Debit cards can also be called deposit access cards.

A debit card enables the cardholder to pay for purchases directly via his or her checking account, replacing cash and checks.

What is an example of a debit card?

One type of debit card is a financial institution's ATM card with point-of-sale features that incorporates a specific acceptance mark (Visa or MasterCard). Payment is completed by signing a sales draft or by entering a

PIN. Then the amount of the sale is deducted from the cardholder's checking account within one to three days. These debit cards are accepted anywhere consumers use their Visa or MasterCard credit cards.

Another type of debit card is an ATM card bearing a PLUS or CIRRUS logo. When cardholders use the card at an ATM or merchant location that accepts PLUS or CIRRUS, the cardholder enters the PIN and the amount of the sale is automatically deducted from the cardholder's checking account. A regular ATM card doesn't have a Visa or MasterCard logo, but instead has a PLUS or CIRRUS logo and is good only where the merchant accepts those brands or at an ATM.

How is a debit card used?

When using a debit card to pay for goods and services, the purchase amount is deducted from the cardholder's checking account. Depending on the type of card, processing a check card transaction requires the cardholder either to sign a sales draft, or to enter a PIN into special terminal equipment, just like at an ATM.

Although accepted at over 10.5 million locations around the world, debit cards cannot be used in all situations (making cash and checks necessary in some situations).

The cardholder must be certain of his or her checking account balance, as it might be possible to make purchases beyond the funds available.

Where are check cards accepted?

Check cards can be used at merchant locations wherever the card logo is displayed.

What do debit cards cost?

Banks determine the fees for each card and/or transaction.

How do you keep track of your check card transactions?

Debit card holders receive receipts at each ATM or merchant location. Users typically record debit card purchases in their checkbook registers. By deducting debit card transactions from their accounts on a regular basis, debit card holders can maintain the most up-to-date available balances.

What if you lose your ATM receipt?

All check card transactions will appear as deductions on your next checking account statement from your financial institution.

Chapter 18

Electronic Banking

Electronic banking means 24-hour access to cash through an automated teller machine (ATM) or direct deposit of paychecks into checking or savings accounts. But electronic banking also involves many other types of transactions.

Electronic banking, also known as electronic fund transfer (EFT), uses computer and electronic technology as a substitute for checks and other paper transactions. EFTs are initiated through devices such as cards or codes that allow you, or those you authorize, to access your account. Many financial institutions use ATM or debit cards and Personal Identification Numbers (PINs) for this purpose. Some use other forms of debit cards such as those that require, at the most, your signature or a scan.

Electronic fund transfers offer several services that consumers may find practical:

• **Automated Teller Machines** or 24-hour Tellers are electronic terminals that let you bank almost any time. To withdraw cash, make deposits, or transfer funds between accounts, you generally insert an ATM

About This Chapter: This chapter begins with text from "Electronic Banking," January 2003, and "Electronic Check Conversion," November 2004, both publications of the Federal Trade Commission. "E-Banking" and "Wireless Banking" are reprinted from "Banking on the Internet," an online financial education publication of the Federal Reserve Bank of New York, http://www.newyorkfed.org, February 2001. "Confirm That An Online Bank Is Legitimate" and "Help Keep Your Transaction Secure" are from "Safe Internet Banking," Federal Deposit Insurance Corporation, January 5, 2005.

card and enter your PIN. Some financial institutions and ATM owners charge a fee, particularly to consumers who don't have accounts with them or on transactions at remote locations. Generally, ATMs must tell you they charge a fee and its amount on or at the terminal screen before you complete the transaction. Check the rules of your institution and ATMs you use to find out when or whether a fee is charged.

- **Direct deposit** lets you authorize specific deposits, such as paychecks and Social Security checks, to your account on a regular basis. You also may pre-authorize direct withdrawals so that recurring bills, such as insurance premiums, mortgages, and utility bills, are paid automatically.

- **Pay-by-phone systems** let you call your financial institution with instructions to pay certain bills or to transfer funds between accounts. You must have an agreement with the institution to make such transfers.

- **Personal computer banking** lets you handle many banking transactions via your personal computer. For instance, you may use your computer to view your account balance, request transfers between accounts, and pay bills electronically.

- **Point-of-sale transfers** let you pay for purchases with a debit card, which also may be your ATM card. The process is similar to using a credit card, with some important exceptions. While the process is fast and easy, a debit card purchase transfers money—fairly quickly—from your bank account to the store's account. So it's important that you have funds in your account to cover your purchase. This means you need to keep accurate records of the dates and amounts of your debit card purchases and ATM withdrawals in addition to any checks you write. Your liability for unauthorized use, and your rights for error resolution, may differ with a debit card.

- **Electronic check conversion** converts a paper check into an electronic payment at the point of sale or elsewhere, such as when a company receives your check in the mail. In a store, when you give your check to a store cashier, the check is processed through an electronic system that captures your banking information and the amount of the check.

Once the check is processed, you're asked to sign a receipt authorizing the merchant to present the check to your bank electronically and deposit the funds into the merchant's account. You get a receipt of the electronic transaction for your records. When your check has been processed and returned to you by the merchant, it should be voided or marked by the merchant so that it can't be used again. In the mail-in situation, you should still receive advance notice from a company that expects to process your check electronically. Be especially careful in telephone transactions, which also could involve e-checks. A legitimate merchant should explain the process and answer any questions you may have. The merchant also should ask for your permission to debit your account for the item you're purchasing or paying on. However, because telephone e-checks don't occur face-to-face, you should be cautious with whom you reveal your bank or checking account information. Don't give this information to sellers with whom you have no prior experience or with whom you have not initiated the call, or to sellers who seem reluctant to discuss the process with you.

> ✔ **Quick Tip**
>
> Some financial institutions and merchants issue cards with cash value stored electronically on the card itself. Examples include prepaid telephone cards, mass transit passes, and some gift cards. These "stored-value" cards, as well as transactions using them, may not be covered for the loss or misuse of the card. Ask your financial institution or merchant about any protections offered for these cards.
>
> Source: From "Electronic Banking," FTC, 2003.

Disclosures

To understand your legal rights and responsibilities regarding your EFT account, read the documents you receive from the financial institution that issued your "access device," that is, a card, code or other means of accessing your account to initiate electronic fund transfers. Although the means varies by institution, it often involves a card and/or a PIN. No one should know your PIN except you and select employees of the financial institution.

♣ It's A Fact!!
E-Filing

More than 47 million taxpayers choose to receive their tax refunds by direct deposit, and nearly 60 million used the Internal Revenue Service's e-file for their federal tax returns during the 2004 tax-filing season. Taxpayers who opt to use direct deposit receive their refunds faster—in as few as 10 days.

- Taxpayers who receive their refunds by direct deposit have significantly fewer problems than with a paper check, and problems can be resolved much faster.

- Benefits of the IRS e-file program include free or low-cost filing; fast, safe refunds; security; and accuracy (an error rate of less than 1%); electronic signatures, proof of acceptance; electronic payment options; and the ability to file both state and federal returns electronically.

- Taxpayers can learn the status of their refunds online by visiting www.irs.gov (click on "Where's My Refund?") or by calling 1-800-829-1954.

—by Eleanor Kelly

Source: Excerpted From "47 Million Can't Be Wrong: Record Number Pick Direct Deposit for Federal Income Tax Refunds as E-File Gets a Big Boost," *Financial Connection*, the online publication of Financial Management Service, a bureau of the U.S. Department of the Treasury, July/August 2004.

Before you contract for EFT services or make your first electronic transfer, the institution must tell you the following information in a form you can keep.

- A summary of your liability for unauthorized transfers.

- The telephone number and address of the person to be notified if you think an unauthorized transfer has been or may be made, a statement of the institution's "business days" (which is, generally, the days the institution is open to the public for normal business), and the number of days you have to report suspected unauthorized transfers.

- The type of transfers you can make, fees for transfers, and any limits on the frequency and dollar amount of transfers.

- A summary of your right to receive documentation of transfers, to stop payment on a pre-authorized transfer, and the procedures to follow to stop payment.

- A notice describing the procedures you must follow to report an error on a receipt for an EFT or your periodic statement, to request more information about a transfer listed on your statement, and how long you have to make your report.

- A summary of the institution's liability to you if it fails to make or stop certain transactions.

- Circumstances under which the institution will disclose information to third parties concerning your account.

- A notice that you may be charged a fee by ATMs where you don't have an account.

In addition to these disclosures, you will receive two other types of information for most transactions: terminal receipts and periodic statements. Separate rules apply to passbook accounts from which pre-authorized transfers are drawn. The best source of information about those rules is your contract with the financial institution for that account. You're entitled to a terminal receipt each time you initiate an electronic transfer, whether you use an ATM or make a point-of-sale electronic transfer. The receipt must show the amount and date of the transfer, and its type, such as "from savings to checking." When you make a point-of-sale transfer, you'll probably get your terminal receipt from the salesperson.

You won't get a terminal receipt for regularly occurring electronic payments that you've pre-authorized, such as insurance premiums, mortgages, or utility bills. Instead, these transfers will appear on your periodic statement. If the pre-authorized payments vary, however, you should receive a notice of the amount that will be debited at least 10 days before the debit takes place.

You're also entitled to a periodic statement for each statement cycle in which an electronic transfer is made. The statement must show the amount of any transfer, the date it was credited or debited to your account, the type of transfer and type of account(s) to or from which funds were transferred, and the address and telephone number for inquiries. You're entitled to a quarterly statement whether or not electronic transfers were made.

Keep and compare your EFT receipts with your periodic statements the same way you compare your credit card receipts with your monthly credit card statement. This will help you make the best use of your rights under federal law to dispute errors and avoid liability for unauthorized transfers.

Errors

You have 60 days from the date a periodic statement containing a problem or error was sent to you to notify your financial institution. The best way to protect yourself if an error occurs—including erroneous charges or withdrawals from an account, or for a lost or stolen ATM or debit card—is to notify the financial institution by certified letter, return receipt requested, so you can prove that the institution received your letter. Keep a copy of the letter for your records.

If you fail to notify the institution of the error within 60 days, you may have little recourse. Under federal law, the institution has no obligation to conduct an investigation if you've missed the 60-day deadline.

Once you've notified the financial institution about an error on your statement, it has 10 business days to investigate. The institution must tell you the results of its investigation within three business days after completing it and must correct an error within one business day after determining that the error has occurred. If the institution needs more time, it may take up to 45 days, in most situations, to complete the investigation, but only if the money in dispute is returned to your account and you're notified promptly of the credit. At the end of the investigation, if no error has been found, the institution may take the money back if it sends you a written explanation.

Limited Stop-Payment Privileges

When you use an electronic fund transfer, you do not have the right to stop payment. If your purchase is defective or your order is not delivered, it's as if you paid cash. That is, it's up to you to resolve the problem with the seller and get your money back.

There is one situation, however, when you can stop payment. If you've arranged for regular payments out of your account to third parties, such as insurance companies, you can stop payment if you notify your institution at least three business days before the scheduled transfer. The notice may be oral or written, but the institution may require a written follow-up within 14 days of the oral notice. If you fail to provide the written follow-up, the institution's responsibility to stop payment ends.

Although federal law provides only limited rights to stop payment, individual financial institutions may offer more rights or state laws may require them. If this feature is important to you, you may want to shop around to be sure you're getting the best "stop-payment" terms available.

E-Checks (Electronic Check Conversion)

The next time you write a check to your local merchant, the cashier may hand it back to you after it's been processed electronically. Or maybe you're mailing a check as payment to a company. That payment, too, may be processed electronically. Why? More merchants and companies are using e-checks, also known as electronic check conversion, which converts a paper check into an electronic payment from your bank account. How does electronic check conversion work?

When you give your check to a store cashier, the check is processed through an electronic system that captures your bank account information and the amount of the check. Once the check is processed, you're asked to sign a receipt and you get a copy for your records. When your check has been processed and returned to you, it should be voided or marked by the merchant so that it can't be used again. The merchant presents the processed check to your bank or other financial institution electronically, and the funds are transferred into the merchant's account.

Electronic check conversion also is being used for checks you mail to pay for a purchase or to pay on an account. The merchant or company sends your check through the electronic system, and the funds are transferred into their account.

If companies you do business with use electronic check conversion, by law you must receive notice if your check will be processed electronically.

Notice can be given in different ways: In a store, a merchant might post a sign at the register or give you a written notice. For a mailed check, the company might include the notice on your monthly statement or under its terms and conditions. The notice also should state if the merchant or company will electronically collect from your account a fee—like a "bounced check" fee—if you have insufficient funds to cover the transaction.

Your financial institution may be unable to give you a duplicate copy of your checks, so it's important to keep your checks—and receipts—that have been processed electronically in a store, especially if you need proof of payment. In the case of merchants and companies that use electronic check conversion for your mailed checks, you won't get your check back because it was transmitted through the process only electronically. However, if you need a copy of the check they processed, you can always ask the merchant or company if they'll provide it to you.

Your bank statement must show the electronic transaction. It should include the name of the merchant or company, the payment amount, and the date the payment was electronically transferred from your account. This information may be included in an area other than where your paper checks are listed, so carefully review the entire statement. It's important to keep your bank statements; they can be used as proof of payment for your transactions.

What electronic check conversion means to the average consumer is that there may be no "float" on your check. That means if you write a check today, you need to have funds in your account today to cover it. If you don't, your check may bounce and you

---

✔ Quick Tips

1. Keep and compare your receipts for all types of EFT transactions with your periodic statements. That way, you can find errors or unauthorized transfers and report them.

2. Make sure you know and trust a merchant before you share any bank account information or pre-authorize debits to your account. Be aware that some merchants use electronic processing of your check if you sign a receipt authorizing the transaction.

Source: From "Electronic Banking," FTC, 2003.

may be charged a fee by the merchant, your financial institution, or both. Bounced checks can blemish your credit record.

Always promptly review your bank statement for errors. For example, did two electronic payments go through instead of one? Were you charged the wrong amount for the item purchased? If you find an error on your account, you have 60 days from the date your statement was sent to you to notify your financial institution. Your financial institution might take up to 45 days from the date you notify it to investigate the situation. In most instances, if it will take more than 10 business days, your financial institution must credit your account while it investigates the error.

If you find unauthorized electronic transfers on your account (or someone has fraudulently obtained your banking account information), notify your financial institution immediately. Your level of loss depends on how quickly you report the problem. Under federal law, if you report the loss within two business days of discovery, you won't be responsible for more than $50 in unauthorized transfers. If you fail to report the loss within two business days, but report it within 60 days after the statement containing unauthorized transfers is mailed to you, you could lose up to $500. If you fail to report the unauthorized transfers within 60 days after your statement is mailed to you, you risk losing all the money in your account and the unused portion of your maximum line of credit for overdrafts.

Keep Close Tabs On Your Account

The Federal Trade Commission suggests that you:

- **Keep track of deposits.** Make sure you record all deposits to your checking account in your checkbook immediately. When you make deposits, save the receipts. They can help resolve mistakes.

- Remember to **record all automatic or Electronic Fund Transfer (EFT) deposits,** such as your paycheck, in your checkbook when they're credited to your account.

- **Keep track of withdrawals.** Immediately record your transactions. This includes: checks you write; ATM withdrawals; all automatic payments, including electronic check conversion, debit card payments at the point of sale, and other direct payments; and fees or service charges, including ATM fees.

- **Promptly balance your account when your statement arrives.** This means reconciling the information you have recorded in your checkbook against the statement your financial institution sends to you. Review your entire bank statement; checks processed electronically may be recorded in an area other than where your paper checks are listed, such as under "other withdrawals."

- **Review your statement** to be sure checks were only processed electronically once and for the correct amount. If your account won't balance, and you can't find the error, promptly call your financial institution for help.

- **Be especially careful with telephone transactions.** If a merchant or company lets you make a payment by e-check for a phone transaction, they should notify you that they will process your payment electronically. They will then ask for your bank and checking account numbers as they appear at the bottom of your check, and for permission to charge the account for the item you're paying for. Your transaction will then be processed and the funds withdrawn from your account and deposited in the merchant or company's account electronically.

✔ Quick Tip

How quickly are on-line transactions processed?

You may discover that online transfers are similar to writing a check and mailing it-transactions may not be processed instantaneously. Be sure to find out from your bank exactly when online or telephone account transfers take place (immediately, end of day, etc.).

If you want to pay bills online, you should ask when electronic payments are deducted from your account, and when they are transferred to third-party billers.

Source: From "E-Banking," Federal Reserve Bank of New York, 2001.

- **Be cautious about sharing your bank and checking account numbers.** Do not give out personal information on the telephone unless you have initiated the contact or know who you're dealing with. Scam artists can use your personal information to commit fraud such as identity theft. (In identity theft, someone uses your personal information, such as your checking or credit card account number, Social Security number, mother's maiden name, or birth date, without your knowledge or permission, to commit fraud or theft.)

E-Banking (Online Banking)

Online banking can help you manage savings and checking accounts, apply for loans, or pay bills quickly and easily. To enjoy the full benefits of online banking, you should understand all that online banking can offer, consider some questions to ask before signing up, and know how to get help if you need it.

Online banking is a service provided by many banks, thrifts, and credit unions that allows you to conduct banking transactions over the Internet using a personal computer, mobile telephone, or handheld computer (such as a personal digital assistant [PDA]). You may be able to:

- Access accounts round-the-clock, even on weekends.

- See balances online and find out whether checks or deposits have cleared.

- Transfer funds between accounts.

- Download information directly into personal finance software.

- Receive and pay bills online (without check writing, envelopes, or stamps).

If you choose an "Internet-only" bank, you may no longer have access to a local "bricks-and-mortar" branch. Some Internet-only banks, however, offer higher interest rates and fewer fees than traditional banks.

To get started, frequently, all you need to do is to log on to your bank's website and follow the instructions.

When choosing an online banking service, use the same good business sense you would in any transaction. Make sure that the online bank has a good reputation before you provide personal information or send money. Also, when purchasing banking products or services online, read agreements carefully before clicking your consent to them or signing the agreements electronically. The time is well spent since you may be legally bound by those agreements. It is also wise to save or print a copy of the agreement for future reference.

The Internet is a convenient place to find bargains in banking products and services. You can often view rates for savings accounts, credit cards, loans, and other financial products and services. Some websites also help you directly compare financial products online.

If you decide to shop for a bank on the Internet, check to see that the Federal Deposit Insurance Corporation (FDIC) insures your bank's deposits. Just as "bricks-and-mortar" banks display the FDIC seal at the branch, most online banks include information on their deposit insurance on their webpages. Keep in mind that the FDIC does not insure non-deposit investment products-mutual funds, money market funds, annuities, life insurance policies, stocks, and bonds-whether they are sold online or through a bank's affiliate.

Also, if you use a bank that is not licensed in the United States, your deposits may not be insured by the FDIC, and you may not benefit from other important consumer protections offered in the United States.

Wireless Banking

Wireless Internet banking, commonly called wireless banking, allows customers to access account information and perform transactions over the Internet using a mobile phone or a personal digital assistant (PDA) instead of a personal computer.

Before you sign up for wireless banking, you should find out exactly how your mobile phone connects to your bank and verify that your information is secure at all times.

♣ **It's A Fact!!**
**Where can I find information if
I am considering wireless banking?**

Your bank's webpage is a good place to start. The
webpage should provide the terms and conditions of wireless services as well as privacy, security, and other basic information. You will need a Web-enabled or Web-ready mobile phone
or PDA; since there are many different kinds, most banks specify the
devices needed for their particular wireless services.

**What if I lose my wireless telephone signal
while in the middle of a banking transaction?**

Contact your particular bank and wireless service provider to determine what happens if a transaction is interrupted, and check
your monthly statements to ensure that all transaction amounts
are correct. It is important to find out how transactions are
completed and verified. You should receive a confirma-
tion number for each completed transaction.

Source: From "Wireless Banking," Federal Reserve Bank of New York, 2001.

Mobile phone service can connect to your bank in a variety of ways. In
some cases, your mobile phone uses your Internet service provider to dial up
and connect to a Web server located at your bank. Alternatively, you may be
given a special access telephone number to dial, and your bank may act as the
Internet service provider. In either case, once you are connected, you enter
your request using the keypad of your mobile phone or PDA.

Wireless banking provides most of the services on-line banking provides,
and may also include:

• Information notification and alerts prompting you to view balances,
see whether checks have cleared, and receive e-mail messages about
deposits and other changes to accounts.

- On-demand transactions allowing you to transfer money from one account to another, make electronic payments, and perform transactions just as in on-line banking, but by using a mobile phone or PDA.

Wireless banking involves the same security and privacy issues as on-line banking with a PC. Unlike PCs, however, mobile phones and PDAs are small and easily lost or stolen, making it even more important that a password be required to access account information or perform transactions. In addition, check to ensure that the information being sent to you is encrypted.

♣ It's A Fact!!
Biometrics

Biometrics is an automated method of recognizing a person based on a physiological or behavioral characteristic. Features with measuring capabilities include the face, iris, retina, vein, fingerprint, voice, hand geometry, and handwriting. Biometric technology offers flexibility and increased levels of security.

The biometric payment process requires multiple validation points between software and security, a digital certificate, a smart card and card reader, and the uniqueness of the certifying officer's and disbursing officer's fingerprints.

The biometric authentication smart card can be used in a broad range of applications that include digitally signing electronic documents, controlling physical access (building entry), and accessing computers and networks. The authorized user's fingerprint template(s) and digital certificate(s) are stored on the card in protected memory, eliminating the need for an external database or processing requirement. The card provides additional functions including system authentication, digital signature ability, public key infrastructure, and related cryptographic processes. The fingerprint card's recognition speed is approximately one-half second.

—by Ethan Cole

Source: Excerpted from "Internet Payment Platform Begins Use of Biometric Technology," *Financial Connection,* the online publication of Financial Management Service, a bureau of the U.S. Department of the Treasury, April/May 2004.

Confirm That An Online Bank Is Legitimate

Whether you are selecting a traditional bank or an online bank that has no physical offices, it's wise to make sure that it is legitimate and that your deposits are federally insured.

Read key information about the bank posted on its website. Most bank websites have an "About Us" section or something similar that describes the institution. You may find a brief history of the bank, the official name and address of the bank's headquarters, and information about its insurance coverage from the FDIC.

Protect yourself from fraudulent websites. For example, watch out for copycat websites that deliberately use a name or website address very similar to, but not the same as, that of a real financial institution. The intent is to lure you into clicking onto their website and giving your personal information, such as your account number and password. Always check to see that you have typed the correct website address for your bank before conducting a transaction.

Verify the bank's insurance status. To verify a bank's insurance status, look for the familiar FDIC logo or the words "Member FDIC" or "FDIC Insured" on the website. Also, you should check the FDIC's online database of FDIC-insured institutions. You can search for an institution by going to the FDIC's home page and selecting "Is My Bank Insured?" Enter the official name, city, and state of the bank, and click the "Find My Institution" button. A positive match will display the official name of the bank, the date it became insured, its insurance certificate number, the main office location for the bank, and its primary government regulator. If your bank does not appear on this list, contact the FDIC. Some bank Web sites provide links directly to the FDIC's Web site to assist you in identifying or verifying the FDIC insurance protection of their deposits.

Remember that not all banks operating on the Internet are insured by the FDIC. Many banks that are not FDIC-insured are chartered overseas. If you choose to use a bank chartered overseas, it is important for you to know that the FDIC may not insure your deposits. Check with your bank or the FDIC if you are not certain.

For insurance purposes, be aware that a bank may use different names for its online and traditional services; this does not mean you are dealing with separate banks. This means, for example, that to determine your maximum FDIC insurance coverage, your deposits at the parent bank will be added together with those at the separately named bank website and will be insured for up to the maximum amount covered for one bank. Talk to your banker if you have questions.

Get more information about FDIC insurance. Don't worry about your deposit insurance coverage if you and your family have less than $100,000 in all your accounts combined at the same FDIC-insured bank. But if your accounts total $100,000 or more, find out if they're within the insurance limit. Contact your bank for more information.

☞ Remember!!

Besides using up-to-date virus protection and encryption software to protect your files and monitoring the security of the websites that you frequent, keep your personal information confidential by using simple precautions:

- Tell no one your password or other confidential information unless you are sure of their identity. Hackers sometimes impersonate technical support workers or others over the phone to obtain private information.

- Keep your password out of plain sight in your work area.

- Select a password that is hard to guess; avoid social security numbers, birth dates, PINs, or other obvious choices.

- Good passwords are unique. Try using capitalization, non-letter characters, and other symbols with significance only to you. Instead of "carrot," for example, use "caRrOt8."

- Be sure to change your password periodically.

Source: Excerpted and reprinted from "Banking on the Internet," an online financial education publication of the Federal Reserve Bank of New York, http://www.newyorkfed.org, February 2001.

It's important to note that only deposits offered by FDIC-insured institutions are protected by the FDIC. Nondeposit investment and insurance products, such as mutual funds, stocks, annuities and life insurance policies that may be sold through websites or at the bank itself are not FDIC-insured, are not guaranteed by the bank, and may lose value.

As in everyday business, before you order a product or service online, make sure you are comfortable with the reputation of the company making the offer. Only then should you give out your credit card or debit card number. And never give the number unless you initiated the transaction.

Help Keep Your Transaction Secure

The Internet is a public network. Therefore, it is important to learn how to safeguard your banking information, credit card numbers, Social Security number and other personal data.

Look at your bank's website for information about its security practices, or contact the bank directly. Also learn about and take advantage of security features. Some examples are:

- **Encryption** is the process of scrambling private information to prevent unauthorized access. To show that your transmission is encrypted, some browsers display a small icon on your screen that looks like a "lock" or a "key" whenever you conduct secure transactions online. Avoid sending sensitive information, such as account numbers, through unsecured e-mail.

- **Passwords or personal identification numbers (PINs)** should be used when accessing an account online. Your password should be unique to you and you should change it regularly. Do not use birth dates or other numbers or words that may be easy for others to guess. Always carefully control to whom you give your password. For example, if you use a financial company that requires your passwords in order to gather your financial data from various sources, make sure you learn about the company's privacy and security practices.

- **General security over your personal computer** such as virus protection and physical access controls should be used and updated regularly. Contact your hardware and software suppliers or Internet service provider to ensure you have the latest in security updates.

If you have a security concern about your online accounts, contact your bank to discuss possible problems and remedies.

Part Four

You And Your Job

Chapter 19

Teens And The Job Market

Child Labor Laws And Enforcement

In America, children have worked, contributing to the well-being of the family unit, since the arrival of the first colonists. European settlers, bringing social values with them that equated idleness with pauperism, were quick to pass laws that actually required children to work. Adopting "poor laws" similar to the English laws, the colonies required the apprenticeship of poor children—some at ages as young as three years. Children worked on family farms and in family cottage industries. The institution of slavery also encompassed the labor of children born or sold into servitude.

Toward Today's Teen Job Market

The industrial revolution ushered in the modern factory system and changed a predominately rural populace into an urban one. Factory towns grew up dependent on a labor supply of women and children, with children seen as a cheap and manageable source of labor. Child labor in this country was so widespread and so much a part of economic reality in the early part of the 19th century that

About This Chapter: This chapter begins with text from "Chapter 2: Child Labor Laws and Enforcement," by Art Kerschner, Jr., in *Report on the Youth Labor Force*, Bureau of Labor Statistics, November 2000. "Choosing a Career" is from the U.S. Department of Education, 2005; and "Teens As Entrepreneurs" is from "Frequently Asked Questions: The Teen Entrepreneur Guide to Owning a Small Business," Small Business Administration, May 17, 2004.

no one looked toward or expected its aboli-
tion. But as the number of factories multi-
plied and the child workforce grew, the
social conscience began to stir—not
against child labor itself, but against
some features of the factory system as
they affected the children.

The earliest concern was that factory
children were growing up without receiving
even a modest education. Long workdays and
workweeks left little time for study. In 1836, Massachusetts passed this
country's first child labor law—legislation that required children under the
age of fifteen employed in manufacturing to spend at least three months
each year in school. A few states soon adopted similar laws.

> **✿ It's A Fact!!**
>
> The Fair Labor Stan-
> dards Act (FLSA) is the
> Federal law governing mini-
> mum wages, overtime, child labor,
> and record keeping.
>
> Source: Bureau of La-
> bor Statistics, 2000.

After the Civil War, industry expanded and became increasingly mecha-
nized. Children as young as six or seven were recruited to work 13-hour
days, for miniscule wages, in hot and dusty factories. Proposals to change
these conditions met with stiff opposition.

The early 1900s saw a growing acceptance of the concept that states should
provide for the general protection of children. By 1913, all but nine states
had fixed 14 years as the minimum age for factory work, and a majority of
the states had extended this minimum to stores and other specified places of
employment. But it was not until 1938, with the passage of the Fair Labor Standards Act (FLSA), that meaningful federal child labor legislation was enacted.

The child labor provisions of the FLSA establish a minimum age of 16
years for covered nonagricultural employment. However, they allow 14- and
15-year-olds to be employed in occupations other than in mining and
manufacturing if it is determined that the employment is confined to periods that will not interfere with their schooling and to conditions that will
not interfere with their health and well-being. The FLSA also prohibits
minors under age 18 from working in occupations that the Secretary of Labor declares to be particularly hazardous for such youths or detrimental to
their health or well-being.

Teens And Jobs

The nature of child labor in the United States has changed over the past fifty years. Child labor now means, almost exclusively, teenagers—teenagers who are generally full-time students and part-time employees. But even with the increased emphasis on education and the improved economic conditions that this century has brought, the nation's young people are still working today, and in large numbers.

The unique history of the United States, which both fostered and overcame some of the most oppressive types of child labor, still helps to create an environment conducive to youth employment that differs considerably from that of other industrialized nations. The most often cited difference is that the proportion of teens who work is relatively high in the United States compared with other developed countries.[1] Americans have always tenaciously believed in the value of work, for themselves and for their children. They believe that positive work experiences during the teenage years can benefit a person's development, maturity, and sense of responsibility. Conversely, idleness is associated with delinquency.

Another difference lies in the reasons why teenagers, who have not yet completed their formal educations, seek employment. For the most part, the jobs held by U.S. teens are not conceived as stepping-stones on a life career path. Other developed countries, such as Germany, Denmark, and Switzerland, have long included adolescent employment as part of formal apprenticeship programs that are closely linked to the educational process and lead to specific adult jobs. Only in the last two decades has there been a concerted effort in the United States to link adolescent work experiences with school curricula to facilitate the transition from student to worker. The little research that has been done on why U.S. teens seek paying jobs suggests that the primary reason is money, not the value of the work experience.[2]

♣ **It's A Fact!!**
Most working teens spend their earnings as discretionary income, rather than helping to meet family expenses.

Source: Bureau of Labor Statistics, 2000.

The nation's roots also affect the types of jobs legally available to young workers. The United States began as a nation of farmers, and agriculture continues to enjoy a special place in the perceptions of its citizens. Growing up on the family farm, learning the value of hard work in the fresh air, is still viewed by many as the perfect childhood. Federal and state child labor laws governing agricultural employment reflect this belief—they are much less restrictive than those applied to other industries.[3]

Federal Child Labor Laws

As mentioned earlier, the Fair Labor Standards Act of 1938 (FLSA) is the framework for federal child labor provisions. Not all employment of young workers is covered under the FLSA. In addition, some jobs held by youths, such as delivering newspapers and performing in motion pictures and theatrical, radio, and television productions, are specifically exempted from the child labor provisions of the FLSA.

♣ **It's A Fact!!**

Children and teens working on farms owned or operated by a parent are completely exempt from federal agricultural child labor provisions, and other teenage farm workers are permitted to perform hazardous jobs at younger ages than are their counterparts who work in other industries.

Source: Bureau of Labor Statistics, 2000.

Nonagricultural employment. Under the FLSA, 16 is the minimum age for nonagricultural employment, but 14- and 15-year-olds may be employed for certain periods—which do not interfere with their schooling—in jobs that the Secretary of Labor has determined will not interfere with their health and well-being. Children under 14 years of age are generally too young for formal employment unless they meet a specific exemption.[4] However, these youths may perform tasks where no covered employment relationship arises—such as baby-sitting on a part-time, irregular basis, or performing minor chores around private homes.

Teenagers 16 years of age and older may work at any time of the day and for unlimited hours. The FLSA prohibits workers under 18 years of age from performing those nonagricultural occupations that the Secretary of Labor declares to be particularly hazardous for the employment of children under 18 years of age or detrimental to their health or well-being.

Agricultural employment. Unlike the rules governing nonagricultural employment, most of the child labor provisions applicable to agricultural employment are statutory. Under federal law:

- A child working in agriculture on a farm owned or operated by his or her parent is exempted from federal agricultural child labor provisions.

- Young farm workers who are not the children of the farmer employing them are subject to federal child labor provisions that differ by age:

  1. Youths are no longer subject to the federal agricultural child labor provisions when they reach 16 years of age.

♣ It's A Fact!!

Federal Limits Type Of Work That 14- And 15-Year-Olds May Perform

- Banned from performing most work but may be employed in retail, food service, and gasoline service establishments.

- Banned from working in manufacturing, processing, or mining, or in any workroom or workplace in which goods are manufactured, processed, or mined.

- Banned from performing any work the Secretary of Labor has declared to be hazardous for young workers by issuing Hazardous Occupations Orders (HOs).

- Banned from occupations involving transportation, construction, warehousing, or communication, or occupations involving the use of power-driven machinery.

- May perform some cooking at snack bars and in fast-food places in full sight of customers, but banned from performing baking.

Source: Bureau of Labor Statistics, 2000.

2. Children aged 14 or 15 may perform any nonhazardous farm job outside of school hours, and, with proper training and certification, they also may perform certain hazardous duties.

3. Children aged 12 or 13 may be employed outside of school hours in nonhazardous jobs, but only on the farm on which their parent works or with the written consent of a parent.

4. Children under 12 may be employed outside of school hours in nonhazardous jobs on farms not subject to the FLSA minimum wage if their parent also is employed on that farm, or with parental consent.

5. Children aged 10 or 11 may be employed to hand-harvest short-season crops outside of school hours under special waivers granted by the U.S. Department of Labor.

There are other labor standards laws, both state and federal, that regulate the hours of work, types of jobs, and working conditions of children and adolescents.

✎ What's It Mean?

Balance Sheet: A document that shows the owners' net equity after calculating the difference between your assets and your liabilities.

Cash Flow: A document which tracks the amount of money that you make and the amount that you pay out.

Entrepreneur: A person who assumes the financial risk of starting, operating, and managing a business or undertaking.

Income Projections: A document which shows how much profit you will make based on the difference between your monthly revenue and your monthly expenses.

Personnel: All employees, including yourself, and a description of their jobs, duties or responsibilities.

Source: Small Business Administration Glossary, 2004.

Teens 14 and 15 years of age may be employed outside school hours in a variety of nonmanufacturing and nonhazardous jobs under specified conditions. There are limits on both the duties they may perform and the hours they may work.

State Child Labor Laws

The adoption of compulsory school attendance laws by the states has done much to curb oppressive child labor in America. Every state also has a child labor law, usually enforced by a state labor department, that strives to preserve the health, education, and well-being of young workers. These laws, which often share extensive overlap in coverage with the FLSA, may contain some provisions that are more or less restrictive than provisions of the federal law. If both the state and federal law apply to the same employment situation, the more stringent standard of the two must be obeyed. The level of enforcement of state laws also varies widely.

✔ **Quick Tip**

For information about specific careers, see the *Occupational Outlook Handbook* at www.bls.gov/oco or in a library.

For a free self-assessment, see www.studentaid.ed.gov (click on "Preparing").

For information about financial aid for college or career school, see www.studentaid.ed.gov.

Source: U.S. Department of Education, 2005.

Federal law is generally more stringent than the state laws with respect to prohibiting work in occupations involving physical hazards and assessing penalties for violations. Federal law also is the same or more restrictive with respect to the minimum age for general employment. On the other hand, many state laws mandate standards that are absent from federal law, such as maximum hours and night work restrictions for 16- and 17-year-olds, prohibitions on employment in occupations or in places detrimental to morals (hotel and liquor service), and mandatory work permits or age certificates.

Though not conceived as labor standards legislation, state laws that establish minimum ages and other criteria for operating motor vehicles on public roads also affect youth employment and the types of jobs available to teens. These rules apply equally to on-the-job driving and to personal, nonemployment situations.

References

1. *Protecting Youth at Work* (Washington, Institute of Medicine/National Research Council, 1998), p. 27.

2. *Protecting Youth at Work*, p. 25.

3. Janice Windau, E. Sygnatur, and G. Toscano, "Profile of Work Injuries Incurred by Young Workers," Monthly Labor Review, June 1999, pp. 3–10.

4. The following types of youth employment are exempt from the child labor provisions of the FLSA: 1) children under 16 who are employed by their parents in occupations other than mining, manufacturing, or those declared hazardous by the Secretary of Labor; 2) children employed as actors or performers in motion pictures or theatrical, radio, or television productions; 3) children engaged in the delivery of newspapers to the consumer; 4) homeworkers engaged in the making of wreaths composed of natural holly, pine, cedar, or other evergreens.

♣ It's A Fact!!

Getting Experience

Teens often work at a sequence of part-time jobs. This is an excellent way not only to earn spending money and save for the future, but also to gain experience that can help them make decisions about future schooling and employment.

The part-time jobs that teens tend to obtain are not usually the kinds of jobs that they want to do for the rest of their lives. Nevertheless, they provide an opportunity to learn basic skills and business practices. Sometimes they can lead to a lifetime career.

As you work at a checkout counter, deliver newspapers, take care of children, or serve tables, you can be thinking about what you would like to do for a living after you graduate from high school.

—KRD

Choosing A Career

A first step in deciding what to do after high school is to talk with your school counselor or a teacher for advice. Ask your counselor about taking an aptitude test or interest inventory to find your strengths, weaknesses, and interests to discover potential career choices that are right for you.

1. Learn about yourself.

- *Values*—What is important to you?
- *Interests*—What appeals to you?
- *Aptitude*—What are you good at?

2. Talk to people.

Once you've narrowed your career choices, talk to people who are working in that field or, if possible, find a part-time job in that field. It's helpful to ask questions such as, "What's good and bad about this job?" "How did you learn your trade?" There are many sources of career and job outlook information available—go to your school library, public library, or school counselor.

✔ **Quick Tip**

What are some ideas for a teen business?

Babysitter Broker, Birthday Party Planner, Computer Teacher, Curb Address Painter, Dog Walker, Face Painter, Game Designer, Homework Helper, Mother's Helper, Photographer, Webpage Designer, etc...

Source: Small Business Administration, 2004

3. Consider how much training you will need for the career you're interested in.

- *High school diploma:* cashier, receptionist, salesperson, security guard, telephone operator, waiter/waitress
- *Special career training:* auto technician, beautician, machinist, medical technician, police officer, computer operator, commercial artist
- *College degree:* accountant, counselor, engineer, nurse, pilot, teacher, public relations specialist
- *Graduate degree:* college professor, doctor, dentist, lawyer, veterinarian, research scientist, architect

Teens As Entrepreneurs

You might decide that you would rather start your own business than work for someone else. You can do this, even while you are in your teens. People who own their own businesses are called *entrepreneurs*.

An entrepreneur is a person who organizes and manages a business undertaking, assuming the risk for the sake of profit. An entrepreneur sees an opportunity, makes a plan, starts the business, manages the business, and receives the profits.

You need to list reasons for wanting to go into business. Some of the most common reasons for starting a business are:

- Being your own boss

- Achieving financial independence

- Having creative freedom

- Utilizing your skills and knowledge.

You will need a *business plan*. A business plan precisely defines your business, identifies your goals and serves as your firm's resume. Its basic components include a current and *pro forma* balance sheet, an income statement and a cash flow analysis. It helps you allocate resources properly, handle unforeseen complications, and make the right decisions. Because it provides specific and organized information about your company and how you will repay borrowed money, a good business plan is a crucial part of any loan package. Additionally, it can tell your sales personnel, suppliers and others about your operations and goals.

> **✔ Quick Tip**
>
> *How do I know when my business is in trouble?*
>
> - You can't pay your bills.
> - You are not keeping business records.
> - You are selling equipment and inventory to get cash.
> - You agree to a business deal for less money than you normally would.
> - You need to keep borrowing money from the business just to get through the day.
>
> Source: Small Business Administration, 2004.

You will also need to *protect your business* from being stolen. There are several ways to protect your business. They include:

- **Patents:** a property right granted by the government to the inventor to make, use and sell the invention for a given period of time.

- **Copyrights:** protects your literary or artistic work, allows you to sell, give away or show your work, and copyrights must be tangible and physical.

- **Trademarks:** name, mark, symbol or motto, legally restricted to the use of the owner or manufacturer, that identifies your company and/or its product.

- **Trade Secrets:** information that you do not want known by your competition because your business would lose significant advantages.

You will need to structure your business for both legal and tax purposes. How you structure your business depends on the management style and financial needs you desire. Your business can be classified under the following business structures:

- Sole Proprietorship

- Partnerships

- Corporations

- Franchises

[Note: It is best to get some expert advice before attempting to establish a business. Organizations such as Junior Achievement, Inc. (www.ja.org) or YoungBiz (www.youngbiz.com) can give you advice. See Chapter 34 for more suggestions.]

Chapter 20

How To Apply For A Job And How To Keep The Job You Get

To apply for a job, you first need to look for employment opportunities.

Job Search Strategies

1. Want ads—need resumes and cover letters

2. Websites/Internet—need electronic resume and cover letters

3. Places—one-stop employment centers

4. Networking—the #1 most effective technique today

5. Employment agencies

6. In-person visits

About This Chapter: This chapter begins with excerpts reprinted with permission from *Jobs for Valley Youth Job Skills Workshop Manual*, Revised June 2003. © 2003 Communities in Schools of Arizona, http://www.cisarizona.org. "Entrepreneurs" is excerpted and reprinted from "Everyday Economics: Entrepreneurs and the Economy," August 2003, a publication of the Federal Reserve Bank of Dallas, http://www.dallasfed.org. "Resigning with Class: How to Diplomatically Resign From Your Job," by Randall S. Hansen, Ph.D., is copyright 2005 by Quintessential Careers. The original article can be found at http://www.quintcareers.com/resigning_job.html. Reprinted with permission.

Workplace Characteristics

- **Trustworthiness:** Standing by commitments, honest, open and ethical in relationships with others, keeping confidences, exhibiting personal integrity.

- **Respect:** Seeking the opinions of others to ensure results, listening and acknowledging the viewpoint of others, treating others with respect and dignity to maintain a positive working environment.

- **Responsibility:** Accountability for quality of work, providing accurate and timely service, accepting ownership of projects, following through to completion, managing time and assignments well.

- **Caring:** Exhibiting empathy and concern in relationships with fellow employees, customers, and others; building positive relationships with customers; sharing (knowledge, time, expertise, etc.) to help others succeed.

- **Boss relationships:** Responding and relating well to bosses, comfortable with being guided and coached.

✔ Quick Tip
Job Seeking: Some Things to Think About Before Starting

- What is your goal? (to find a job that pays or that is located in ____ or in which you can use skills ...)

- How will you meet that goal? Who would you contact to help you?

- Have you composed a resume?

- Do you have a portfolio?

- Do you have letters of recommendation?

- Who are potential employers?

- Who will you contact for an informational interview?

- What kind of jobs are available?

- What are the requirements for these positions?

- Do you have to be 18?

- Do you require a HS diploma or GED?

- Where have you applied?

- Have you followed up with your possibilities?

Source: Reprinted with permission from *Jobs for Valley Youth Job Skills Workshop Manual*, Revised June 2003. © 2003 Communities in Schools of Arizona, http://www.cisarizona.org.

- **Composure:** Cool under pressure, not becoming defensive or irritated when times are tough, mature, able to handle stress, confident.

- **Conflict management:** Good at focused listening, able to find common ground and get cooperation.

- **Creativity:** Suggesting new and unique ideas.

- **Customer focus:** Dedicated to meeting the expectations and requirements of customers, acting with customers in mind, gaining trust and respect of customers.

- **Managing diversity:** Managing relationships with all kinds of people equitably.

- **Humor:** Positive and constructive sense of humor, able to laugh at yourself and with others, appropriately funny, using humor to ease tension.

- **Listening:** Attentive and active, with the patience to hear people out, able to restate the opinions of others accurately even when in disagreement.

- **Perseverance:** Energy, drive to the finish, seldom giving up, especially in the face of resistance or setbacks.

- **Problem solving:** Using logic to solve difficult problems with effective solutions.

- **Team player:** Contributing to group effort, communicating ideas, able to persuade others, capable of negotiating toward agreement.

Turning In An Application

When dropping off an application, ask (1) if they are hiring, (2) who will be doing the hiring, and for a business card if available, and (3) when you might hear from them.

After dropping off an application, if you have not heard from the company in a week, call back, ask for the person in charge of hiring and ask about the status of your application. Ask when you might hear from them. Some possible questions are: "Are you still considering applicants for the position?"

"Have you had a chance to look over my application and if so, do you have any additional questions?" "Do you know when you might be making a decision about who you will be hiring?"

Verbal Communication

From the start, you will need to communicate well. There are three parts of verbal communication:

1. *Speaking:* Establishing rapport through small talk, conversation, asking proper questions, and rephrasing words that are too casual or slang (i.e.,

---

✔ Quick Tip
Key Words For Scannable Resumes

In today's world, many companies are taking advantage of technology by using scanners as the first filtering method for applications. Scanners are programmed to "look for" certain words that describe the types of skills needed for a certain position. It is important for the word or phrase to be written exactly the way the scanner was programmed. Here is a list of some "key words" that are commonly searched for today:

• Computer skills	• Child care
• Access	• First aid
• Excel	• Typing
• Word	• Retail sales
• Publisher	• Janitorial
• Customer service	• Carpentry
• Phone experience	• Accounting
• Cash handling	• Auto mechanics
• Machine operation	• Cleaning
• Painting	• Team player
• Assembly	• Organizational skills

Source: Reprinted with permission from *Jobs for Valley Youth Job Skills Workshop Manual*, Revised June 2003. © 2003 Communities in Schools of Arizona, http://www.cisarizona.org.

"Whassup?; "And she was, like, go ahead and call that lady."; "It don't matter.")

2. *Listening:* Pay close attention. Ask questions for clarification. Remember names. Look a person in the eye when listening. Don't get distracted by other things or thoughts.

3. *Body Language:* Be alert and interested. Smile. Dress appropriately. Shake hands firmly while looking at the other person. Do *not* glare, roll your eyes, slouch, or cross your arms.

✔ **Quick Tip**

Application Tips

Fill out completely

Print neatly

Use black ink

Make sure spelling is correct

Sign your full name

Turn in unfolded and unwrinkled

Source: Reprinted with permission from *Jobs for Valley Youth Job Skills Workshop Manual*, Revised June 2003. © 2003 Communities in Schools of Arizona, http://www.cisarizona.org.

Preparing For Your Interview

1. Know yourself

   • Before the interview review in your mind previous work, school information, relative experiences, skills, accomplishments, and your strengths and weaknesses.

   • Be ready to answer questions about things that are important to that job, about your personality, and your past successes

2. Know the company

3. Bring the right materials. Necessary documents include:

   • driver's license

   • photo ID

   • social security card

   • school and work records

   • resume

Interview Do's And Don'ts   ✔ Quick Tip

Things to *do* in an interview:

- Be on time or early
- Use a firm handshake and smile appropriately
- Be polite, use proper greeting, have a positive attitude
- Stay interested, alert and enthusiastic
- Smile
- Keep good eye contact with occasional affirmative nodding of the head
- Build rapport with the interviewer
- Relax and be yourself
- Be honest and realistic
- Sit with hands, feet and arms unfolded, and erect in the chair
- Do not fiddle
- Think before you speak
- Give strong answers and back them up with examples
- Thank the interviewer for his or her time.

Things *not* to do in an interview:

- Chew gum, smoke or eat candy
- Bring a cell phone or pager
- Bring friends or family members
- Ask about salary, vacation time, holidays, etc.
- Sit until offered a chair
- Make derogatory remarks about previous employers or co-workers
- Answer questions with only "yes" or "no" (give open-ended answers)

Things to do *after* the interview:

- Debrief yourself: Write down everything you feel you handled right and wrong; note any information you may need to include in the thank you letter; note all information that is key when speaking with the interviewer in the future.
- Write a thank you letter.

Source: Reprinted with permission from *Jobs for Valley Youth Job Skills Workshop Manual*, Revised June 2003. © 2003 Communities in Schools of Arizona, http://www.cisarizona.org.

- portfolio
- references
- A black ink pen
- Paper to take notes on
- A calendar of your available days and date when you will be available to start work

4. Think about your appearance
   - Be well rested and alert
   - Dress appropriately and be well groomed
   - Look like you are excited about the job you are applying for

Commonly Asked Interview Questions

Questions About Yourself

- Tell me about yourself. What are your hobbies and interests?
- What are your major strengths and weaknesses?
- How would you describe yourself? How would a friend describe you? How would your previous employer describe you?
- What motivates you?
- What three accomplishments have given you the most satisfaction and why?
- Have you ever done any volunteer work? Explain.
- Where do you see yourself in five years?
- What classes did you like most in school? Least?
- What activities did you participate in at school?

Questions About Your Previous Experience

- What did you like most/least about your last job?
- Why did you leave your last job? What have you learned from previous work experience?
- Have you ever spoken before a group of people? Explain.

Questions Specific To The Company

- What do you know about this company? Why do you want to work for this company?

- Why do you think you would be a good match for this position?

- What kind of boss do you like to work for?

- What kind of work environment makes you the most comfortable?

- Why should I hire *you*?

Behavior-Based Questions

- Describe a time when you were faced with problems or stresses in school or at work that tested your coping skills. What did you do?

- Tell me about an experience in which you had to speak up and tell other people what you thought or felt.

- Give an example of a time when you used your fact-finding skills to gain information needed to solve a problem. Tell me how you analyzed the information and came to a decision.

- Describe the most creative project you have completed.

- Discuss a situation during the past year in which you had to deal with an angry and upset customer, co-worker, or classmate.

- Describe a project that was difficult for you to lead. What did you do to keep the project on track.

- Give an example of how you contributed in a teamwork environment in school or on the job.

- Describe the most difficult supervisor or teacher you have had and tell me how you dealt with that person.

- What have you learned from your mistakes?

- Do you have any questions?

Illegal Questions

- With whom do you live? Are you married? Do you have any children? What does your spouse do?

- What is your native language? Where were your parents born?

- How tall are you? How much do you weigh?

- Do you need any accommodations to perform the job?

- Have you ever been arrested?

- What organizations or clubs do you belong to?

- Do you own or rent your home?

To Ask

- Does your company encourage further education? Is financial assistance available?

- Please describe the duties involved with the position.

- Can you tell me more about the company?

- Is there a formal training program or on-the-job training?

- Are there plans for this company to expand?

- Have you had layoffs or cut positions in the last three years?

- Do you fill positions from the outside or promote from within first?

- Are there performance reviews? How often?

- To whom would I report?

- What is the next course of action? When should I expect to hear from you or should I contact you?

Not To Ask

- What is the salary? When can I expect a raise?

- How much vacation do I get? How much sick pay is allowed?

- How long are breaks and lunch?

Entrepreneurs

Entrepreneurs And The Economy

An entrepreneur is a person who comes up with a new idea or invention and brings together a country's resources (land, labor, and capital) to take the idea to the marketplace. Entrepreneurs manage and assume the risk of a

---

♣ It's A Fact!!

Amy Glass, job trainer and coach at Brody Communications Ltd., shares her opinions on body art and how it impacts your job.

Do employers discriminate against tattooed/pierced job applicants?

I have a friend in his late 20s who has an earring in each ear. He has a master's degree and a good job history. He went recently to interview for a job with a financial company. He was recommended by someone high up in the company and that's how he got the job interview.

He thought the interview went well and he wrote them a thank you note. He did all the things you're supposed to do, but he didn't get a call back from them. Finally, someone from the company called him to say that they had found someone else.

The person he knew there said the reason he didn't get the job was because of the piercings. But obviously, that can't be said directly to him because it would be illegal. In his job, he'd have to work directly with the public and it wasn't acceptable. Her suggestion: take the earrings out if he applied for another job there. He decided that he didn't want the job bad enough to do that.

Interns and other people in job training programs that are just entering the work force often ask about piercings and tattoos. They're saying, "Why can't I keep my nose pierced or my eyebrow pierced?" In most industries, especially Fortune 1000 companies, it is not considered acceptable to do it. I'm not suggesting that it won't change at some point. Less than 10 years ago women couldn't wear pant suits at many banks. You had to wear a skirt suit. But, as things stand right now if you're interested in working in a large corporation, having any visible piercings or body tattoos can be an issue.

business enterprise. They improve established products and services, or they create new ones. Entrepreneurs, like everyone else, respond to incentives. In a free market economy, one of the strongest incentives that drive entrepreneurs is to please customers and thereby earn a profit. To flourish, entrepreneurs need an economic environment that encourages private property and free markets.

What about tattooed/pierced people who apply for professional jobs where they're not dealing directly with clients?

If you work in information technology, usually there's a lot more freedom in how you can look. The dress code at IT is quite lax compared to other departments because they only work internally and it's known that they have a very specific skills set. It's hard enough to get people who are very good at computer technology so [body art] is more acceptable. But people who work in sales have to dress in business casual to business professional attire.

Can someone hide a tattoo under a long sleeve shirt during the interview?

For someone with a very visible tattoo or who's just decided to wear a nose ring when they've never worn one before, human resources could definitely say that they don't want to send that message out to clients. They may interpret that wrong. We prefer you to wear a long sleeve shirt when you work with our clients. It is the company's full right to say that. Now, it is not their full right to terminate. They would have to come up with a work-producing reason to terminate, not the tattoo, because otherwise that is a basis for a lawsuit.

Does the type of industry you work in affect the office dress code?

I want to make a distinction between working in a large corporate environment and working in a more or an artsy environment, which could be advertising, certain kinds of journalism, or parts of public relations. In those types of creative industries, especially if you're a creative type and not an account manager, you get a lot more flexibility.

Reprinted with permission of InCharge Education Foundation, Inc., Spring 2003 issue of YOUNG MONEY, www.youngmoney.com.

What Is An Entrepreneur?

We admire and appreciate people who venture forth to try something new and end up benefiting a host of other people. These qualities describe the essence of entrepreneurship. An entrepreneur is one who asserts, "There is a better way, and I will find it." Being entrepreneurial means having energy, vision, optimism, and daring to try something new. An entrepreneur is anyone with both an idea and the willingness to take the idea to the marketplace. Creativity and risk taking are two essential elements of entrepreneurship.

Entrepreneurs As Vital Resources

Entrepreneurs concoct the recipe, design the machine, develop the process, and organize the workers who create and package the delicious chocolate bar on the grocery store shelf. In most cases, all we see is the final product, and thus we take entrepreneurs for granted. But entrepreneurs play the crucial role in the marketplace of making something that others will value. They are like the spark in an engine, igniting new ideas and discoveries that move the economy forward. They seek new ways to improve current products, processes, and services, and they create entirely new ones.

Entrepreneurs can be found everywhere, doing just about everything—from starting a new restaurant to creating a new technology or invention. These people often put their money or their reputations on the line. Some wish to become rich and famous. Others wish to make themselves, their families or their communities better off. And some seek pure adventure—to challenge the limits of their capability. Regardless of motive, the entrepreneur's goal is to improve things. [See Chapter 33, Websites About Money/Job and Career for more information.]

Resigning With Class: How To Diplomatically Resign From Your Job
—by Randall S. Hansen, Ph.D.

Are you preparing to resign from your current job? Some job-seekers have a hard time doing so, either because they love the job and their co-workers or because they can't stand the job and can't wait to leave. Curious? Then read on. The first part of this section discusses the strategies behind making a graceful departure from your employer and the second part shows you how to write a letter of resignation.

Strategies For Resigning With Class

The most important job-search rule to remember when resigning from any job is that you never want to leave on bad terms—if possible. Courtesy, etiquette, and professionalism go a long way. So, as much as you may want to tell off your boss or a co-worker, you should never burn any bridges. And don't spend time bragging to co-workers about your great new opportunity. Job-hunting is a funny process, and you never know when you'll run smack right into your former supervisor, a former co-worker, or a former employer through a merger or other circumstance.

So, once you are ready to announce your resignation, how can you make as smooth a transition from your current employer to your new one? You'll again want to act professionally—and follow company guidelines. Specifically, you need to consider:

- *Timing.* Give enough notice. The standard notice has traditionally been two to four weeks, but you should consult your employee handbook in case your employer expects more (or less) advance warning.

- *Negotiating.* Be sure to get a fair settlement for any outstanding salary, vacation (and sick and personal) days, and commission payments or other compensation due to you.

- *Hiring.* Offer to help your current employer find your replacement.

- *Training.* Volunteer to train or work with your replacement to show him or her "the ropes."

- *Working.* Don't disappear during the last weeks on the job. Stay an active member of the team. Avoid taking a short-timer's attitude or aligning yourself with any discontented co-workers.

- *Completing.* Be sure to do your best to complete all open assignments and leave detailed progress reports for your supervisor and co-workers.

- *Leaving.* Before walking out the door for the last time, be sure you have contact information for key supervisors and co-workers that you want to keep part of your network of contacts—and be sure to thank them again for their support.

Here are some other issues you need to be prepared for once you announce your resignation:

- *Escorted out of the building.* In some industries and with some professions (such as sales), once an employee resigns, the employer asks the person to leave on the spot. Be prepared for this scenario by clearing personal files and removing personal software from your computer, removing personal information and belongings, and getting your workspace organized.

- *Guilt from co-workers or your boss.* It's only natural, especially if you are leaving an unpleasant work environment, that your co-workers may be a bit envious and try to make you feel a little guilty. And no matter how great your boss may be, s/he may also make you feel a little guilty for "deserting" the team. Try not to let these things bother you; instead, concentrate on making the final weeks/days pleasant and professional.

- *A counter-offer to entice you to stay.* Be very wary of counteroffers. No matter how good it makes your ego feel to have your current employer respond with a counteroffer, most career experts advise against taking it because studies show that the vast majority of employees who accept counteroffers from current employers aren't in those jobs for very long. Whether the employer admits it or not, your dedication will be questioned, and once that happens, your time on the job is limited. It's better to tactfully decline the offer and focus on your new job with your new employer.

- *An exit interview.* Some employers like to have all departing employees meet with someone from the human resources department for an exit interview. Be careful—but be professional. Some employers want to know the "real" reason you are leaving. Again, remember not to burn any bridges by saying anything negative or petty.

Writing A Professional Resignation Letter

What should you do once you've made the decision to take a job with another employer? You should take the time to write a letter of resignation to your current employer. It's best to have written documentation of your resignation and planned last day of work.

The most important thing to remember when writing your letter of resignation is to be professional—there is just no sense in making enemies. Regardless of whether you loved or hated your job or your employer, the outcome should be the same: a short, polite, and professional letter stating your intention to leave.

People leave their jobs for all sorts of reasons, and you certainly do not need to provide any details on why you are leaving the company. Resignation letters are a courtesy to your employer, so you simply need to state that you are leaving your current position to pursue other opportunities.

As you are composing your letter, please again remember that your job history follows you around, and that frequently the world is much smaller than we think. You never ever want to leave on bad terms with any employer—mainly because doing so could come back to haunt you later in your career.

When should you submit your letter of resignation? And to whom? You should submit your resignation two or more weeks before your planned resignation date (depending on company/profession policy). And you should submit the letter/memo to your direct supervisor, with a copy to your human resources office.

What exactly should you say in your letter of resignation? Here's a basic outline:

First Paragraph: State your intention of quitting your job and leaving the company. Give a specific last day of work.

Second paragraph: If you feel comfortable, give a reason why you are leaving—relocating, better job, career change, graduate school, etc. Or, reinforce your value by mentioning your key accomplishments with the employer (though doing so may trigger a counter offer).

Third Paragraph: Thank both your supervisor and the company for the opportunities you had working for them. Be sure to end the letter on a positive note.

One final note: Assuming you leave on a positive note with your supervisor and co-workers, once you have settled into your new job, remember to contact your former supervisor and co-workers and give them your updated contact information so that you can continue to keep them as a part of your job search network (because you never know when you'll be job-hunting again).

Chapter 21

Avoid These Jobs

Multi-Level Marketing Or Pyramid Scheme?

A Maryland woman answered a help wanted ad for a marketing director that promised a six-figure income. When she arrived for the interview, she was led into a room with twenty other people. They were subjected to a high-pressure sales presentation about a company that was looking for distributors to market nutritional supplements, vitamins and jewelry.

The speaker told the woman that she could get rich by recruiting new people to become distributors. He explained that she just needed to develop a "downline" of people she would recruit into the program, people those recruits would bring in, and so on. She would earn a percentage of the sales made by all of these people, and she could eventually retire on the commissions on this ever-growing downline. She was convinced. She bought thousands of dollars worth of the company's products on credit—and became part of the speaker's downline.

This story is a composite of several actual complaints made to the Maryland attorney general's office. It illustrates a common sales pitch for a type of

About This Chapter: This chapter includes "Multi-Level Marketing or Pyramid Scheme," © 2000 Maryland Office of the Attorney General, Consumer Protection Division. Reprinted with permission; and, "Tip-Offs to Rip-Offs," © 2003 Maryland Office of the Attorney General, Consumer Protection Division. Reprinted with permission

illegal "pyramid scheme" that has cost some people a lot of money, time and effort. The woman in this story would almost certainly have lost the thousands of dollars she invested as a distributor. She would have spent more money and many hours trying to recruit new people into her downline. Ultimately, she would have given up, much poorer, but wiser.

Some pyramid schemes call themselves "multi-level marketing programs," but there is a difference. If you are looking for an opportunity that will allow you to work at home or be your own boss, you should be aware of the differences between a legitimate multi-level marketing company and an illegal pyramid scheme.

♣ **It's A Fact!!**
Examples Of Business Opportunity Scams

Lured by deceptive promises of independence and easy income, many would-be entrepreneurs are jumping into the arms of con artists who claim: "We are not just selling you a business, we put you IN business." The following examples illustrate the nature and extent of the business opportunity fraud epidemic in America:

Major Financial Losses. A Pennsylvania woman responded to an advertisement for a pizza vending machine business opportunity. The promoter promised huge earnings and the best locations in the area. The woman ended up losing her entire investment of $72,000.

Promises Of Instant Riches. One trademark of a business opportunity scam is an overblown promise of easy money. A brochure for a Utah snack vending machine company reads: "Many People Earn $36,000/year in Income, But ... Very Few Earn $30,000/year working only five-six hours per week." In another case, a promoter for a gumball machine business opportunity claimed that one operator had earned $14,000 from four machines ... in just seven days!

Source: Excerpted from "Major State-Fed Crackdown Targets Business Opportunity Scan 'Epidemic'," Federal Trade Commission, July 1995.

What's The Difference?

"Multi-level" or "network" marketing is a form of business that uses independent representatives to sell products or services to family, friends and acquaintances. A representative can earn commissions from sales that he or she makes, and also from sales made by other people he or she has recruited into the program. Examples of well-known multi-level marketing companies include Amway and May Kay Cosmetics.

Some companies call themselves multi-level marketing when they are really pyramid schemes. They may market a product or service, but they teach their representatives to spend most of their time and effort recruiting new people to join the program. If the company focuses primarily on recruitment rather than sales, it is a pyramid scheme.

Pyramid schemes are not only illegal, they are a waste of money and time. Because pyramid schemes rely on recruitment of new members to bring in money, the schemes inevitably collapse when the pool of potential recruits dries up. When the plan collapses, most people, except the few at the top of the pyramid, lose their money.

The simplest form of pyramid scheme is the chain letter that asks the recipient to pay $1.00 to each of five names on a list, copy the letter, and then send it out to new people with the recipient's name added to the list. In recent years, pyramid schemes have become more sophisticated, and many have surfaced on the Internet.

Pyramid Tip-Offs

The pyramid scheme disguised as a multi-level marketing opportunity is not always easy to spot, but is just as much of a scam as the chain letter. Here are some tips to consider before participating in a multi-level marketing program:

- Avoid any program that focuses more on recruitment of new people rather than the sale of a product or service. If the program offers to pay commissions solely for recruiting new members, look elsewhere.

- Be cautious about participating in any program that asks distributors to purchase expensive inventory.

- Be skeptical about specific income or earnings claims. Many programs boast about the incredibly high earnings of a few top performers ("thousands per week" or "six figure-income"). The reality is that most of the people recruited into the organization are not making anywhere near those amounts.

- Make sure the product or service offered by the company is something you would buy and is competitively priced. Illegal pyramid schemes often sell products at prices well above retail or sell products that are difficult to value, such as health and beauty aids, new inventions or "miracle" cures.

- Don't believe statements from a program that it has been "approved" by the state or the attorney general's office.

- Never sign a contract or pay any money to participate in a multi-level marketing program, or any business opportunity, without taking your time and reading all of the paperwork. Talk the opportunity over with a spouse, knowledgeable friend, accountant or lawyer. If you feel that you are being subjected to high-pressure sales tactics or are not being given enough time to review the details, go elsewhere.

- If you join a pyramid scheme disguised as a multi-level marketing program, your decision will affect not only you, but everyone you bring into the program. Many people devote a substantial amount of time trying to market these ultimately worthless ventures.

Tip-Offs To Rip-Offs

You Could Be A Model

You're in the mall when a person says "I'm a talent scout for a modeling agency. You look like the type we're looking for. Come to an audition." Or maybe you get a postcard in the mail or see an ad in the paper announcing an audition.

Guess what? The "audition" is just a way to try to get you to buy modeling lessons or expensive photos for "your portfolio." Some teens and their parents have been pressured into signing contracts for a couple of thousand dollars worth of lessons. Afterwards, the school didn't help them get any modeling work.

✔ Quick Tip

The Federal Trade Commission (FTC) suggests that you use common sense, and consider these tips before you decide to sign up for a multilevel marketing job:

1. Avoid any plan that includes commissions for recruiting additional distributors. It may be an illegal pyramid.

2. Beware of plans that ask new distributors to purchase expensive products and marketing materials. These plans may be pyramids in disguise.

3. Be cautious of plans that claim you will make money through continued growth of your downline, that is, the number of distributors you recruit.

4. Beware of plans that claim to sell miracle products or promise enormous earnings. Ask the promoter to substantiate claims.

5. Beware of shills— "decoy" references paid by a plan's promoter to lie about their earnings through the plan.

6. Don't pay or sign any contracts in an "opportunity meeting" or any other pressure-filled situation. Insist on taking your time to think over your decision. Talk it over with a family member, friend, accountant, or lawyer.

7. Do your homework. Check with your local Better Business Bureau and state attorney general about any plan you're considering—especially when the claims about the product or your potential earnings seem too good to be true.

8. Remember that no matter how good a product and how solid a multilevel marketing plan may be, you'll need to invest sweat equity as well as dollars for your investment to pay off.

Source: Excerpted from "The Bottom Line about Multilevel Marketing Plans," Federal Trade Commission, October 2000.

Poet And Don't Know It?

Ever see ads for contests like "Win $10,000 for Poetry"? If you enter, you'll probably get a letter saying you are a "semifinalist" and your poem is so great that they want to publish it in a book. Would you like a copy of the book?... Just send $59.95.

It's flattering to be told that you have great talent—except when it seems that everyone who enters is told the same thing. If you don't mind paying $59.95 for a book with your poem in it, go ahead. But think about it. You were hoping to get money from them, but instead—they get money from you.

👉 Remember!!

Investigations show that business opportunity scams are most often promoted at trade shows and through small ads that appear in the classified sections of newspapers and magazines. Once touted almost strictly on a face-to-face basis, business opportunities are increasingly being promoted through slick telemarketing. Most of the schemes:

- Use classified ads that urge the prospect to call an "800" number.

- Make wild and unsubstantiated claims about potential earnings. Include claims about "proven" concepts.

- Suggest that no experience is necessary.

- Promise exclusive territories.

- Rely on high-pressure telemarketing sales techniques to pressure a victim into turning over his or her money.

- Make assurances about good locations for vending machines or display racks, or the assistance of a professional locator.

- Hype references handpicked by the company (instead of providing a list of all current business opportunity owners in the region).

- Fail to provide prospective investors with a complete disclosure document containing pre-sale disclosures about their experience, lawsuit history, audited financial statements, and substantiation for any representations made about earnings

Source: Excerpted from "Major State-Fed Crackdown Targets Business Opportunity Scan 'Epidemic'," Federal Trade Commission, July 1995.

Scholarship Scams

Teens sometimes get scammed by con artists who offer help in getting college scholarships or financial aid in return for fees. Watch out for companies that say things like this:

"The scholarship is guaranteed or your money back."

"You can't get this information anywhere else."

"I need your credit-card or bank-account number to hold this scholarship."

For free information about scholarships and financial aid, talk to your high school guidance counselor or the financial aid officer at the college you plan to attend. Also, check out FinAid: SmartStudent Guide to Financial Aid (http://www.finaid.org).

Chain Letters

You get a letter that says, "You can get $46,000 or more in the next 90 days." It says you should send $5 to each of ten other people at the top of a list, and add your name to the list.

Don't fall for it! That's a chain letter. Chain letters that promise a reward are a scam, and they are against the law. People who get suckered into sending money just lose it.

Chains and other kinds of "pyramid schemes" don't work. A pyramid scheme is called that because of the shape of the layers of people it involves. If a con artist recruits 10 people, and they are supposed to recruit 10 people, and so on, it makes this shape:

You can see that in only 11 layers it would require 10 billion people to make it work, many more people than live on the entire earth! With no more recruits, the people at the bottom wouldn't get what was promised to them.

1
10
100
1,000
10,000
100,000
1,000,000
10,000,000
100,000,000
1,000,000,000
10,000,000,000

Actually, pyramids fall apart long before then, because many people will not take part because they know it's a scam. But there are always some people who get fooled. Pyramid schemes keep making the rounds because of greed and wishful thinking.

Chapter 22

You As A Wage-Earner

"How much does this job pay?"

Although you hold back the urge to blurt this question out during the interview, it is on top of your mind as you scan the want ads, consider a career change, or prepare for the first leap from school to work.

You already know what it costs to live; you know what kind of work you are interested in (at least for now)—now you need to know if a particular job will support you (and any other people who depend on your paycheck).

You may have to negotiate a salary after you have been offered a job. Or, you may take a job knowing exactly what the starting and experienced-worker wages are. Either way, you will want to understand exactly how you are to be compensated for your work.

There are two main types of compensation, or "earnings," that you will receive for your skills, efforts, production, and time. They are *wages* and *benefits*.

About This Chapter: Text in this chapter is from "Know about Wages," © 2002 Idaho Career Information System. Reprinted with permission. Additional information from the Idaho CIS can be found online at www.cis.idaho.gov.

Wages

Wages are actual money or payment that you receive for your time. You may be compensated in wages, commissions, tips, or salary.

A salary (often expressed in an annual or monthly amount) is a fixed amount of money that you are paid to do your job—whether or not you work late evenings, or make other sacrifices for your job. A fixed wage, on the other hand, will include overtime pay for time spent working beyond eight hours a day or 40 hours a week. A wage is often expressed in hourly terms, and may be already set for the job you apply for, or open to negotiation.

A commission is payment workers receive instead of, or in addition to, their wages. People whose job it is to sell expensive items such as cars or houses may be paid only by commission (a percentage of each sale), or may be paid a commission on top of a minimal wage.

If you are starting work in a field in which you haven't worked before, expect to be paid a starting wage or salary. After you show your ability, you may automatically receive an increase in pay or you may need to ask for a raise. It is a good idea to keep track of your accomplishments and challenges met in a portfolio, similar to the portfolio you may have kept through high school, so that you are prepared when you are ready to ask for a raise.

✎ What's It Mean?

Fringe Benefit: An indirect, non-cash benefit provided to employees by employers in addition to regular wage or salary compensation, such as health insurance, life insurance, profit-sharing, and the like.

Source: From "Glossary of Economic Terms," U.S. State Department, 2001.

Benefits

Another type of compensation workers receive from their employers is *benefits*. Typical benefits for full-time workers may be paid health insurance, a retirement plan, paid vacation time or sick leave, meals, or transportation. Benefits may be clear-cut or may be in the form of a less formal agreement between you and your employer.

Your Net And Gross Pay

Your paycheck will be for your "net" pay: the amount of your wages or salary (your "gross pay"), minus any deductions. (Deductions are money that is subtracted from your income and put toward federal income tax, state taxes, Medicare, Social Security, and possibly other accounts that you approve such as uniforms or parking.) The amounts of these deductions will appear on your paycheck stub. Your pay stub may also show vacation time or sick leave that

---

♣ It's A Fact!!

Employee Benefits

Different benefits appeal to different people. The list of possible employee benefits and their applications is nearly unlimited. To achieve the maximum value, employers should tailor the benefit to both the employee and the job as well as to their business requirements and financial capabilities.

Here are some of the more common flexible benefits that may be included as part of a benefits program:

- pre-tax thrift-savings programs
- recreational programs
- discounts
- scholarships
- personal financial planning
- loans
- tuition refund
- profit sharing
- company car

- personal expense account
- parking privileges
- legal assistance
- flex-time
- extra vacation
- child care
- job titles
- professional or trade association memberships
- travel

A benefit not only satisfies the employee's needs, but it also communicates the employer's concern to meet those needs, creating the kind of work environment that contributes to increased employee productivity.

Source: Office of Women's Business Ownership, U.S. Small Business Administration, 1997.

you have used and/or earned, the time period covered by that check, your social security number, and other information. Each company's paycheck and pay stub style is a little different.

If you are earning *tips* on top of your wages, they will not show on your pay stub. A tip, also called a gratuity, is money the customer pays over and above the cost of the item or service. Tips make up a significant portion of income for waiters and waitresses, hairdressers and barbers, cab drivers, and some other workers. (These jobs are sometimes exempt from minimum wage laws.) A tipped employee has to keep track of the tips he or she earns for when it is time to pay income taxes.

More Than Wages

Keep in mind that some intangible benefits may also enhance your working experience. Some jobs have flexible work hours while others provide opportunities to earn more money and/or promotion within the company. Still others are quite stable, and provide a high amount of job security. Others provide opportunities to further your education or training. Consider the things that are important to you, and don't forget to think about them when considering a particular job.

Whatever job you end up taking, know what to expect from your employer, as well as what your employer expects from you.

Chapter 23

What Happens Between "Gross" And "Net"?

You have probably heard the terms *gross* and *net* linked with wages for employment. What do they mean?

Gross means "all"—all of your pay, before any deductions have been made.

Net means your pay after deductions have been made.

As you begin working for a paycheck, you need to understand the difference between your gross and net income—and where those deductions are going.

An Example Of Paycheck Deductions

A single person who claims one exemption would have this money deducted from his or her paycheck:

1.   Federal Income Tax (FIT): For those earning under about $24,600 per year, the tax rate is approximately 15% of gross earnings. Between $24,600 and about $60,000, the tax rate jumps to 28%. Above $60,000 the tax rate is 31%, 36%, or 39.6%.

About This Chapter: This chapter includes "An Example of Paycheck Deductions," from *Practical Money Skills for Life*, a financial literacy education program from Visa, http://www.practicalmoneyskills,com. © Visa U.S.A. All rights reserved. Reprinted with permission; "Social Security and You," published by the Social Security Administration, August 1995; "What Is A Social Security Statement?" published by the Social Security Administration, August 4, 2004.

2. Federal Insurance Compensation Act (FICA), the official name for Social Security: The tax rate is 6.2%, up to a maximum tax of about $4,100 for Social Security. The tax rate is 1.45% for Medicare on all wages earned.

3. State Income Tax (SIT): The tax rate ranges from 0% to 9.3%, depending on (1) your state and income, and (2) where you live.

4. State Disability Insurance (SDI): The tax rate is 1%, up to a maximum tax of about $320.

See Figure 23.1 for an example of a paycheck stub.

Waist not! Want not!	EMPLOYEE	JONATHAN R. DOE	
	SSN	123-45-6789	
	PAY PERIOD	3/4/99 TO 3/15/99	
	PAY DATE	3/15/99	NET PAY $644.41
PAYROLL ACCOUNT	CHECK NO.	060432	

EARNINGS			TAXES WITHHELD			OTHER DEDUCTIONS	
Description	Hrs.	Amount	Tax	Current	YTD	Description	Amount
REGULAR	80	800.00	FED INCOME TAX	102.40	307.20	401(K)	35.00
OVERTIME	5	75.00	SOCIAL SEC	54.25	130.20		
			MEDICARE	12.69	30.45		
			STATE INCOME TAX	26.25	63.00		
CURRENT		875.00					
YTD		2100.00					

Figure 23.1. Reading A Paycheck Stub. Source: From Practical Money Skills for Life, *a financial literacy education program from Visa, http://www.practicalmoneyskills,com.* ©Visa U..S.A. All rights reserved. Reprinted with permission.

Social Security And You

Social Security affects everyone, directly or indirectly. Virtually every working American pays Social Security taxes. And one in six Americans receives monthly Social Security benefits.

Remember!!
Adding Up The Benefits

Benefits cost your employer between 33% and 50% of your pay. These may include:

- Paid vacation days

- Paid sick days (usually 5–10 per year)

- Health, dental, and eye care insurance

- Life insurance

- Disability insurance

- Retirement benefits

- Tax-deferred retirement plan

- Parental leave

- Stock purchase plan

- Employee assistance plans

- Employee fitness programs

- Employee discounts

Source: From *Practical Money Skills for Life*, a financial literacy education program from Visa, http://www.practicalmoneyskills.com. © Visa U.S.A. All rights reserved. Reprinted with permission.

Yet Social Security is probably one of the least understood programs in the country. Most people, including students, tend to think of it in terms of retirement, something for the distant future. They are unaware that the program pays important survivors and disability benefits to workers and their families. Or they think disability and premature death are calamities that happen only to other people. In fact, one out of every four female students and one out of every three male students will become severely disabled or die before reaching retirement age. Nearly 28 percent of current Social Security beneficiaries are under the age of sixty-two.

It is important for people to have a basic understanding of Social Security. They should know what it is, how it works, and how it may help them at various stages in life. Social Security should play a key role in a person's financial planning. It can be the basis for financial security for growing families and for future retirement. It's never too early to start thinking about this.

The basic idea of Social Security is simple. During working years, employees, their employers, and self-employed people pay Social Security taxes. This money is used only to pay benefits to Social Security beneficiaries and the administrative costs of the program. Then, when today's workers' earnings stop or are reduced because of retirement, disability, or death, benefits will be paid to them and their eligible family members from

Social Security taxes. The system functions like a pipeline, with workers paying in one end and beneficiaries receiving at the other. As workers retire, become disabled, or die, they and/or their families move to the receiving end of the pipeline.

Part of the "FICA" tax goes for hospital insurance under Medicare. It helps pay hospital bills for workers and eligible family members at age 65 or if they receive Social Security disability benefits for two years or more. A second part of Medicare is Supplementary Medical Insurance. Approximately one-fourth of the cost is financed by premiums paid by people who have enrolled for this protection and the balance is paid by general tax revenues.

♣ It's A Fact!!
What Does FICA Mean?

Social Security payroll taxes are collected under authority of the Federal Insurance Contributions Act (FICA). The payroll taxes are sometimes even called "FICA taxes."

In the original 1935 law, the benefit provisions were in Title II of the Social Security Act (which is why we sometimes call Social Security the "Title II" program.) The taxing provisions were in a separate title, Title VIII. As part of the 1939 Amendments, the Title VIII taxing provisions were taken out of the Social Security Act and placed in the Internal Revenue Code. Since it wouldn't make any sense to call this new section of the Internal Revenue Code "Title VIII," it was renamed the "Federal Insurance Contributions Act."

The payroll taxes collected for Social Security are of course taxes, but they can also be described as contributions to the social insurance system that is Social Security. Hence the name "Federal Insurance Contributions Act." So FICA is nothing more than the tax provisions of the Social Security Act, as they appear in the Internal Revenue Code.

Source: Social Security Administration (www.ssa.gov), 2004.

The government's share of the cost of the medical insurance part of Medicare comes from general revenues of the federal treasury, not from payroll taxes. All Social Security and Medicare funds not required for current benefit payments and expenses are invested in interest-bearing U. S. government securities.

Social Security benefits are a statutory right in the United States. A worker's entitlement to Social Security is based on past work and there is no test of need to determine the right to claim benefits. Taxes and benefits are related to a worker's level of earnings during working years. In general, the higher a person's earnings, the higher the benefits.

The benefit formula is weighted in favor of workers with lower average lifetime earnings. The program also is weighted in favor of workers with families by providing benefits to a worker's family based on his or her work under Social Security.

The program is compulsory; no one may opt out; workers are required by law to participate in the program. If it were not compulsory, those who need it most would be the least likely to replace it with private resources.

Social Security is financed primarily from the taxes that workers (and the self-employed) pay, matched by employers. The fact that the program is financed by those who will receive benefits is credited with its widespread public acceptance and support.

Who Can Get Benefits And How

Social Security pays monthly cash retirement, survivors, and disability benefits to workers and their families.

Retirement. The age for receiving full benefits is increasing gradually from 65 to 67. Workers who retire as early as age 62 receive a permanently reduced amount. Once a person starts receiving benefits, most other types of retirement income will not affect payments (for example, savings, investments, and private insurance). Only earned income—from working—over a certain annual limit affects retirement benefit payments. However, the annual limit does not apply to beneficiaries who are 70 years of age and over.

Disability. Disability benefits are paid to workers who suffer a physical or mental condition that prevents them from performing any significant kind of work and is expected to last at least a year or to result in death. This is a more strict definition of disability than that used by some other programs that also pay for partial disability.

Disability benefits continue as long as a person is disabled and unable to work. They may also continue under certain conditions if a person attempts to work while still disabled until he or she can work on a regular basis. The work does not necessarily have to be the kind of work done before disability—it can be any kind of gainful work found in the national economy.

Benefits also may be paid to the worker's children under age 18 (or 19 if still in high school) or those disabled before age 22 who continue to be disabled, and to a wife or husband caring for children who are under 16 or disabled.

Survivors. Unmarried children under 18, or 19 if still in high school, or those disabled before age 22 who continue to be disabled, may qualify for benefits if a parent dies. A widow or widower may also qualify for benefits if he or she is at least 60 years of age, or has the worker's child under 16 or disabled in his or her care, or is disabled at age 50 or later. A divorced spouse may qualify for a benefit if the marriage lasted at least 10 years, or if he or she is caring for the worker's child who is under 16 or disabled.

Medicare. Most people 65 or older are eligible for Medicare benefits. People receiving disability benefits for 24 months or who suffer permanent kidney failure may also receive Medicare coverage. Medicare has two parts: hospital insurance and medical insurance. The hospital part of Medicare helps pay the cost of inpatient care and certain kinds of follow-up care. It is financed by a part of the Social Security tax. The medical insurance part of Medicare helps pay the cost of doctors' services, outpatient hospital services, and for certain other medical items and services. It is financed partly from monthly premiums paid by those covered, and partly from general revenues of the federal government.

> ✎ **What's It Mean?**
>
> Earnings Record: A chronological history of the amount you earn each year during your working lifetime. The credits you earn remain on your Social Security record even when you change jobs or have no earnings.
>
> FICA Tax: FICA stands for "Federal Insurance Contributions Act." It's the tax withheld from your salary or self-employment income that funds the Social Security and Medicare programs.
>
> Social Security: Social Security is based on a simple concept: While you work, you pay taxes into the Social Security system, and when you retire or become disabled; you, your spouse and your dependent children receive monthly benefits that are based on your reported earnings. Also, your survivors can collect benefits if you die.
>
> Social Security Number: Your first and continuous link with Social Security is your nine-digit Social Security Number (SSN). Your SSN helps us to maintain an accurate record of your wages or self-employment earnings that are covered under the Social Security Act, and to monitor your record once you start getting Social Security benefits.
>
> Wages: All payment for services performed for an employer. Wages do not have to be cash. The cash value of all compensation paid to an employee in any form other than cash is also considered wages
>
> Source: From "A Glossary of Social Security Terms," Social Security Administration (www.ssa.gov), n.d.

Social Security Credits

Before a worker can get benefits, he or she must have credit for a certain amount of work under Social Security. The amount of work credits needed varies with the type of benefit and the year at which the worker will become 62, or the age he or she becomes disabled or dies. Under current law, no one will need more than 40 credits for any type of benefit.

A young worker and his or her family have disability and survivors' protection after the worker has worked under Social Security for at least a year and a half (six credits). For retirement benefits, no one will need more than 10 years of work (40 credits).

A credit of work is based on a specified amount of earnings which increases each year with increases in general wage levels. A worker earns a maximum of four credits a year. The earnings and work credits are recorded under the worker's name and Social Security number in a lifetime earnings record in Social Security computers.

Amount Of Benefits

The amount of the benefit is based on the worker's average annual earnings over his or her working life. In general, the higher the earnings, the higher the benefit. Benefits increase annually with increases in the cost of living.

Social Security does not do it all. It provides a base on which people can build financial security for themselves and their families through savings, investments, earnings, insurance, and other means. To use Social Security in financial planning, a person needs to know:

1. *How much a worker and his/her family can expect from Social Security in retirement, disability, or survivors' benefits.* Social Security is designed to replace only a portion of the earnings a person loses as a result of retirement, death, or disability:

✤ It's A Fact!!
History Of Social Security

The Social Security system was developed as a result of the lessons learned from the Great Depression, to supply support for the aged and to protect themselves from external economic forces in an industrialized society.

The program grew to include survivors' and dependents' insurance (1939), disability insurance (1956), and Medicare (1965).

While all of these programs still exist today, the Old-Age, Survivors, and Disability programs became what is known as Social Security. The health insurance program is known as Medicare and is now administered by the Health Care Financing Administration. In 1972, the state-administered public assistance programs for the aged, blind, and disabled were transferred to the federal government under the Social Security Administration. The resulting federal program, Supplemental Security Income (SSI), provides a nationwide, uniform floor of income protection for people who are 65 and over or blind or disabled with limited income and resources. It is funded from federal general revenues, not the Social Security taxes.

Source: Social Security Administration (www.ssa.gov), 2004.

- Low wage earner—60 percent
- Average wage earner—42 percent
- High wage earner—26 percent

2. *How other income affects Social Security benefits.* In general, other types of retirement income—pensions, savings, investments—do not affect Social Security benefits. There is a limit on how much earnings a person can have and still collect benefits, however. In addition, another government pension may cause Social Security retirement benefits to be reduced. Workers' compensation and disability benefits from other public programs may affect disability benefits.

3. *How Social Security relates to private pensions.* In general, pensions from private insurance will not affect Social Security benefits. Note that many employers count Social Security benefits in setting the level of their pension plan benefits.

Retirement planning is an important part of financial planning. It should start as early as possible. A person should start early to build additional sources of income to supplement Social Security, such as savings, private insurance, a pension, stocks and bonds, rental income, IRA (Individual Retirement Account), and other investments. You can get a Personal Earnings and Benefit Estimate Statement from Social Security that will tell you how much you can expect from Social Security at retirement, or if you become disabled or die. It will also show the earnings credited to your record and the estimated Social Security taxes paid. The form can be requested from the Social Security office.

How Tax Rates Are Set

The tax rates are set in the law, and are intended to ensure sufficient income to pay current benefits plus a reserve to make up for any shortfall in income and to help pay future benefits. Future demographic trends will require either higher tax rates, lower program expenditures, or some combination to keep the Social Security and Medicare programs in financial balance. The maximum amount of annual earnings subject to Social Security taxes and creditable for Social Security benefits increases each year with increases in earnings levels.

When you work for more than one employer in a year and pay Social Security taxes on wages over the maximum amount, you may claim a refund of the excess amount on your federal income tax return for that year. If you work for only one employer who deducts too much in taxes, you should apply to the employer for a refund. A refund is made only when more than the required amount has been paid. Questions about taxes or refunds should be directed to the Internal Revenue Service.

What Is A Social Security Statement?

Your Social Security statement is a concise, easy-to-read personal record of the earnings on which you have paid Social Security taxes during your working years and a summary of the estimated benefits you and your family may receive as a result of those earnings. Statements are provided in two ways: in automatic annual mailings to workers and former workers aged twenty-five and older and at any time to workers of any age who request them. You can see a sample statement by going to http://www.socialsecurity.gov/mystatement/statsamples.htm.

You should keep your statement with your other important papers and use it in several ways:

- First, the benefit estimates in your statement can play an important role in your financial planning. When combined with your savings, investments and other pensions, your Social Security benefits can help you build a secure future for yourself and your family.

- Second, the statement can help you make sure your reported earnings and other important information such as your name and date of birth are correct on your record. Mistakes could keep you from getting all the Social Security benefits you have earned. The sooner you identify mistakes, the easier it will be to help us correct them.

- And finally, the general information on the statement tells you about all the protection you are earning under Social Security. Many people think of Social Security only as a retirement program. The Statement shows how even young workers are building valuable protection in case they become disabled or die before they reach retirement age.

☞ **Remember!!**
How To Apply For A Social Security Card

When to apply. Apply if you need to replace a lost Social Security card, change the name shown on your card, or request a replacement card.

How to apply. Obtain form SS-5 by downloading it from the Social Security website (at http://www.ssa.gov/replace_sscard.html), by calling 1-800-772-1213, or by visiting your local Social Security office.

What you need. To get a replacement card, you usually need one identifying document (originals only, not photocopies, even if notarized). Your replacement card will have the same number as your old card. Documents accepted as proof of identity are:

- Driver's license
- Marriage or divorce record
- Military records
- Employer ID card
- Adoption record
- Insurance policy
- Passport
- Health Insurance card (not a Medicare card)
- School ID card

For a name change, you also need documentation that shows your old name and your new name. Your new card will show your new name but will have the same number as your old card. Your old Social Security card cannot be accepted as evidence of identity.

For a new card, you should provide documents that show your age, citizenship or lawful alien status, and who you are; for example, a birth certificate and a school record.

You will need an in-person interview if you are age 12 or older and are applying for an original number. If you were born in the U.S. and are age 12 or older, you must explain why you do not already have a Social Security number. If you were born outside the United States, you also generally must show proof of U.S. citizenship or lawful alien status.

Source: Social Security Administration (www.ssa.gov), 2004.

Starting about three months after your twenty-fifth birthday, you should begin to receive your Social Security statement every year. The Social Security Administration is required by law to send these statements automatically to eligible people:

- who have worked in Social Security-covered employment or self-employment,

- who are not yet receiving benefits, and for whom the Social Security Administration can find a current mailing address.

If you wish to request a copy of your Social Security statement prior to your twenty-fifth birthday, or at any other time, you can send your request by Internet (www.socialsecurity.gov); download a paper version of the request form to mail in; or call, toll-free, 1-800-772-1213 and ask to have a paper request form mailed to you. The forms are also available at local Social Security offices.

Whether you make your request online or by mail, you will receive your statement by mail. It takes about two to four weeks if you request the statement electronically and about four to six weeks if you send your request by mail.

If you are automatically receiving a Social Security Statement about three months before your birthday each year, this request will stop your next scheduled mailing. You won't receive another automatic statement until the following year.

How Social Security Taxes Are Collected

If you are employed, your Social Security and Medicare taxes are deducted from wages each payday. A portion of every dollar earned—up to a certain maximum amount—is deducted from a worker's pay for Social Security. Your employer matches your payment and sends the combined amount to the Internal Revenue Service. In addition, Social Security beneficiaries who have high outside income in addition to their benefits (about 15–20 percent of all beneficiaries) pay income tax on a portion of their benefits to help finance the program.

If you are self-employed and your net earnings are $400 or more in a year, you must report your earnings and pay the self-employment tax each year when you file your federal income tax return. This is true even if you owe no income tax.

Your wages and self-employment income are entered on your Social Security record throughout your working years. This record of your earnings will be used to determine your eligibility for benefits and the amount of cash benefits that you and your eligible family members will receive. As long as you have earnings that are covered, you continue to pay Social Security and Medicare taxes—regardless of your age and even if you are receiving Social Security and Medicare benefits.

Social Security, the nation's primary means of providing a continuing income to a family when a worker dies, becomes disabled, or retires, accounts for less than half of the difference between your "gross" and "net" income. The larger portion of your deducted pay goes to pay your income taxes. Read more about that in the next chapter.

♣ It's A Fact!!
Social Security Office

Your local Social Security office is the place where you can:

• Apply for a Social Security number,

• Check on your earnings record,

• Apply for Social Security benefits, black lung benefits, Supplemental Security Income (SSI), and hospital insurance (Medicare) protection,

• Enroll for medical insurance,

• Get help applying for food stamps, and

• Learn everything you need to know about your rights and obligations under the Social Security law.

There is no charge for any services. You can also call 1-800-772-1213, to receive all these services, or go to http://www.socialsecurity.gov. You can find the location of your local office at http://www.socialsecurity.gov/locator.

Source: Social Security Administration
(www.ssa.gov), 2004.

Chapter 24

Yes, You Are A Taxpayer

Hannah's Story

It is March in Hannah's senior year of high school. She is going to college in the fall and has a scholarship that covers two-thirds of her tuition. Her parents have agreed to pay the remaining one-third of her tuition and her room and board. Hannah must pay for her books each semester and for her miscellaneous expenses such as pizza, movies, and other entertainment. Hannah has been looking for a job for several weeks and has finally found one. Let's listen while Hannah tells her mother about her new job.

"Mom! I did it! I found a job. I'll earn $7.50 per hour at Toys for You. The manager said I could work weekends until school is out. That will be about twelve hours a week. She said that I could work at least twenty-five hours a week during the summer. Mom, I'll have almost $2000 before college starts in the fall. If I combine that with what I've already saved, I'll have more than enough money for school. Can you believe it? I start next week—that's spring break. The manager said to count on twenty-five hours."

About This Chapter: This chapter begins with "Hannah's Story," excerpted from "Math and Taxes: A Pair to Count On," from *Money Math: Lessons for Life*, Copyright © 2001 The Curators of the University of Missouri, a public corporation, Center for Entrepreneurship & Economic Education, University of Missouri-St. Louis. "How Fair Are Taxes," excerpted and reprinted with permission from *OnPoint Economics*, Volume 10, Spring 2004, copyright © 2004, publication of Junior Achievement. Text under the heading "Full-Time Students And Taxes" is from Internal Revenue Service (IRS) fact sheets and Publication 501, 2003-2004.

"Hannah that's great. Be careful though, before you start counting your money you need to remember that you have to pay taxes."

"Yeah, yeah, I know. They gave me some forms to fill out. I have to take them back tomorrow when I start. What's the big deal about taxes? All I have to do is fill out some forms. No problem."

☞ **Remember!!**

What's Significant About April 15th?

April 15 is the annual deadline for filing federal taxes and some state taxes.

Source: Junior Achievement (www.ja.org), 2004.

"Hannah, it is more than just forms. Toys for You will take money from your check each week. That money will be sent to the state and federal governments. So don't plan to receive as much money as you expected each week."

"Come on, Mom. No matter what happens, you always have to talk about the negative stuff. Just be happy I have a job and that I start tomorrow. Now, I have to figure out what to wear for my first day. Maybe I'll go buy something new. After all, I am going to have a lot of money!"

Two weeks later: "Mom, Mom, where are you?" Hannah shouted. "I have a really big problem."

"Hannah, for heaven's sake, what are you yelling about?" Mom replied.

"I just got my first paycheck from Toys for You. Mom, they didn't pay me as much as they said they would. I've been cheated."

"Hannah, they paid you what they said they would. You worked thirty hours last week and your gross income is $225."

"But Mom, the check is only for $162. That's the gross part, if you ask me. They cheated me out of $63."

"Hannah, gross income means the total amount you earned before taxes are withheld. The $162 is your net income. That's the amount left after you pay taxes. Remember, I tried to tell you about taxes. Gross income is the actual amount you earned before taxes were withheld."

"Oh, yeah, those forms I filled out, right?"

"Yes, you filled out forms so that Toys for You could withhold federal income tax, Social Security and Medicare/Medicaid tax, and state income tax. Look at your pay receipt."

"Well, Mom, this is ridiculous. I am just a kid. Why do I have to pay taxes? What do I get from the government? This just isn't fair. I shouldn't have to pay taxes."

"Hannah, think. You get some goods and services from the government. Plus, you won't earn much income during the year, so you'll probably get a refund. This means that the state and federal government may give back part or all of the income tax you paid. The Social Security taxes won't be refunded."

How Fair Are Taxes?

Ask most Americans about the significance of April 15 and a common response might be, "That's the date taxes are due." It's true that April 15 is the deadline for filing federal and, where applicable, state taxes.

The fact is, most Americans pay taxes nearly every day. When was the last time you stopped at a convenience store to purchase snacks or other products? Did you pump gas into your car this week? Did you pay for tickets to a concert or athletic event? Did an employer recently hand you a paycheck?

If you answered "yes" to any of these questions, then you made a tax payment to your local and state governments, and perhaps to the federal government. Because so many transactions involve paying taxes to some governmental body, we often are unaware that we're doing this.

Why Do We Pay Taxes?

The federal government, state governments, local governments, and other taxing bodies collect taxes to fund programs and services. If you attend a public school, taxes pay for the building, equipment, furniture, and salaries of teachers and administrators. Through income and payroll taxes, the federal government finances "entitlement" programs, such as Medicare and Social Security.

Tax policy also can be used to promote a social objective that government believes is important. One of the largest tax deductions for many Americans is the interest paid on home mortgages. Federal tax policy encourages homeownership. On the other hand, tax policy also may attempt to discourage certain behavior. Taxes on tobacco and alcohol are intentionally high to curb use of these two products.

High taxes are intended to discourage cigarette smoking and use of alcoholic beverages, while taxes on gasoline are meant to lower fuel use. Government has used tax policy to discourage behavior it believes is harmful to individuals and the national interest. According to the Centers for Disease Control and Prevention, obesity resulting from a poor diet and physical inactivity is now the second highest cause of death among Americans. Cigarette smoking is ranked first.

Finally, tax policy is an instrument used to manage the economy. During the recent recession, congress and the president reduced federal taxes to stimulate the economy. Lower taxes provide consumers and business with more money to spend. Policy makers hope that the additional spending will result in more jobs, production, and profits. In times of high inflation, the federal government may raise taxes to slow spending. The use of taxes and federal spending to manage economic growth is referred to as "fiscal policy."

Taxes That You Pay

The most common tax paid by middle grades and high school students is a sales tax that is paid on most purchases. Sales tax is typically a revenue source for states, although some local governments (cities and counties) also may raise money through a sales tax. You'll notice that income taxes are withheld from your paycheck if you have a summer job or are employed during the school year. The first time you were paid, you [like Hannah] may have been surprised at how much was taken out for taxes.

♣ It's A Fact!!
The most common tax paid by teens is sales tax, which is paid on most purchases.

Source: Junior Achievement, 2004

Federal withholding will depend partly on the employee's annual salary. Since federal income tax is a progressive tax, higher paid employees will have a greater percentage of their pay withheld. Some states have no state income taxes, while other state income taxes are fairly high. The Medicare and Social Security tax are set at a fixed rate (up to a certain income level). Check on the Internet or in the school library to learn more about these federal programs.

> ✎ **What's It Mean?**
>
> Budget Deficit: When the government's annual revenues (primarily taxes) are less than expenditures.
>
> Budget Surplus: When a government's annual revenues exceed expenditures.
>
> Fiscal Policy: The use of taxes and federal spending to manage economic growth.
>
> Income Tax: Taxes paid on personal income.
>
> National Debt: The total accumulation of all deficits in the national budget.
>
> Sales Tax: Taxes paid on purchases.
>
> Source: Junior Achievement, 2004.

The Issue Of Fairness

The issue of tax fairness relates to who pays the taxes and how much he or she pays. There are two different principles used to approach this fairness question.

The benefits-received principle asserts that whenever possible, people who use a service should pay for it. For example, most cities have public golf courses that are available to residents of the community. Benefits-received advocates believe that golfers using that facility should finance the maintenance and improvement of the golf course, not citizens who don't play the sport. As a practical matter, golfers do pay for the rounds they play at public courses, but those fees don't cover all expenses. The remaining expenses are supported by taxing the entire community.

If all public golf course expenses had to be paid exclusively by golfers, many citizens could not afford to golf. Does a public golf course offer benefits to a community that justifies all citizens partially supporting the facility through taxes?

The ability-to-pay principle contends that taxes should be paid according to one's income and wealth. Wealthier individuals should bear a greater tax burden than less affluent citizens regardless of how much they use services or programs. Supporters of the ability-to-pay principle argue that taxing the poor beyond their ability to pay deprives them of necessities, while taxing the wealthy may only deprive them of some luxuries.

The Politics Of Taxes

Current debate on the tax cut and future tax policy is being triggered by the projected budget deficit and a decision on whether tax cuts should be renewed or be allowed to expire. A budget deficit occurs when the nation's annual revenues (primarily taxes) are less than expenditures. A budget surplus results when annual revenues exceed expenditures.

Similar to a household, the federal government needs to match expenditures with income. In cases when expenditures exceed income, both governments and households need to borrow. Households may take out a loan from a bank, tap into savings, or use credit cards to pay for expenditures. The federal government sells treasury bonds and notes to finance the deficit. The national debt is the total accumulation of all deficits.

Full-Time Students And Taxes

If you are a full-time student, are you exempt from federal taxes?

No. Every U.S. citizen or resident must file a U.S. income tax return if certain income levels are reached. There is no exemption from tax for full-time students. But if you are a full-time student, you may not be working full time. Factors that determine whether you have an income tax filing requirement include:

• the amount of your income (earned and unearned),

• whether you are able to be claimed as a dependent,

• your filing status, and

• your age. If your income is below the filing requirement for your age, filing status, and dependency status, you will not owe income tax on the income and will not have to file a tax return. You may choose to file if you have withholding that you would like refunded to you.

✔ Quick Tip
How long
should your refund take?

If you file a complete and accurate paper tax return, your refund should be issued in about six to eight weeks from the date IRS receives your return. If you file your return electronically, your refund should be issued in about half the time it would take if you filed a paper return—even faster when you choose direct deposit, if you used accurate routing and account numbers on the "refund" section of your tax form. (A word of caution—some financial institutions do not allow a joint refund to be deposited into an individual account. Check with your bank or other financial institution to make sure your direct deposit will be accepted.)

Refund delays may be caused by a variety of reasons. For example, a name and Social Security number listed on the tax return may not match the IRS records. You may have failed to sign the return or to include a necessary attachment, such as Form W-2, Wage and Tax Statement. Or you may have made math errors that require extra time for the IRS to correct.

To check the status of a refund you are expecting, go to www.irs.gov and find *Where's My Refund?* or call the IRS Refund Hotline at 1-800-829-1954.

If it has been at least four weeks since you filed your return, you can check on the status of your refund by calling the toll-free IRS TeleTax System at 1-800-829-4477. When you call, you will need to provide your Social Security number shown on the return, your filing status and the amount of the refund. If the IRS has processed your return, the system will tell you the date your refund will be sent.

Source: IRS (www.irs.gov),
2003.

You may have given your employer a Form W-4, *Employee's Withholding Allowance Certificate,* claiming exemption from withholding. To claim exemption from withholding, you generally would have to have had no tax liability the previous year and expect none in the current year. An exemption certificate is good for the calendar year.

If you are an individual who may be claimed as a dependent on another person's return and you are single and under age sixty-five, you must file a return if any of the following circumstances apply:

- Your unearned income was more than $750. Unearned income includes taxable interest, dividends, capital gains, and trust distributions of interest, dividends, capital gains, and survivor annuities. If you had an investment loss, your unearned income could be a negative amount.

- Your earned income was more than $4,750. Earned income includes wages, tips, taxable scholarship and fellowship grants, and salaries.

- Your total income was more than the larger of $750 or your earned income (up to $4,750) plus $250. If you file Form 1040EZ, Income Tax Return for Single and Joint Filers With No Dependents, your total income is the same as your adjusted gross income.

Even if you do not have to file, you should file a federal income tax return to get money back if you had income tax withheld from your pay.

Who Must File

If you are a U.S. citizen or resident, whether you must file a federal income tax return depends upon your gross income, your filing status, your age, and whether you are a dependent. Even if you do not have to file, you should file a tax return to get money back if you had income tax withheld from your pay. For information on what form to use—Form 1040EZ, Form 1040A, or Form 1040—see the instructions in your tax package.

You may have to pay a penalty if you are required to file a return but fail to. If you willfully fail to file a return, you may be subject to criminal prosecution.

Dependents

A person who is a dependent may still have to file a return. This depends on the amount of the dependent's earned income, unearned income, and gross income. Even with extenuating circumstances such as being blind, if your gross income was $3,050 or more, you usually cannot be claimed as a dependent unless you were under age nineteen or a full-time student under age twenty-four.

If a dependent child who must file an income tax return cannot file it for any reason, such as age, a parent, guardian, or other legally responsible person must file it for the child. If the child cannot sign the return, the parent or guardian must sign the child's name followed by the words "By (signature), parent for minor child."

How To Get More Information

You can order free publications and forms, ask tax questions, and get more information from the IRS in several ways.

Personal Computer. You can access the IRS on the Internet at www.irs.gov, or by using File Transfer Protocol at ftp.irs.gov. At the IRS website, you can select:

- *Frequently Asked Tax Questions* (located under Taxpayer Help & Ed) to find answers to questions you may have.

✎ What's It Mean?

Child's Earnings: The amounts of money that a child earns by performing services are his or her gross income. This is true even if under local law the child's parents have the right to the earnings and may actually have received them. If the child does not pay the tax due on this income, the parent is liable for the tax.

Earned Income: Salaries, wages, professional fees, and other amounts received as pay for work you actually perform. Earned income (only for purposes of filing requirements and the standard deduction) also includes any part of a scholarship that you must include in your gross income.

Gross Income: Gross income is all income you receive in the form of money, goods, property, and services that is not exempt from tax.

Self-Employed Persons: If you are self-employed in a business that provides services (where products are not a factor), your gross income from that business is the gross receipts. If you are self-employed in a business involving manufacturing, merchandising, or mining, your gross income from that business is the total sales minus the cost of goods sold. To this figure, you add any income from investments and from incidental or outside operations or sources.

Unearned Income: This is income such as interest, dividends, and capital gains. Trust distributions of interest, dividends, capital gains, and survivor annuities are considered unearned income also.

Source: IRS (www.irs.gov), 2004.

- *Forms & Pubs* to download forms and publications or search for forms and publications by topic or keyword.

- *Fill-in Forms* (located under Forms & Pubs) to enter information while the form is displayed and then print the completed form.

- *Tax Info For You* to view Internal Revenue Bulletins published in the last few years.

- *Tax Regs in English* to search regulations and the Internal Revenue Code (under United States Code [USC]).

- *Digital Dispatch and IRS Local News Net* (both located under Tax Info For Business) to receive electronic newsletters on current tax issues and news.

- *Small Business Corner* (located under Tax Info For Business) to get information on starting and operating a small business.

TaxFax Service. Using the phone attached to your fax machine, you can receive forms and instructions by calling 703-368-9694. Follow the directions from the prompts. When you order forms, enter the catalog number for the form you need. The items you request will be faxed to you.

Phone. Many services are available by phone:

- To order current and prior year forms, instructions, and publications, call 1-800-829-3676.

- To ask tax questions, call the IRS at 1-800-829-1040.

- To listen to pre-recorded messages covering various tax topics, call 1-800-829-4477.

Walk-In. You can walk in to many post offices, libraries, and IRS offices to pick up certain forms, instructions, and publications. Also, some libraries and IRS offices have:

- An extensive collection of products available to print from a CD-ROM or to photocopy from reproducible proofs.

- The Internal Revenue Code, regulations, Internal Revenue Bulletins, and Cumulative Bulletins available for research purposes.

Mail. You can send your order for forms, instructions, and publications to the Distribution Center nearest to you and receive a response within ten workdays after your request is received. Find the address that applies to your part of the country.

Western part of U.S.:

Western Area Distribution Center
Rancho Cordova, CA 95743-0001

Central part of U.S.:

Central Area Distribution Center
P.O. Box 8903
Bloomington, IL 61702-8903

Eastern part of U.S. and foreign addresses:

Eastern Area Distribution Center
P.O. Box 85074
Richmond, VA 23261-5074

CD-ROM. You can order IRS Publication 1796, Federal Tax Products on CD-ROM, and obtain:

- Current tax forms, instructions, and publications.

- Prior-year tax forms, instructions, and publications.

- Popular tax forms which may be filled in electronically, printed out for submission, and saved for record keeping.

- Internal Revenue Bulletins.

The CD-ROM can be purchased from National Technical Information Service (NTIS) by calling 1-877-233-6767 or by going on the Internet to www.irs.gov/cdorders. The first release each year is available in mid-December and the final release is available in late January.

Part Five

Understanding Loans And Credit Cards

Chapter 25

How To Borrow The Money You Need

Manage Credit Wisely

Borrowing money can help you meet your long-term goals for an education or an automobile. But borrowing for day-to-day needs and wants gets many people into financial trouble. Before using your credit card or applying for a loan of any kind, ask yourself if you really need to borrow the money. Avoid spur-of-the-moment purchases and set a monthly limit on your credit card charges.

When you borrow money, you have a right and a responsibility to know all the loan's terms and conditions. Ask questions and compare interest rates and fees. Know what's at stake if you don't make your payments.

About This Chapter: This chapter begins with "Manage Credit Wisely," excerpted from "There's a Lot to Learn about Money: Get the Best Deal," Federal Reserve Board of Governors, November 2002. "Automobile Loans" is excerpted from "First Car Loan" and "Your Future Mortgage" is excerpted from "Mortgage Basics," both © 2002 Illinois Division of Banks and Real Estate. (Neither the State of Illinois, nor any of its agencies, is liable for any improper or incorrect use of the information contained herein and assumes no responsibility for anyone's use of the information.) "Financing College," 2003, is reprinted from the Teen Consumer Scrapbook, http://www.atg.wa.gov/teenconsumer/index.htm, a project of Ellensburg High School, Ellensburg, Washington, and sponsored by the Washington State Attorney General. Reprinted with permission. "Cosigning A Loan" is adapted from a publication of the same name produced by the Federal Trade Commission, March 1997.

Before you borrow money, ask these questions:

- What is the interest rate?

- What are all the fees?

- How much will I have paid in interest when the loan is paid off?

- Can I pay it off early without penalty?

Shop around and compare. Don't get taken.

- Question an offer that makes borrowing sound too good to be true.

- Always read and understand the fine print.

- Seek help if you need it.

Save money with the right loan. See Table 25.1 for information about comparing loans at different interest rates and different terms.

Table 25.1. Save Money With The Right Loan: Get the lowest rate; choose the shortest term.

$15,000 Car Loan For Five Years

Lender	Interest Rate	Total Interest
Pixley Bank	6.5%	$2,609.53
ABC Car Loan	7.5%	$3,034.15
XYZ Finance Company	8.75%	$3,573.51

$15,000 Car Loan at 10% Interest

	3-year	4-year	5-year
Number of payments	36	48	60
Payment	$484	$380	$318
Total paid	$17,424	$18,261	$19,122
Interest saved	$1,698	$861	—

Source: Federal Reserve Board of Governors, 2002.

Automobile Loans

Getting an automobile loan is also referred to as financing the automobile. An auto loan can be used to purchase a new or used automobile. The automobile becomes collateral for the loan, which means the lender will hold the automobile title until the loan is paid off. The title indicates who owns the automobile. If the loan is not paid off, the bank can sell the automobile. New automobile loans typically exist for three to seven years, while loans for used automobiles remain for two to four years.

An auto loan might be one of your first big expenses. When considering an auto loan, be sure to shop around for the best deal before making a commitment.

An auto loan can be obtained from a bank, credit union, or another financial institution. Most lenders can pre-approve a car loan. This means the financial institution calculates how much money can be borrowed to buy the car. This is typically a free service and does not obligate anyone to accept a loan offer from that institution. These sources of financing will usually offer the lowest rates, and credit unions are generally lower than banks.

Financing can also be from the dealer or auto manufacturer. In most cases the dealer/manufacturer financing will cost more. But there will be occasions where a dealer will actually give the best deal. Unfortunately, those occasions are not predictable (despite endless "must sell" and "no money down" advertising by dealers) and the only way to be sure is by comparison shopping. To get the lowest advertised rates, usually there are requirements that must be met, such as:

- Make a large down payment

- Agree to a short loan term, usually three years or less

- Have excellent credit history

- Pay a participation fee, which is a fee that must be paid up front to get the low rate advertised.

Financing College

Congratulations, you've decided to go to college—now you need to know how to pay for it. As you realize, thousands of pre-college and college students search for scholarships, government loans, and grants each year.

According to the College Cost Book, the estimated cost to attend a public four-year college in the academic year 2000-2001 is at least $12,914 for one year, while for a private four-year college the cost more than doubles. This figure includes tuition, room, and board. A student must also consider the cost of books and personal expenses when figuring college expenses. One source estimates that figure to be over $600 annually. This makes it easy to understand the need for financial aid among many college students.

Types Of Financial Aid

Grants And Scholarships: This type of aid is generally provided by the federal government or private organizations. Grants and scholarships do not have to be paid back but usually require qualifications in certain areas. (i.e. music, sports, academics, etc.)

Work-Study: This is a program where a student in college may earn income and gain work experience at the same time. It is usually

> **✔ Quick Tip**
> **Scholarship Scams**
>
> Too many scholarship search services and financial aid advice services charge high rates to provide information that can be found elsewhere for free.
>
> Charging a lot for a service isn't illegal—what makes some of these companies fraudsters is that they collect money to find scholarships for students but never provide the information, or they misrepresent themselves as a government agency in order to appear legitimate, or they guarantee they'll get the student full funding for college (and then don't).
>
> If you're searching the Internet for scholarships and visit a site that asks for your credit card or another form of payment before it'll help you find funding, keep searching. Similarly, if you or your parents are contacted by an unfamiliar organization that invites you to an "interview" or "seminar" about preparing and paying for college, ask your high school counselor or a college financial aid administrator if the organization is legitimate. In many cases, such invitations are a way to get you to come listen to a sales pitch: the company wants you to pay for advice on scholarships and other funding.
>
> Don't believe anyone who tells you the information they offer can't be found anywhere else. You can get free advice from a variety of sources. The best places to start are your high school counselor or a college financial aid administrator.
>
> Source: U.S. Department of Education (www.ed.gov), 2004.

provided by the Federal Work Study program (http://faid.tamu.edu/main.cfm?Section=2). The college financial aid office can assist you in finding a job.

Loans: Based on financial need, this type of aid may carry low interest rates and accommodating repayment plans. However, every loan will require you to pay interest for as long as the debt exists.

Requirements For Eligibility

There are certain requirements a person must meet to be eligible for financial aid:

- high school diploma or GED certificate

- proof of financial need

- U.S. citizenship or proof of eligibility as a non-citizen

- a social security number

- a specific GPA

- affiliation with a group

- financial need

When searching and applying for financial aid, remember to apply every year because you might become eligible even though you were not eligible the previous year. Make a note of all deadlines for financial aid; registering early for aid is best. Also, avoid scholarship online services that want money in return for the service. College is expensive, but there are free sources that can help you pay for school if you spend some time and effort looking.

Your Future Mortgage

Buying a home is probably the single largest purchase a consumer makes. Most people cannot afford to buy a home outright. A mortgage is necessary to give a consumer the means to purchase a home. However, it is important to understand that until the mortgage is paid off, the bank owns the house. Monthly mortgages usually include the following, known as the PITI: Principal, Interest, real estate Taxes, and property Insurance.

Common types of mortgages include:

30-year fixed rate mortgage
- Monthly payments are lower
- Interest rates are higher than with a shorter mortgage
- Accumulated interest is tax deductible

15-year fixed rate mortgage
- Monthly payments are larger than with a longer term mortgage
- The interest rates are lower
- Accumulated interest is lower (Less money saved on taxes than with a 30-year fixed rate mortgage.)

Adjustable rate mortgage (ARM)
- Interest rate reflects a market index
- Lender adds a margin to the index (usually 2 to 4 percent)
- Interest rate is usually slightly lower than with the fixed rate mortgage
- Some lenders adjust the rate every year
- The shorter the term of the loan the more volatile it becomes
- Some lenders adjust the rate only once in the lifetime of the loan (at three, five, seven, or ten years).
- Some ARMs have build in caps to help curb the volatility of the loan:
    1. Lifetime cap—Limits the interest over the entire lifetime
    2. Periodic rate cap—Limits how much payments can increase at one time
    3. Payment cap—Limits payments of the lifetime of the loan

Cosigning A Loan

A lender may be reluctant to loan money to a young person, especially if this is your first loan. They may require you to provide a "cosigner" for your loan. Do you understand what cosigning involves?

Under federal law, creditors are required to give cosigners a notice that explains his or her obligations. The cosigner's notice states:

You are being asked to guarantee this debt. Think carefully before you do. If the borrower does not pay the debt, you will have to. Be sure you can afford to pay if you have to, and that you want to accept this responsibility.

You may have to pay up to the full amount of the debt if the borrower does not pay. You may also have to pay late fees or collection costs, which increase this amount.

The creditor can collect this debt from you without first trying to collect from the borrower. [*Depending on your state, this may not apply. If state law forbids a creditor from collecting from a cosigner without first trying to collect from the primary debtor, this sentence may be crossed out or omitted altogether.*] The creditor can use the same collection methods against you that can be used against the borrower, such as suing you, garnishing your wages, etc. If this debt is ever in default, that fact may become a part of your credit record.

This notice is not the contract that makes you liable for the debt.

Cosigners Often Pay

Studies of certain types of lenders show that for cosigned loans that go into default, as many as three out of four cosigners are asked to repay the loan. In other words, cosigners are being asked to take a risk that a professional lender won't take. If the borrower met the criteria, the lender wouldn't require a cosigner.

In most states, if you miss a loan payment, the lender can immediately collect from the cosigner without first pursuing you, the borrower. In addition, the amount of the loan may be increased—by late charges or by attorneys' fees—if the lender decides to sue to collect. If the lender wins the case, the cosigner's wages and property may be taken.

Despite the risks, there may be times when cosigning is the right choice. Your parents may cosign for your first loan, or you may turn to a close friend when you need help. Before someone cosigns for you, they should consider this information:

- Can the person afford to pay off your loan? If it's not feasible to pay off your loan, the person could be sued or his or her credit rating could be damaged.

- Even if the person is not asked to repay your debt, the liability for your loan may keep him or her from getting other credit because creditors will consider the cosigned loan to be an obligation.

- Before someone pledges personal property to secure the loan, such as a car or furniture, the person needs to understand the consequences. If you, the borrower, default, your parent, relative, or friend could lose these items.

- The person can ask the lender to calculate the amount of money that might be owed. The lender isn't required to do this, but may if asked. The cosigner may be able to negotiate the specific terms of the obligation. For example, the liability could be limited to the principal on the loan, not including late charges, court costs, or attorneys' fees. In this case, the lender can be asked to include a statement in the contract similar to: "The cosigner will be responsible only for the principal balance on this loan at the time of default."

- The cosigner can ask the lender to agree, in writing, to be notified if you, the borrower, miss a payment. That will give the cosigner time to deal with the problem or to make back payments without having to repay the entire amount immediately.

- The cosigner should sure to get copies of all important papers, such as the loan contract, the Truth-in-Lending Disclosure Statement, and warranties (if the loan is for a purchase). The cosigner may need these documents if there's a dispute between you and the seller. The lender is not required to give the cosigner these papers; the cosigner may have to get copies from you.

- State laws vary; cosigners should check the laws in their own state.

Chapter 26

Avoiding Abusive Lending

Advance-Fee Loan Scams Most Frequently Reported Type Of Consumer Fraud

A survey by the Federal Trade Commission shows that nearly 25 million adults in the United States—11.2% of the adult population—were victims of fraud during the year studied. American Indians and Alaska Natives were the ethnic group most likely to be victims: nearly 34% had experienced one or more frauds in the preceding year. Of African Americans, 17% were victims; over 14% of Hispanics were victims; and over 6% of non-Hispanic whites were victims.

The survey of 2,500 randomly chosen consumers shows that consumers with high levels of debt were more likely to be victims of fraud. Three of the top four categories of fraud related to credit, including credit-repair scams often targeted at those carrying high debt loads or having bad credit.

About This Chapter: This chapter begins with "Advance-Fee Loan Scams Most Frequently Reported Type Of Consumer Fraud," excerpted from "FTC Releases Consumer Fraud Survey," Federal Trade Commission (FTC), August 5, 2004. "Payday Loans = Costly Cash" is from an FTC *Consumer Alert* dated February 2000. "How Pawnshops Work," is excerpted from an article by Marshall Brain, © 2005 How Stuff Works, Inc. Reprinted with permission. "Scholarship Scams" is reprinted from the Teen Consumer Scrapbook, http://www.atg.wa.gov/teenconsumer/index.htm, a project of Ellensburg High School, Ellensburg, Washington, and sponsored by the Washington State Attorney General. Reprinted with permission.

The most frequently reported type of consumer fraud was *advance-fee loan scams,* in which consumers pay a fee for a "guaranteed" loan or credit card. Four and a half million consumers—2.1% of the U.S. adult population—paid advance fees but did not receive the promised loan or card. In fact, some consumers reported that more than once during the last year they paid fees to get loans or credit cards they did not get.

Buyers' club memberships or *bills for unordered publications* was the second most commonly reported fraud category in the survey. Some four million consumers—1.9% of the U.S. adult population—were unwittingly billed for memberships they did not authorize or publications they did not order.

Credit card insurance scams and *credit repair* were the third and fourth most common frauds identified in the survey. While federal law limits consumers' credit card fraud liability to $50, fraudsters sell credit card insurance by falsely claiming that cardholders face significant financial risk if their credit cards are misused. An estimated 3.3 million consumers bought unnecessary insurance against the unauthorized use of their credit cards.

Some fraudsters convince consumers that they can help them remove truthful, negative information from their credit report, or establish a new credit record. They can't, and credit repair schemes are illegal, but two million consumers paid for "credit repair" services the year prior to the survey.

In addition, the survey found that an estimated 13.9 million consumers were victims of telephone "slamming"—unauthorized and illegal changes in long distance telephone service.

The survey reveals that 33% of fraud victims first learned about a fraudulent offer or product from print advertising in newspapers, magazines, direct mail, catalogs, or posters. Telemarketing was the first source of contact in 17% of the frauds. Only 14% of fraudulent offers were promoted using Internet and e-mail; television or radio advertising account for only 10.6% of fraudulent offers.

Women and younger consumers are more likely to complain if they have been victims of fraud, the survey found. An estimated 74.5% of female victims complained. For males, the complaint rate was ten percentage points lower. Similarly, almost 75% of consumers under the age of 35 complained, compared to only 55.4% of consumers between 55 and 64. Consumers between the ages of 25 and 44 are most likely to be fraud victims; 11% of them were victims, compared to 8.7% in the 45- to 54-year bracket, 6.1% of consumers aged 55 to 64, and only 4.7% of consumers 65 years and older.

Payday Loans = Costly Cash

"I just need enough cash to tide me over until payday."

"GET CASH UNTIL PAYDAY!...$100 or more...FAST."

The ads are on the radio, television, the Internet, even in the mail. They refer to payday loans—loans which come at a very high price.

Check cashers, finance companies and others are making small, short-term, high-rate loans that go by a variety of names: payday loans, cash advance loans, check advance loans, post-dated check loans or deferred deposit check loans.

Usually, a borrower writes a personal check payable to the lender for the amount he or she wishes to borrow plus a fee. The company gives the borrower the amount of the check minus the fee. Fees charged for payday loans are usually a percentage of the

♣ **It's A Fact!!**

The top ten frauds include:

- Advance-fee loan scams—4.55 million victims;
- Buyers clubs—4.05 million victims;
- Credit card insurance—3.35 million victims;
- Credit repair—2 million victims;
- Prize promotions—1.8 million victims;
- Internet services—1.75 million victims;
- Pyramid schemes—1.55 million victims;
- Information services—8 million victims;
- Government job offers—65 million victims; and
- Business opportunities—45 million victims.

Source: FTC, 2004.

face value of the check or a fee charged per amount borrowed—say, for every $50 or $100 loaned. And, if you extend or "roll-over" the loan, say for another two weeks, you will pay the fees for each extension.

Under the Truth in Lending Act, the cost of payday loans—like other types of credit—must be disclosed. Among other information, you must receive, in writing, the finance charge (a dollar amount) and the annual percentage rate or APR (the cost of credit on a yearly basis).

A cash advance loan secured by a personal check, such as a payday loan, is very expensive credit. Let's say you write a personal check for $115 to borrow $100 for up to fourteen days. The check casher or payday lender agrees to hold the check until your next payday. At that time, depending on the particular plan, the lender deposits the check, you redeem the check by paying the $115 in cash, or you roll-over the check by paying a fee to extend the loan for another two weeks. In this example, the cost of the initial loan is a $15 finance charge and 391 percent APR. If you roll-over the loan three times, the finance charge would climb to $60 to borrow $100.

Alternatives To Payday Loans

There are other options. Consider the possibilities before choosing a payday loan:

- When you need credit, shop carefully. Compare offers. Look for the credit offer with the lowest APR—consider a small loan from your credit union or small loan company, an advance on pay from your employer, or a loan from family or friends. A cash advance on a credit card also may be a possibility, but it may have a higher interest rate than your other sources of funds: find out the terms before you decide. Also, a local community-based organization may make small business loans to individuals.

- Compare the APR and the finance charge (which includes loan fees, interest and other types of credit costs) of credit offers to get the lowest cost.

- Ask your creditors for more time to pay your bills. Find out what they will charge for that service—as a late charge, an additional finance charge or a higher interest rate.

- Make a realistic budget, and figure your monthly and daily expenditures. Avoid unnecessary purchases—even small daily items. Their costs add up. Also, build some savings (even small deposits can help) to avoid borrowing for emergencies, unexpected expenses or other items. For example, by putting the amount of the fee that would be paid on a typical $300 payday loan in a savings account for six months, you would have extra dollars available. This can give you a buffer against financial emergencies.

- Find out if you have, or can get, overdraft protection on your checking account. If you are regularly using most or all of the funds in your account and if you make a mistake in your checking (or savings) account ledger or records, overdraft protection can help protect you from further credit problems. Find out the terms of overdraft protection.

- If you need help working out a debt repayment plan with creditors or developing a budget, contact your local consumer credit counseling service. There are non-profit groups in every state that offer credit guidance to consumers. These services are available at little or no cost. Also, check with your employer, credit union or housing authority for no- or low-cost credit counseling programs.

- If you decide you must use a payday loan, borrow only as much as you can afford to pay with your next paycheck and still have enough to make it to the next payday.

How Pawnshops Work

Pawnshops and pawnbroking have been around for thousands of years. The basic idea behind any pawnshop is to loan people money. It goes like this:

1. You bring in something you own and give it to the pawnbroker as collateral for a loan (this act is called pawning).

2. The pawnbroker loans you money against that collateral.

3. When you repay the loan plus the interest, you get your collateral back.

4. If you don't repay the loan, the pawnbroker keeps the collateral.

☞ Remember!!

Predatory Lending Characteristics

While there is no single definition for predatory lending, federal banking regulators, the financial services industry, and consumer advocates generally agree that predatory lending refers to abusive practices involving deception, fraud or unfairness. In some instances, a loan product may not seem predatory initially but could develop predatory characteristics if used to trap or mislead borrowers. These characteristics include:

- Aggressive solicitations to targeted neighborhoods or individuals.

- Home improvement scams.

- Yield-spread premiums—kickbacks to mortgage brokers.

- Shifting unsecured debt into loans.

- Reverse redlining—steering elderly, minority or low-income borrowers to high-cost loans.

- Flipping—repeated refinancing.

- Balloon payments.

- Negative amortization—monthly payments don't pay off accrued interest, thus increasing the principal balance.

- Single-premium credit insurance.

- Excessive prepayment penalties.

- High loan-to-value (LTV) loans—loans in excess of 100% LTV.

- Rolling excessive fees into the loans.

Source: Excerpted from *e-Perspectives Online*, Volume 3, Issue 2, 2003 with permission from the Federal Reserve Bank of Dallas, http://www.dallasfed.org.

How Much Will You Give Me?

To try this out, I went to Rick's Music & Pawn and asked, "How much will you loan me for my wedding ring?"

It's a nice wedding ring—a standard gold ring with my wife's name and our wedding date engraved inside. Bought new in 1994, the ring cost about $140.

Your jewelry might hold special value to you, but you'd be surprised to learn of what little value it is in a pawnshop. The answer was, "$10."

In return for pawning my wedding ring, I would receive $10 and a pawn ticket. The ticket would indicate the following:

- The item that I pawned.

- The amount of money loaned to me for the item.

- The amount of money due in 30 days to get the item back.

My ticket would tell me that, for my wedding ring, I received $10 and that I need to pay $12.20 (that's 2 percent interest plus 20 percent in fees on my $10) in 30 days to get the ring back. Within 30 days, I have three options:

1. I can return to the pawnshop and pay the full amount ($12.20 in this case) to retrieve my wedding ring.

2. I can return to the pawnshop and pay the monthly fee ($2.20 in this case) to extend my loan for another 30 days. At this point, I'd have to enter into a new contract for the next 30 days. Here's where some pawnshops differ on the second-month contract: Some would make you pay 22 percent on the new principal, $12.20, (for a total of $14.88), while other pawnshops will allow you to continue paying 22 percent on the original principal.

3. I can do nothing, in which case the pawnshop keeps my ring and sells it.

That, in a nutshell, is the basic pawnshop transaction. In a busy pawnshop, that sort of transaction happens hundreds of times every day. In many communities, the pawnshop is pretty much the only easy way to borrow small amounts of money. If you need $100 to make it through the week to your next paycheck, where are you going to get the money? A bank is not going to touch a small loan like that, and even if it did it would take a week or two to process the application. A pawnshop is a quick, easy way to get a loan.

Of course, $2.20 fees due in 30 days for a $10 loan is a pretty steep rate. That's 264 percent per year!

Scholarship Scams

Graduating from high school is an exciting time in your life, but it can also be a stressful time. There are many preparations to be made: figuring out what your future plans are, finding the right college, and applying for all those scholarships. Be aware, in the middle of this confusion, there are many scholarship scams out in the "real world". Businesses or consultants may offer to help you find scholarship dollars, and according to the Federal Trade Commission, they lure you in with promises of easy money.

The scholarship might not be legitimate if it:

• Promises or guarantees free money.

• Encourages you to act quickly before you lose out.

• Announces money has been reserved for you.

• States millions of dollars in scholarship funds go unused each year, and they are just waiting for you.

• Guarantees a scholarship or your money back.

✎ What's It Mean?

As defined by the North Carolina General Statutes, 91A-3 (Pawnbrokers Modernization Act of 1989):

Pawnbroker: Any person engaged in the business of lending money on the security of pledged goods and who may also purchase merchandise for resale from dealers and traders.

Pawnshop: The location at which, or premises in which, a pawnbroker regularly conducts business.

Pawn/Pawn Transaction: A written bailment of personal property as security for a debt, redeemable on certain terms within 180 days, unless renewed, and with an implied power of sale on default.

Source: © 2005 How StuffWorks, Inc.

- Boasts "we do all the work" or "you will not find this opportunity anywhere else."

These are just some statements that you may run into. While not all of these statements indicate you are being scammed, it is important to be aware of the lines con artists commonly use.

Tips

For those of you who are up to your neck in scholarship applications, here are some helpful tips. First, read all the information and keep a record for yourself. Never give out financial information over the phone, and don't pay anyone who says they are holding a scholarship for you. Check to make sure that the foundation or program offering the scholarship is legitimate before sending money to apply. Last, don't be afraid to ask questions; legitimate scholarships are eager to give you all the information you want.

Following these suggestions can save a lot of stress in the long run and can make the time and effort you spend rewarding.

If you believe you have been scammed, the best thing to do is contact the National Fraud Information Center by calling their toll-free number: 1-800-876-7060.

Chapter 27

Understanding Credit Cards

Credit Cards

A fistful of credit cards is a good thing, right? Well, maybe yes and maybe no. With a credit card you are able to receive money, goods, or services in the present, in exchange for a promise to pay in the future.

Used wisely, credit cards enable people to expand their income, immediately enjoy the results of their labor, and manage short-term money problems. Although a credit card may seem like the perfect answer to your money problems, if used unwisely you can get into a lot of trouble. If you are unable to pay off your credit cards you may end up in a debt hole that you dug for yourself. Don't take the promise of "easy payment plans" too literally. Using more credit than you can afford is a trap.

About This Chapter: This chapter begins with "Credit Cards," reprinted from the Teen Consumer Scrapbook, http://www.atg.wa.gov/teenconsumer/index.htm, a project of Ellensburg High School, Ellensburg, Washington, and sponsored by the Washington State Attorney General. Reprinted with permission. "Credit Cards = Borrowing" is excerpted from "Credit Cards," © 2002 Illinois Division of Banks and Real Estate. (Neither the State of Illinois nor any of its agencies, is liable for any improper or incorrect use of the information contained herein and assumes no responsibility for anyone's use of the information.) "Using Credit Responsibly" from the *Credit Center* is reprinted with permission from http://www.choicenerd.com. © 2005 ChoiceNerd.com. All rights reserved. "Credit Card Fees Often Go Unnoticed Even As They Increase" is from *FDIC Consumer News*, 2001, Federal Deposit Insurance Corporation. "Choosing a Credit Card" is from the Federal Reserve Board of Governors, May 3, 2002.

According to the experts, the primary purpose of a credit card should be convenience. Buying by phone, over the Net or just for the ease of not carrying cash are all examples of appropriate card use. If you use your credit card properly you will pay off the total you charged each month. If you do not pay off the balance owed, you will have to pay interest.

Credit card bills state clearly what your minimum payment must be, but beware—minimum payments are a trap; they are often designed so that it takes months or years to pay off the balance.

There are many different types of credit cards. A department store or chain of stores may issue retail credit cards for use in the main store or in any of its branches. The store handles the processing and the billing. Bank cards, like MasterCard and Visa, are credit cards issued by banks and accepted by millions of businesses in the United States and abroad. They can be used at hotels, restaurants, department stores, theaters, and airline ticket offices—just about anywhere. Major oil companies issue credit cards that provide credit for gas, oil, and other products. Interest charges and fees vary with each type of credit card.

Excessive credit debt is a serious problem that frequently begins right after high school. It is important to remember the differences between wants and needs. Pay close attention to your spending habits, refuse to charge things that are not essential and plan to pay your credit card off every month.

Credit Cards = Borrowing

Credit cards are a convenient form of borrowing. People generally use credit cards to purchase goods and services. Credit cards represent a revolving line of credit. This means there is an unlimited number of purchases that can be made with a credit card, up to a pre-approved limit. At least some portion of the bill must be paid every month. This is called a minimum payment, which is often a percentage of the balance.

Credit card companies start soliciting students in high school. Often, credit card companies will send pre-approved credit card offers to students. Before accepting the offer, always remember to review all the terms. Pre-approved credit offers are subject to verification of income, employment, and credit history. Remember to shop for the best possible deal.

Make sure the terms of the plan are understood. Read the fine print. Beware of introductory rates. A credit card might not have an annual fee for the first year but will charge a fee for the second year. Also a card might start off with a low interest rate, but the interest rate might rise after a few months. If the monthly bill is expected to be paid in full each month, it will be more important to compare the annual fee and other charges than the interest rate.

Beware of credit card issuers who require application fees. Most credit card issuers don't charge fees to open accounts.

Once the basics of credit are learned, as a young adult it is important to have a credit card in your own name. It's a fact that credit becomes increasingly difficult to obtain once a person graduates from college. One way to build a good credit history is to obtain a major credit card and then use it responsibly. Responsibility means making payments on time, according to the terms and conditions of the lender. Avoid paying minimum balances, as with other forms of credit, credit cards become a problem when someone spends more then they can afford. The higher the credit balance climbs, the faster the interest will grow.

✎ What's It Mean?

Annual Percentage Rate (APR): The APR represents the rate of interest charged plus fees, expressed as a yearly rate. If a balance is kept on a credit card it is best to look for a low APR. If the bill is paid in full every month than it will be more important to compare the annual fee and other charges.

Fees: It is important to check annual fees, late fees, or over-the-limit fees. If good credit history is present then most credit card issuers will waive the annual fee.

Grace Period: The grace period is the number of days the balance must be paid until a creditor starts charging interest.

Interest Rates: Interest rates can be fixed or variable. Fixed rates means the interest rate will not change. Variable rates means the rate can increase or decrease based on the terms of the contract.

Source: © 2002 Illinois Division of Banks and Real Estate.

Using Credit Responsibly

Credit can be a very convenient; yet, tempting form of payment to use. People typically use credit as a way to pay for items that cost more than they can afford to take out of their current income or savings. Credit purchases offer the advantage of delayed billing, because you are given a grace period before you are responsible for making a payment. People frequently use credit to live beyond their means. Overspending is the biggest danger of using credit, because it's so easy to do. Many credit card companies target young consumers due to their impulsive buying habits and inexperience. Unlike paying cash, credit purchases do not take an immediate dent out of your pockets. Therefore, you can go on a shopping spree at your local mall without having to take a dollar out of your pocket. Overspenders assume they can afford to buy the things they charge, because they are able to make the minimum payment. Yet the minimum payment does little to pay off your debts and prolongs your credit payoff due to the accumulation of finance charges.

> ♣ **It's A Fact!!**
>
> A credit card balance of $1,000 takes 12 years to pay off if only the minimum required payment (2.5% of the balance) is made. By adding just $25 every month the payment time is only two years and seven months.
>
> Source: © 2002 Illinois Division of Banks and Real Estate.

In order to establish and maintain a good credit history it is important to be very disciplined with your purchases. Here are some suggestions to follow when handling your credit:

- Choose credit cards that offer the most benefits including: low interest rates, no annual fees, insurance protections, and other special offers like a 0% introductory interest rate.

- Periodically use credit to purchase items even if you have the cash to pay for them which will enable you to maintain a current credit history. However, pay the full amount when you receive your statement.

- Make the largest payment you can afford when you receive a credit statement. If you can pay off the payment every month, do it. By making a considerable payment, you lessen the interest charges that accumulate.

- Avoid purchases from high interest rate cards such as department stores.

- As you start to receive better credit offers, close higher interest rate cards and take advantage of low interest balance transfer rates. (Beware of fees associated with the transfer.)

- Consult creditors and make payment arrangements immediately if you cannot meet payments as agreed.

Credit Debt Limits

One of the best ways to avoid credit problems is to monitor your overall credit exposure. A useful credit guideline is not exceeding 20% of your monthly take-home pay. Most experts consider the 20% rule as the "maximum" debt burden and recommend debt safety ratios closer to 10% to 15%.

Too many people forget they must eventually pay for the items they charge. Don't make the mistake of charging up credit cards and applying for more credit cards, just to max them out also. Try not to use credit while paying down other excessive balances. Runaway debt can be very difficult to get your hands around, and will only impair your financial outlook in the long run.

Establishing Credit

The benefits of establishing good credit are numerous:

- Access to large amounts of money for emergencies and other special purchases from higher credit limits

- Assurance for potential employers or lenders that you are a responsible person

- Realized savings from low interest rates on purchases and delayed outlays of large sums of money

- Personal satisfaction of managing your own affairs

The following are suggestions on establishing a good credit history. It is important not to get yourself in credit debt while trying to establish a strong credit history.

1.	The first step to establishing good credit is to open both a checking and savings account. By opening bank accounts you begin to establish stability and express to creditors that you handle your finances in a professional manner.

2.	Next, open a credit card account, if you do not already have one, and make a few credit purchases a month. By purchasing through credit, you begin to establish your credit history. Remember to pay your balances off each month.

3.	Next, if you do not already have a history of paying off personal loans, take out a small loan ($500) and pay it off to demonstrate you can responsibly handle a loan. Even if you do not need a loan, you could put the borrowed money in an interest-bearing account and pay it off over a six-month period. This tactic will come in handy when you go to make a major purchase such as a car.

The best way to build a strong credit history is to consistently make payments on time month after month. When you accept a credit card or other financial obligations, you are pledging to pay your bills in a timely fashion.

Credit Card Finance

Your APR or Annual Percentage Rate is usually the advertised rate of interest you will pay over the lifetime of your credit loan. However, you must also know what your effective annual rate is because it truly defines what you will pay in interest per year, and takes into account the compounding of interest. For example, an APR of 18% would actually equal an effective annual rate of 19.6%.

It is your federal right as a consumer to be told the dollar amount of interest charges (where applicable) and the APR on any financing you are considering. According to the Truth in Lending Act, credit lenders must disclose the amount of interest they charge and their method of computing finance charges. The following finance calculations will show you the various ways how credit card companies determine your monthly statements.

Average Daily Balance Method. The ADB is a method of figuring the specific balance on your monthly purchases to apply interest to. There are four common methods of calculating (ADB):

1. *ADB (including new purchases).* This is the most common form of calculation. For each day of the billing cycle: add the outstanding balance including new purchases, subtract payments and credits, then divide by the number of days in the billing cycle.

2. *ADB (excluding new purchases).* Calculated the same way as the method above; however, new purchases are not added in.

3. *Two-cycle ADB (including new purchases).* Calculated the same way as above; yet, using the average daily balance for both the current and previous billing cycles.

4. *Two-cycle ADB (excluding new purchases).* Calculated like the above two cycle method, but excluding new purchases.

Out of the four methods that have just been described, ADB (including new purchases) is the most commonly used method that you will be exposed to. Table 27.1 shows an example of how the finance charge works for a credit card using this method at the end of the month with a 12% APR:

Table 27.1. How A Finance Charge Works

Days In Billing Cycle		Balance		Total
first 5	x	$200	=	$1000
next 15	x	$500	=	$7500
last 10	x	$600	=	$6000
(sum)				($14,500)
ADB	=	$14,500 / 30 days	=	$483.33

$483.33 x .02 (24% APR / 12 mos.) = $9.67 in finance charges

Source: Reprinted with permission from http://www.choicenerd.com. © 2005 ChoiceNerd.com. All rights reserved.

Credit Card Fees Often Go Unnoticed Even As They Increase

Credit cards offer great convenience to consumers, but that convenience comes at a price. In recent years, card issuers have raised or added new fees for their products and services. While these costs are described in the mailings and card agreements (contracts) consumers receive from card companies, too many people forget about these fees or aren't aware of them until after they've run up a sizable bill. Here are some examples of fees that are becoming more common or more costly, yet still go unnoticed by many cardholders:

Monthly Maintenance Fees. Rather than charge an annual fee, some lenders impose a monthly fee, often from $6 to $12 a month, whether you use the card that month or not. "Many people don't blink twice over $6 a month—it doesn't seem so bad," says Janet Kincaid, a credit card specialist with the Federal Deposit Insurance Corporation (FDIC). "But if they stopped to think that they're paying $72 a year just to be able to carry a card, they'd realize they could have done better by paying a lower annual fee."

Balance Transfer Fees. You've probably received mail from a credit card issuer trumpeting a "can't-beat-this" low Annual Percentage Rate (APR) of, say, 2.9% on any balance you transfer to that card from a competitor's card. But, there also could be a fee for the balance transfer that could outweigh the benefit of the low interest rate. In addition, there may be no grace period on the balance you transfer. "Interest often begins accruing the moment the balance transfer is completed," Kincaid explains. "Even if you paid off the balance by the due date, you may still incur interest charges."

Suppose you transfer a $100 balance at a special 2.9 % APR to a card that otherwise charges a 15% APR, and you already have a $200 balance on that card from your previous purchases. Then let's say you send in a $50 card payment at the end of the month. It's important to know how that $50 payment will be applied. Will the payment go to reduce the "old" high-rate $200 balance or the "new" low-rate $100 balance you transferred? The card issuer can decide how to allocate your payment, and unless you know the card issuer's policy by calling the company or checking your card agreement, you can assume the procedures will benefit the card issuer.

Cash Advance Fees. When you use your credit card to get cash from an ATM, that's considered a loan, and you will incur interest charges immediately, without a grace period. But in addition, you may be charged a transaction fee by both the financial institution that holds your credit card and by the bank that owns the ATM you're using. The fee can either be a flat dollar amount or a percentage (perhaps 3%) of the cash advance. The fee can make a simple cash withdrawal fairly expensive.

Fees For Late Payments. If you mail in your payment too close to the due date and miss the deadline, you could face a late-payment fee. These fees have increased in recent years from about $15 to as much as $29. You may face other penalties, such as having your interest rate raised or your card canceled. Here's another alternative to mailing a payment late: Consider calling your card company to authorize it to "debit" (deduct) your payment directly from your bank account before the deadline. "This convenience will cost you more than a postage stamp, usually as much as $10," says Kincaid, "but it's usually a better, cheaper option than paying late and incurring a penalty."

Fees For Sending In Less Than The Minimum Monthly Payment. Suppose you're expected to pay at least $50 for a card payment but you only have $25 available, so you send it in anyway. "Yes, you've made a payment," Kincaid says, "but anything less than the minimum can be considered a late payment, subject to a late-payment fee." Again, those fees have increased to as much as $29 at many institutions. And, because an insufficient payment is considered a late payment, you could be subject to other penalties, such as having your interest rate raised or your card canceled.

The lesson here? Read and understand a credit card offer before you commit to anything. And monitor your monthly billings or other mailings for notices of fee increases or rule changes by your card company.

Choosing A Credit Card

Shopping around for a credit card can save you money on interest and fees. You'll want to find one with features that match your needs.

How will you use your credit card?

The first step in choosing a credit card is thinking about how you will use it.

If you expect to always pay your monthly bill in full—and other features such as frequent flyer miles don't interest you—your best choice may be a card that has no annual fee and offers a longer grace period.

If you sometimes carry over a balance from month to month, you may be more interested in a card that carries a lower interest rate (stated as an annual percentage rate, or APR).

♣ It's A Fact!!

Most credit cards charge fees under certain circumstances:

- *Annual fee* (sometimes billed monthly): Charged for having the card.

- *Cash advance fee:* Charged when you use the card for a cash advance; may be a flat fee (for example, $3.00) or a percentage of the cash advance (for example, 3%).

- *Balance-transfer fee:* Charged when you transfer a balance from another credit card (Your credit card company may send you "checks" to pay off the other card. The balance is transferred when you use one of these checks to pay the amount due on the other card.)

- *Late-payment fee:* Charged if your payment is received after the due date.

- *Over-the-credit-limit fee:* Charged if you go over your credit limit.

- *Credit-limit-increase fee:* Charged if you ask for an increase in your credit limit.

- *Set-up fee:* Charged when a new credit card account is opened.

- *Return-item fee:* Charged if you pay your bill by check and the check is returned for non-sufficient funds (that is, your check bounces).

- *Other fees:* Some credit card companies charge a fee if you pay by telephone (that is, if you arrange by phone for payment to be transferred from your bank to the company) or to cover the costs of reporting to credit bureaus, reviewing your account, or providing other customer services. Read the information in your credit card agreement to see if there are other fees and charges.

Source: Federal Reserve Board of Governors, 2004.

If you expect to use your card to get cash advances, you'll want to look for a card that carries a lower APR and lower fees on cash advances. Some cards charge a higher APR for cash advances than for purchases.

What are the APRs?

The annual percentage rate (APR) is the way of stating the interest rate you will pay if you carry over a balance, take out a cash advance, or transfer a balance from another card. The APR states the interest rate as a yearly rate.

Multiple APRs: A single credit card may have several APRs:

- *One APR for purchases, another for cash advances, and yet another for balance transfers:* The APRs for cash advances and balance transfers often are higher than the APR for purchases (for example, 14% for purchases, 18% for cash advances, and 19% for balance transfers).

- *Tiered APRs:* Different rates are applied to different levels of the outstanding balance (for example, 16% on balances of $1–$500 and 17% on balances above $500).

- *A penalty APR:* The APR may increase if you are late in making payments. For example, your card agreement may say, "If your payment arrives more than ten days late two times within a six-month period, the penalty rate will apply."

- *An introductory APR:* A different rate will apply after the introductory rate expires.

- *A delayed APR:* A different rate will apply in the future. For example, a card may advertise that there is "no interest until next March." Look for the APR that will be in effect after March.

If you carry over a part of your balance from month to month, even a small difference in the APR can make a big difference in how much you will pay over a year.

Fixed vs. variable APR: Some credit cards are "fixed rate"—the APR doesn't change, or at least doesn't change often. Even the APR on a "fixed rate" credit card can change over time. However, the credit card company must tell you before increasing the fixed APR.

Other credit cards are "variable rate"—the APR changes from time to time. The rate is usually tied to another interest rate, such as the prime rate or the Treasury bill rate. If the other rate changes, the rate on your card may change, too. Look for information on the credit card application and in the credit card agreement to see how often your card's APR may change (the agreement is like a contract—it lists the terms and conditions for using your credit card).

How long is the grace period?

The grace period is the number of days you have to pay your bill in full without triggering a finance charge. For example, the credit card company may say that you have "25 days from the statement date, provided you paid your previous balance in full by the due date." The statement date is given on the bill.

The grace period usually applies only to new purchases. Most credit cards do not give a grace period for cash advances and balance transfers. Instead, interest charges start right away.

If you carried over any part of your balance from the preceding month, you may not have a grace period for new purchases. Instead, you may be charged interest as soon as you make a purchase (in addition to being charged interest on the earlier balance you have not paid off). Look on the credit card application for information about the "method of computing the balance for purchases" to see if new purchases are included or excluded. Information on methods of computing the balance is in the section "How is the finance charge calculated?"

How is the finance charge calculated?

The finance charge is the dollar amount you pay to use credit. The amount depends in part on your outstanding balance and the APR.

Credit card companies use one of several methods to calculate the outstanding balance. The method can make a big difference in the finance charge you'll pay. Your outstanding balance may be calculated:

- Over one billing cycle or two,

- Using the adjusted balance, the average daily balance, or the previous balance, and

- Including or excluding new purchases in the balance.

Depending on the balance you carry and the timing of your purchases and payments, you'll usually have a lower finance charge with one-cycle billing and either:

- The average daily balance method excluding new purchases,

- The adjusted balance method, or

- The previous balance method.

Minimum finance charge: Some credit cards have a minimum finance charge. You'll be charged that minimum even if the calculated amount of your finance charge is less. For example, your finance charge may be calculated to be 35¢—but if the company's minimum finance charge is $1.00, you'll pay $1.00. A minimum finance charge usually applies only when you must pay a finance charge—that is, when you carry over a balance from one billing cycle to the next.

What are the cash advance features?

Some credit cards let you borrow cash in addition to making purchases on credit. Most credit card companies treat these cash advances and your purchases differently. If you plan to use your card for cash advances, look for information about:

- *Access:* Most credit cards let you use an ATM to get a cash advance. Or the credit card company may send you "checks" that you can write to get the cash advance.

- *APR:* The APR for cash advances may be higher than the APR for purchases.

- *Fees:* The credit card company may charge a fee in addition to the interest you will pay on the amount advanced.

- *Limits:* Some credit cards limit cash advances to a dollar amount (for example, $200 per cash advance or $500 per week) or a portion of your credit limit (for example, 75% of your available credit limit).

- *How payments are credited:* Many credit card companies apply your payments to purchases first and then to cash advances. Read your credit card agreement to learn how your payments will be credited.

How much is the credit limit?

The credit limit is the maximum total amount—for purchases, cash advances, balance transfers, fees, and finance charges—you may charge on your credit card. If you go over this limit, you may have to pay an "over-the-credit-limit fee."

What kind of card is it?

Most credit card companies offer several kinds of cards:

- *Secured cards*, which require a security deposit. The larger the security deposit, the higher the credit limit. Secured cards are usually offered to people who have limited credit records—people who are just starting out or who have had trouble with credit in the past.

- *Regular cards*, which do not require a security deposit and have just a few features. Most regular cards have higher credit limits than secured cards but lower credit limits than premium cards.

- *Premium cards* (gold, platinum, titanium), which offer higher credit limits and usually have extra features—for example, product warranties, travel insurance, or emergency services.

> ✔ **Quick Tip**
> Before you sign up to pay for any of special credit card features, think carefully about whether it will be useful for you. Don't pay for something you don't want or don't need.
>
> Source: Federal Reserve Board of Governors, 2004.

Does the card offer incentives and other features?

Many credit card companies offer incentives to use the card and other special features:

- Rebates (money back) on the purchases you make

- Frequent flier miles or phone-call minutes

- Additional warranty coverage for the items you purchase

- Car rental insurance

- Travel accident insurance or travel-related discounts

- Credit card registration, to help if your wallet or purse is lost or stolen and you need to report that all your credit cards are missing

Credit cards may also offer, for a price:

- Insurance to cover the payments on your credit card balance if you become unemployed or disabled, or die. Premiums are usually due monthly, making it easy to cancel if the payments are higher than you want to pay or you decide you don't need the insurance any longer.

- Insurance to cover the first $50 of charges if your card is lost or stolen. Under federal law, you are not responsible for charges over $50.

How do I find information about credit cards?

You can find lists of credit card plans, rates, and terms on the Internet, in personal finance magazines, and in newspapers. The Federal Reserve System surveys credit card companies every six months. You'll need to get the most recent information directly from the credit card company—by phoning the company, looking on the company's web site, or reading a solicitation or application.

Under federal law, all solicitations and applications for credit cards must include certain key information, in a disclosure box similar to the one shown in Figure 27.1.

What are your liability limits?

If your credit card is lost or stolen—and then is used by someone without your permission—you do not have to pay more than $50 of those charges.

This protection is provided by the federal Truth in Lending Act. You do not need to buy "credit card insurance" to cover amounts over $50.

If you discover that your card is lost or stolen, report it immediately to your credit card company. Call the toll-free number listed on your monthly statement. The company will cancel the card so that new purchases cannot be made with it. The company will also send you a new card.

Make a list of your account numbers and the companies' phone numbers. Keep the list in a safe place. If your wallet or purse is lost or stolen, you'll have all the numbers in one place. Take the list of phone numbers—not the account numbers—with you when you travel, just in case a card is lost or stolen.

Annual percentage rate (APR) for purchases	2.9% until 11/1/06 after that, **14.9%**
Other APRs	Cash-advance APR: 15.9% Balance-transfer APR: 15.9% Penalty rate: 23.9% See explanation below. *
Variable-rate information	Your APR for purchase transactions may vary. The rate is determined monthly by adding 5.9% to the Prime Rate **
Grace period for repayment of balances for purchases	25 days on average
Method of computing the balance for purchases	Average daily balance (excluding new purchases)
Annual fees	None
Minimum finance charge	$.50
Transaction fee for cash advances: 3% of the amount advanced Balance-transfer fee: 3% of the amount transferred Late-payment fee: $25 Over-the-credit-limit fee: $25	
* Explanation of penalty. If your payment arrives more than ten days late two times within a six-month period, the penalty rate will apply. ** The Prime Rate used to determine your APR is the rate published in the *Wall Street Journal* on the 10th day of the prior month.	

Figure 27.1. Sample Credit Card Solicitation/Application (Source: Federal Reserve Board of Governors, 2004).

✎ What's It Mean?

The following terms may appear in the disclosure box on a credit card solicitation or application form (Note: These terms are listed in the order in which they occur in the example shown in Figure 27.1):

APR for purchases: The annual percentage rate you'll be charged if you carry over a balance from month to month. If the card has an introductory rate, you'll see both that rate and the rate that will apply after the introductory rate expires.

Other APRs: The APRs you'll be charged if you get a cash advance on your card, transfer a balance from another card, or are late in making a payment. More information about the penalty rate may be stated outside the disclosure box—for instance, in a footnote. In the example shown in Figure 27.1, if you make two payments that are more than ten days late within six months, the APR will increase to 23.9%.

Variable-rate information: Information about how the variable rate will be determined (if relevant). More information may be stated outside the disclosure box—for instance, in a footnote.

Grace period for repayment of balances for purchases: The number of days you'll have to pay your bill for purchases in full without triggering a finance charge.

Method of computing the balance for purchases: The method that will be used to calculate your outstanding balance if you carry over a balance and will pay a finance charge.

Annual fees: The amount you'll be charged each twelve-month period for simply having the card.

Minimum finance charge: The minimum, or fixed, finance charge that will be imposed during a billing cycle. A minimum finance charge usually applies only when a finance charge is imposed, that is, when you carry over a balance.

Transaction fee for cash advances: The charge that will be imposed each time you use the card for a cash advance.

Balance-transfer fee: The fee that will be imposed each time you transfer a balance from another card.

Late-payment fee: The fee that will be imposed when your payment is late.

Over-the-credit-limit fee: The fee that will be imposed if your charges exceed the credit limit set for your card.

Source: Federal Reserve Board of Governors, 2004.

What can you do about billing errors?

The federal Fair Credit Billing Act covers billing errors. Examples of billing error are:

- A charge for something you didn't buy.

- A bill for an amount different from the actual amount you charged.

- A charge for something that you did not accept when it was delivered.

- A charge for something that was not delivered according to agreement.

- Math errors.

- Payments not credited to your account.

- A charge by someone who does not have permission to use your credit card.

What if the item you purchase is damaged?

The federal Fair Credit Billing Act allows you to withhold payment on any damaged or poor-quality goods or services purchased with a credit card—even if you have accepted the goods or services—as long as you have made an attempt to solve the problem with the merchant.

The sale must have been for more than $50 and must have taken place in your home state or within 100 miles of your home address. You should notify the credit card company in writing and explain why you are withholding your payment.

You may withhold the payment while the credit card company investigates your claim. If you pay the charges for the goods on your credit card bill before the dispute is resolved, you will lose your right to make a claim.

Chapter 28

Protecting Your Credit Rating

Stay Afloat—Don't Let Those Credit Card Blues Get You Down

One thing you have to learn is how to live within your means. You may be learning how to deal with rent payments, monthly bills and other expenses. At the same time, you'll want to spend money on other things like concerts, movies, CDs, and parties. This becomes a problem when your paycheck or budget aren't enough to cover everything. What do you do?

When you have a credit card, it's so easy to spend money you do not have. You might buy things without hesitation that you never would if you had to pay cash. In less than a blink, you can make purchases way beyond your ability to pay. How are you going to pay the credit card bills? You can easily be on the way to huge financial problems.

About This Chapter: This chapter includes "Stay Afloat—Don't Let Those Credit Card Blues Get You Down," © 2005 Pennsylvania Office of the Attorney General, Bureau of Consumer Protection. Reprinted with permission. "Credit Rating," is excerpted from "Credit Cards," © 2002 Illinois Division of Banks and Real Estate. (Neither the State of Illinois nor any of its agencies, is liable for any improper or incorrect use of the information contained herein and assumes no responsibility for anyone's use of the information.) "Credit Bureaus" and "The Road to Credit Recovery" are excerpted from "Credit Center" and are reprinted with permission from http://www.choicenerd.com. © 2005 ChoiceNerd.com. All rights reserved.

By now you've probably received many credit card offers. Credit card companies are always looking for new customers. They would like you to become a cardholder as early as possible in order to keep you as a satisfied customer for many years. There are a lot of businesses willing to let you have their credit card, despite your being a student. It's easy to get credit cards. And they can help you develop a healthy financial record if used sparingly and responsibly. Unfortunately, you can also get trapped with huge debt and no way out.

Who Defaults On Credit Card Payments?

According to studies, the vast majority of people who default on their credit card payments earn less than $30,000 per year. Most college students make considerably less than that amount. If you don't have a reliable source of income, think long and hard before getting a credit card. If your income is low and you do get a credit card, keep your purchases low so that you can fit your payments into your budget.

It's enticing to use your credit card and run up a tab you cannot pay. The credit card companies recognize that many people are unable to pay the full balance each month. Instead, they will allow you to make a minimum monthly payment. Although this sounds enticing, it can be the start of serious financial problems.

First, when you do not pay off the entire balance, you pay interest on the unpaid amount. Often, interest can be at an annual rate of 18% or more. Credit card interest is among the highest allowed by law. It is not an economical way to borrow.

Second, when you only pay the minimum monthly payment, you are paying interest on almost all of the balance. The interest makes the amount

Remember!!

"Students are getting the hard sell [from credit card companies] and getting into a lot of financial trouble as a result."

—U.S. Rep. Joseph P. Kennedy, Chair, House Banking Subcommittee on Consumer Credit.

Source: Pennsylvania Office of the Attorney General, Bureau of Consumer Protection, 2005.

owed grow at an extremely fast rate. If you continue to pay only the minimum, the amount you owe gets bigger all the time. It is not unusual to pay as much in interest than the cost of your purchases! It can also take you a long, long time to pay off the debt.

For example, if you spend or charge $2,000.00 by credit card in one month, at the interest rate of 18.5%, and only make the minimum monthly payment, it will take you 11 years to pay off the bill. And you will pay a total of $1,934.00 in interest.

Bad Credit Really Can Go On Your Permanent Record

Your history of late payments and missed payments will get sent to the major credit reporting agencies, and forwarded to local "credit bureaus." That information is used to indicate a poor credit history. That can be passed on to anyone from whom you want credit, such as banks, stores, and even landlords.

A poor credit history will follow you everywhere. It is almost impossible to get rid of it. Years from now, it can hurt your chances of getting credit cards, bank loans, or a mortgage to buy a house. Your credit history can even be examined by a potential employer when you are looking for a job.

Credit Rating

Credit is part of life, and should be managed responsibly. Three major credit reporting agencies (Equifax, Experian, TransUnion) monitor and maintain records of every person's credit. Their reports are compiled and comprise a person's credit rating. A credit report is a collection of credit information. It is how creditors predict whether a person will make regular payments on their loans. A financial institution will ask the credit reporting agencies for credit information for a person who is applying for a loan.

Basic information found on a credit report:

- *Identifying Information:* name, social security number, current and previous address, telephone number, birth date, current and previous employers, and spouse's name.

- *Credit History:* Shows how much credit has been extended and how it has been repaid.

- *Public Record Information:* Matters of public record; collection accounts, bankruptcies, foreclosures, tax liens, civil judgments, and late child support payments.

- *Inquiries:* List that identifies creditors and other authorized parties who have requested and received the credit report.

Credit reports can be obtained at any time from any of the three agencies, Equifax, Experian, or TransUnion. It is a good idea to regularly (about every year) request a credit report. The request for a credit report can be done over the phone, in writing, or through the Internet. Be sure to call the credit reporting agencies or look up information on the Internet to verify specific requirements needed to get a credit report.

If you think there is an error on your credit report, contact the credit-reporting agency and write a dispute letter. Remember to keep a copy of the dispute letter. The credit reporting agencies are required to conduct an investigation within 30 days of receiving the letter. [See Chapter 31 for detailed

> **✔ Quick Tip**
> *If You Do Get A Credit Card...*
>
> If, despite the risks, you decide to get a credit card, there are a lot of matters to consider. There are many types of cards, a variety of ways of calculating interest, and other variables. Before you sign up, find out the answers to these questions:
>
> - What type of card is it? Credit? Debit? Secured?
> - What up-front payments are required? An annual fee? A deposit as security?
> - What is the interest rate? How is it calculated? Can it change?
> - What is the maximum you can charge?
> - Can you get a cash advance? What fees and interest rates apply?
> - What credit reporting services does the company use? How often does it report?
>
> Source: Pennsylvania Office of the Attorney General, Bureau of Consumer Protection, 2005.

contact information for the three agencies, including contact information for correcting errors.]

Having good credit is not difficult, but it does take perseverance and diligence. Here are some important tips to keep in mind:

Pay On Time: This is the most crucial part of maintaining good credit. When using a credit card it does not matter how much of the balance is paid, but it does matter when the check gets to the card issuer. Make sure all of the credit cards' specific policies regarding "timely" payments are known to you.

Closing An Account: An account not closed will stay open on the credit report, even if the account is not in use. As a result, creditors will see that account as potential debt, which will hurt your credit rating. To close an account, notify the credit card company. Once the decision to close an account is made, cut the credit card into pieces and throw it in the garbage.

Keep Information Private: Keep all credit card and PIN numbers private. Do not share them with anyone.

Pay More Than The Minimum: Minimum payments, as they are a percentage of your total balance, are engineered so the balance is never paid off. By paying more then the minimum balance your debt will be erased more quickly.

Keep Your Spending Within A Budget: It's hard to stay out of debt when overspending occurs. Create a budget for yourself and make sure you follow it. Clearly define your goals and define your financial plan.

Maintain Good Records: Overdrawing a checking account can be reported to the credit agencies. Keep track of all finances.

Credit Bureaus

As already stated, it is very important to manage your credit responsibly. Credit bureaus are agencies that collect and sell your financial information to credit card companies and other financial entities. They create credit reports, which grade your financial fitness. If you have ever wondered why you

Table 28.1. Credit Scoring

Variances	Score	Variances	Score
Marital Status		*Annual Income*	
Married	2	Under 25,000	4
Not Married	0	25-35,000	8
Residence		35-65,000	12
Live with Parents	0	65,000+	16
Rent	3	*Financial Accts.*	
Own-Mortgage	8	Checking	3
Own-No Mortgage	13	Savings	3
Age		Paid Loans	5
Under and 25	2	*Monthly Debt*	
26 to 64	8	$0-200	4
65+	2	200-500	2
Length/Employment		500-1,000	0
0-1 Yr.	0	1,000+	-2
2-5 Yrs.	5	Source: © 2005 ChoiceNerd.com.	
5+ Yrs.	10	Reprinted with permission.	

received a pre-approved credit card or similar offers from telemarketers, it is because they have bought access to your financial information and feel you qualify for their product. Information in your file comes from these sources:

• creditors who have done business with you

• creditors who supply information at your request

• public recorded court documents

Your credit file does not contain all of your personal information. There is no information on: religious/political affiliations, lifestyle, or race. However, the typical information displayed on a credit report is as follows:

- Your name, social security number, birth date, employer, and current/ previous addresses

- Public records information involving bankruptcies, tax liens, and court judgments

- Your credit history including a list of credit cards you have opened or closed, your payment history and timeliness, and account balances

- The dates and names of institutions that have requested your financial information

Credit reports help financial institutions paint a picture of your financial history. A couple of late payments may not scare off potential creditors; however, a pattern of 30 to 60 days late

✔ **Quick Tip**

To order a copy of your credit report, contact one or all of the following agencies:

- Equifax: www.equifax.com
  1-800-685-1111
  P.O. Box 740241
  Atlanta, GA 30374-0241

- Experian: www.experian.com
  1-888-397-3742
  P.O. Box 2104
  Allen, TX 75013

- TransUnion:
  www.transunion.com
  1-800-916-8800
  P.O. Box 1000
  Chester, PA 19022

payments or greater will show an inability to responsibly handle your credit obligations. Consequently, it is important to use your credit wisely, because a poor credit payment history can scar your credit capability for up to 10 years. Also, it is important to know that some employers request a copy of your credit report to determine your character as an individual. *Do not avoid credit collectors, because your unpaid balance will not go away and will make you look highly irresponsible when your credit file is pulled.* If you cannot pay your credit bills on time it is essential that you make arrangements to pay down the balance. Additionally, you can place statements on your credit report to explain your financial circumstances. For example if your creditor canceled your credit card, you could insert a statement that reads "I lost my job due to company downsize; however, I made arrangements to pay off the balance in full." Inserting a statement does not guarantee consideration from potential creditors; yet, it does allow them to better understand your circumstances. Lastly, mistakes that appear on your credit report can be investigated and corrected by each credit bureau; however, you will have to contact all three major credit bureaus because they do not release their findings to each other.

The Credit Report

As you can see, credit agencies give higher scores to people who are more established, which is difficult for a young person just getting started. You must focus on controlling the controllables such as opening a savings and checking account and staying current on all loans. How many points would you have using Table 28.1? [Note that a high number is better.]

Your credit report, collected information from your financial activities, is like a snapshot of your credit rating.

☞ **Remember!!**

Get a copy of your credit report from more than one credit bureau. Check for inaccuracies.

Don't share personal information with anyone who doesn't have the right to know. Among other things, that means you shouldn't write down your social security, credit card, or telephone numbers on checks if it's not appropriate to do so. And don't offer this information to store clerks and unknown telephone marketers.

Be aware that almost every time you call an 800, 888, or 900 number, your name and address are captured by the company you dialed. This information becomes part of your electronic profile.

Ask your bank to notify you in writing when someone requests your records. Examine your automated teller receipts to make sure that the balance is correct and that nobody is tapping your account electronically.

Source: Excerpted from "Frequently Asked Questions," United States Secret Service, 2002.

The Road To Credit Recovery

Getting over your head in credit debt is very easy to do. Every day we are constantly bombarded with commercials and advertisements, which entice us to buy the latest products. Many of us get into credit card debt because we consistently increase our expenses without a comparable increase in our income. If you find yourself over your head in credit debt, you should consider taking the following steps:

1. Stop spending—When you cannot pay your current bills, it only makes sense not to keep spending. If you are in credit trouble only buy things that are a necessity with cash.

2. Calculate exactly how much debt you are in. You can't develop a plan without knowing what you are up against.

3. Request a credit report to verify your total debt.

4. Be responsible—Map out a plan to begin repaying your debts. If you are behind on payments, call the creditor and set up a repayment schedule. Avoiding creditors and bill collectors will only hamper your ability to obtain credit in the future.

5. After you pay off your debts discontinue usage of high interest cards. Also insert statements on your credit report explaining any unordinary reasons for your credit problems.

Chapter 29

Use Your Card—Don't Let It Use You

How To Avoid Common College Debt Traps

College is a time of many firsts for students: the first time you are living without your parents and the first time you decide on your own schedule. It is also the first time you have to make financial decisions for yourself. It can be frightening, and without proper planning, you could easily find yourself burdened with debts beyond just your student loans.

The most dangerous pitfall for many college students is the overuse of credit cards. Many banks do their best to entice new card holders with low or zero-interest cards. Gary Schatsky, a certified financial planner in New York, says that certain companies specifically prey on the vulnerability of students with no income.

"Just because the kids are approved, it doesn't mean the companies are confident that they can pay their bills," he said. "They are signing on for large debts with low initial interest rates that can skyrocket ultimately."

About This Chapter: This chapter includes text from "How To Avoid Common College Debt Traps," by Eri Kaneko, reprinted with permission of InCharge Education Foundation, Inc., October-November 2003 issue of YOUNG MONEY, www.youngmoney.com. All rights reserved. "Build Your Credit and Your Future" by Keisha Richards and "Get Rid of Debt!," by Samantha Edmondson, are reprinted with permission of InCharge Education Foundation, Inc., Spring 2003 issue of YOUNG MONEY, www.youngmoney.com. "Fiscal Fitness: Choosing A Credit Counselor" is excerpted from a *Facts for Consumers* document produced by the Federal Trade Commission, November 2003.

Kara Marmion, 20, a junior at Pennsylvania State College, understands the dangers of overusing a credit card. "I don't have a credit card," she said. "A lot of my friends have them, but use them sparingly, and they're usually given to them by their parents to use for necessary stuff, like books."

Marmion, a public relations and advertising major, says that her biggest expenses are eating out several times a week, buying clothes, and her sorority dues, which she pays every semester. "I use a check card and stuff adds up," she said. "I don't even realize that until I check my balances."

Schatsky says that sticking to a budget in college may be difficult, but he suggests making a list of your needs versus your wants.

"If anything, it can get you thinking about your purchasing decisions. It's painful, but definitely a positive experience," he said.

He says that it is almost impossible to live within your means as a college student, and he acknowledges that spending sparingly by eating pizza for breakfast, lunch, and dinner for four or more years is not fun.

"You should give yourself the occasional luxury, but still try to live as frugally as possible," he said.

Shelly R. Plumb, an educational consultant based in Pennsylvania who runs a company called A+ College Financial Planning, agrees that keeping to a budget can be challenging. But she says that students should strive to set out at least a loose budget based on the money they have, and alter it based on their needs.

"You can revamp your budget every semester if your expenses are higher than you anticipated," she said. "Look at how much money you have. Then, take less than what you want with you to school, and base your budget off of that."

Plumb also suggests that students ask their parents, who have already had significant experience in planning out finances, for help in mapping out a budget.

"College kids are going to have to learn it the hard way if they don't learn it from their parents," she said.

Build Your Credit And Your Future

Some financial lessons are learned the hard way. Just consider what happened to Shawn Buchanan, a graduate student from Ohio University.

"During my freshman year, I used my credit card to make a purchase for approximately $500 on behalf of an adult who I trusted and who promised to reimburse me upon receipt of the bill," says Buchanan. "However, when the bill came, the person had no money to do so and I was unable to make the monthly payments on time."

Unfortunately, Buchanan is not alone when it comes to making poor money management decisions. Many young adults are ill prepared to take charge of their personal finances. Results from the 2002 Students in Free Enterprise report (SIFE) show that only 38 percent of college students prepare a monthly budget, 32 percent are currently in credit card debt and less than half understand how the stock market works.

Students tend to apply for credit cards, unaware of Annual Percentage Rates (APR) and interest charges because most college campuses and credit card companies fail to educate them about loans and credit card finances.

Because of prior lack of knowledge about APR and grace periods for repayment of purchases, many students do not consider comparing credit cards to determine which credit card is the best and/or the safest one to have.

Colleges don't want to alienate the credit card companies that pay them rebates based on how much each cardholder spends with an affinity card, which allow cardholders to make a contribution to a organization each time the card is used, according to Shannon Buggs of the *Houston Chronicle*, so the more a student charges, the more money a university can make. Some colleges have established codes of conduct for credit card solicitors; however, others choose to continue with this distribution for their own benefit.

"Because most credit card companies are competing for business, they may think that by educating the students, they will lose business to other companies that offer better rates or services than they do," says Donna Hazel, a sophomore at Delaware University. "Schools should perhaps begin to look at how they can assist students in making wise credit card choices."

Rasheed Hodge, a senior at Barry University in Miami, Fla., says, "Applying for a credit card helped me when I was in quite a few financial predicaments, and they also helped to build my credit history because I was being told by car dealers and a few other financial companies that I had insufficient credit history."

Organizations such as SIFE (www.sife.org) have also developed programs like Credit-Wise Cats, a student-run counseling service designed to teach students about reducing debt, increasing savings, and creating budgets. Last year, the team facilitated workshops for 790 graduates and undergraduates. Test results have shown that students' knowledge of credit and debt management improved by one-third after attending the SIFE counseling sessions.

> ♣ **It's A Fact!!**
> There are some students who have been educated about spending wisely, especially during their college years when building good credit is so important. Those students learned that credit cards could serve users well during emergency situations, and by helping them to build their credit history.
>
> Source: From "Build Your Credit and Your Future" by Keisha Richards; reprinted with permission of InCharge Education Foundation, Inc., Spring 2003 issue of YOUNG MONEY, www.youngmoney.com.

Get Rid of Debt!

Three thousand dollars in major credit card debt and all he got was a lousy T-shirt. During his sophomore year at Southern Illinois University in Carbondale, Neal Papich signed up for a major credit card in order to get a free T-shirt for a fund-raiser. Papich, now a senior in child psychology, has maxed out his $3,000 credit card limit.

"I try to cut down on what I use, but my one [card] has a zero percent interest rate for a year," Papich said.

Along with weekend party expenses, school loans, and paying monthly bills, credit card debt is one of many financial problems students obtain during their time at college. According to MSN Money writer Liz Pulliam

Weston, most credit-card carrying households, which hold more than $8,000 in credit-card debt, pay about $1,400 a year in interest at a 17 percent interest rate.

Jim Musumeci, an associate finance professor at SIUC, said students often make the minimum payments on their debt, unaware of the increased interest rate after certain amount of time. He compares it to other situations that occur on campus, such as students who park their cars in restricted lots.

"I ask them, 'Don't you know you will get a ticket?' They say, 'I will worry about it later,'" Musumeci said. "But eventually those tickets add up, preventing them from graduating or even being enrolled the next semester. The same happens with debt."

But there are ways that students can combat debt, purchase their own T-shirts, and not have to sign up for another credit card in order to clothe themselves through four years of higher learning.

Mark Hoaglund, a SIUC senior in mathematics and computer science, said he keeps a fairly tight budget, refusing to carry any major credit cards and using his check card to pay for items only in an emergency.

☞ **Remember!!**

Students can avoid going into debt and protect their credit ratings by staying within their budget. And if they happen to max out their card, it is not wise for them to open another charge account until they have paid off the current one. Card users should try to pay more than the monthly minimum due on their bill in order to avoid accumulating high interest rate charges. They should also avoid using their credit cards for cash advances as those often carry costly transaction fees.

Most importantly, students should never make a purchase on a credit card that they can't afford to make with cash, unless it is a life or death emergency.

Source: From "Build Your Credit and Your Future" by Keisha Richards; reprinted with permission of InCharge Education Foundation, Inc., Spring 2003 issue of YOUNG MONEY, www.youngmoney.com.

Chris Labyk, assistant director of the SIUC Wellness Center, said that students should manage their time, create a balanced budget, and not give into to all types of spending impulses.

"A lot of students eat out or go out with friends," she said. "Some people spend money when they get bored or are depressed, but it is a temporary feeling."

Papich, who is still not accustomed to balancing a budget, often spends $40 to $50 in one night out with his friends. But he said he is trying to watch what he spends more, since he knows it will catch up with him when he graduates with his master's degree in three years.

MSN's Weston states that although credit card distributors contribute to increasing debt loads by setting high rates, the consumer is the one who is ultimately responsible. Papich's parents have also reminded him of this.

"They said, 'you are going to have to clean up this mess,'" he said. "And it's true."

Fiscal Fitness: Choosing A Credit Counselor

Living paycheck to paycheck? Worried about debt collectors? Can't seem to develop a workable budget? If this sounds familiar, you may want to consider the services of a credit counselor. Many credit counseling organizations are nonprofit and work with you

✔ Quick Tip

Liz Pulliam Weston, an eight-year veteran in writing about personal finance, offers three keys to defeating debt.

Get all the facts: Get intimate with your debt. Find out everything about your debts, including balances on every account, the interest rates, whether the interest is deductible, and when and how those rates can change.

Prioritize your bills: Credit cards, car loans, and personal loans—which are nondeductible—mortgages, home equity loans, and some student loans—which are deductible—should be divided into piles, then ranked from highest rate to lowest.

Pay high interest debts first: Start with the highest rate, typically starting with nondeductible debt, then moving onto the next.

Source: "Get Rid of Debt!," by Samantha Edmondson; reprinted with permission of InCharge Education Foundation, Inc., Spring 2003 issue of YOUNG MONEY, www.youngmoney.com.

to solve your financial problems. But beware—just because an organization says it is "nonprofit" doesn't guarantee that its services are free or affordable, or that its services are legitimate. In fact, some credit counseling organizations charge high fees, some of which may be hidden, or urge consumers to make "voluntary" contributions that cause them to fall deeper into debt.

Most credit counselors offer services through local offices, the Internet, or on the telephone. If possible, find an organization that offers in-person counseling. Many universities, military bases, credit unions, housing authorities, and branches of the U.S. Cooperative Extension Service operate nonprofit credit counseling programs. Your financial institution, local consumer protection agency, and friends and family also may be good sources of information and referrals.

✔ Quick Tip

A reputable credit counseling agency should send you free information about itself and the services it provides without requiring you to provide any details about your situation. If a firm doesn't do that, consider it a red flag and go elsewhere for help.

Source: Federal Trade Commission, 2003.

Reputable credit counseling organizations advise you on managing your money and debts, help you develop a budget, and usually offer free educational materials and workshops. Their counselors are certified and trained in the areas of consumer credit, money and debt management, and budgeting. Counselors discuss your entire financial situation with you, and help you develop a personalized plan to solve your money problems. An initial counseling session typically lasts an hour, with an offer of follow-up sessions.

Once you've developed a list of potential counseling agencies, check them out with your state Attorney General, local consumer protection agency, and Better Business Bureau. They can tell you if consumers have filed complaints about them. (If they don't have complaints about them, it's not a guarantee that they're legitimate.) Then, it's time for you to interview the final "candidates."

Questions To Ask

Here are some questions to ask to help you find the best counselor for you:

• What services do you offer?

(Look for an organization that offers a range of services, including budget counseling, and savings and debt management classes. Avoid organizations that push a debt management plan [DMP] as your only option before they spend a significant amount of time analyzing your financial situation.)

• Do you offer information? Are educational materials available for free? (Avoid organizations that charge for information.)

• In addition to helping me solve my immediate problem, will you help me develop a plan for avoiding problems in the future?

• What are your fees? Are there set-up and/or monthly fees? (Get a specific price quote in writing.)

• What if I can't afford to pay your fees or make contributions? (If an organization won't help you because you can't afford to pay, look elsewhere for help.)

• Will I have a formal written agreement or contract with you? (Don't sign anything without reading it first. Make sure all verbal promises are in writing.)

• Are you licensed to offer your services in my state?

• What are the qualifications of your counselors? Are they accredited or certified by an outside organization? If so, by whom? If not, how are they trained? (Try to use an organization whose counselors are trained by a non-affiliated party.)

• What assurance do I have that information about me (including my address, phone number, and financial information) will be kept confidential and secure?

• How are your employees compensated? Are they paid more if I sign up for certain services, if I pay a fee, or if I make a contribution to your organization? (If the answer is yes, consider it a red flag and go else-where for help.)

Debt Management Plans

If your financial problems stem from too much debt or your inability to repay your debts, a credit counseling agency may recommend that you enroll in a debt management plan (DMP). A DMP alone is not credit counseling, and DMPs are not for everyone. Consider signing on for one of these plans only after a certified credit counselor has spent time thoroughly reviewing your financial situation, and has offered you customized advice on managing your money. Even if a DMP is appropriate for you, a reputable credit coun-seling organization still will help you create a budget and teach you money management skills.

Here's how a DMP works: You deposit money each month with the credit counseling organization. The organization uses your deposits to pay your unse-cured debts, like credit card bills, student loans, and medical bills, according to a payment schedule the counselor develops with you and your creditors. Your credi-tors may agree to lower your interest rates and waive certain fees, but check with all your creditors to be sure that they offer the concessions that a credit counsel-ing organization describes to you. A successful DMP requires you to make regu-lar, timely payments, and could take forty-eight months or longer to complete. Ask the credit counselor to estimate how long it will take for you to complete the plan. You also may have to agree not to apply for—or use—any additional credit while you're participating in the plan.

In addition to the questions already listed, here are some other important ones to ask if you're considering enrolling in a DMP:

- Is a DMP the only option you can give me? Will you provide me with on-going budgeting advice, regardless of whether I enroll in a DMP? (If an organization offers only DMPs, find another credit counseling organization that also will help you create a budget and teach you money management skills.)

- How does your DMP work? How will you make sure that all my credi-tors will be paid by the applicable due dates and in the correct billing cycle? (If a DMP is appropriate, sign up for one that allows all your creditors to be paid before your payment due dates and within the correct billing cycle.)

- How is the amount of my payment determined? What if the amount is more than I can afford? (Don't sign up for a DMP if you can't afford the monthly payment.)

- How often can I get status reports on my accounts? Can I get access to my accounts online or by phone? (Make sure that the organization you sign up with is willing to provide regular, detailed statements about your account.)

✔ Quick Tip
How To Make A Debt Management Plan (DMP) Work For You

The following steps will help you benefit from a DMP, and avoid falling further into debt:

- Continue to pay your bills until the plan has been approved by your creditors. If you stop making payments before your creditors have accepted you into a plan, you'll face late fees, penalties, and negative entries on your credit report.

- Contact your creditors and confirm that they have accepted the proposed plan before you send any payments to the credit counseling organization for your DMP.

- Make sure the organization's payment schedule allows your debts to be paid before they are due each month. Paying on time will help you avoid late fees and penalties. Call each of your creditors on the first of every month to make sure the agency has paid them on time.

- Review monthly statements from your creditors to make sure they have received your payments.

- If your debt management plan depends on your creditors agreeing to lower or eliminate interest and finance charges, or waive late fees, make sure these concessions are reflected on your statements.

Source: Federal Trade Commission, 2003.

- Can you get my creditors to lower or eliminate interest and finance charges, or waive late fees? (If yes, contact your creditors to verify this, and ask them how long you have to be on the plan before the benefits kick in.)

- What debts aren't included in the DMP? (This is important because you'll have to pay those bills on your own.)

- Do I have to make any payments to my creditors before they will accept the proposed payment plan? (Some creditors require a payment to the credit counselor before accepting you into a DMP. If a credit counselor tells you this is so, call your creditors to verify this information before you send money to the credit counseling agency.)

How will enrolling in a DMP affect my credit? (Beware of any organization that tells you it can remove accurate negative information from your credit report. Legally, it can't be done. Accurate negative information may stay on your credit report for up to seven years.

- Can you get my creditors to "re-age" my accounts—that is, to make my accounts current? If so, how many payments will I have to make before my creditors will do so? (Even if your accounts are "re-aged," negative information from past delinquencies or late payments will remain on your credit report.)

Debt Negotiation Programs

Debt negotiation is not the same thing as credit counseling or a DMP. It can be very risky and have a long term negative impact on your credit report and, in turn, your ability to get credit. That's why many states have laws regulating debt negotiation companies and the services they offer.

Debt negotiation firms may claim they're nonprofit. They also may claim that they can arrange for your unsecured debt—typically, credit card debt—to be paid off for anywhere from 10 to 50% of the balance owed. For example, if you owe $10,000 on a credit card, a debt negotiation firm may claim it can arrange for you to pay off the debt with a lesser amount, say $4,000.

The firms often pitch their services as an alternative to bankruptcy. They may claim that using their services will have little or no negative impact on your ability to get credit in the future, or that any negative information can be removed from your credit report when you complete the debt negotiation program. The firms usually tell you to stop making payments to your creditors, and instead, send your payments to the debt negotiation company. The firms may promise to hold your funds in a special account and pay the creditors on your behalf.

However, just because a debt negotiation company describes itself as a "nonprofit" organization, there's no guarantee that the services they offer are legitimate. There also is no guarantee that a creditor will accept partial payment of a legitimate debt. In fact, if you stop making payments on a credit card, late fees and interest usually are added to the debt each month. If you exceed your credit limit, additional fees and charges also can be added. All this can quickly cause a consumer's original

Remember!!

Tip-Offs To Rip-Offs

Steer clear of companies that:

• guarantee they can remove your unsecured debt.

• promise that unsecured debts can be paid off with pennies on the dollar.

• claim that using their system will let you avoid bankruptcy.

• require substantial monthly service fees.

• demand payment of a percentage of savings.

• tell you to stop making payments to or communicating with your creditors.

• require you to make monthly payments to them, rather than with your creditor.

• claim that creditors never sue consumers for non-payment of unsecured debt.

• promise that using their system will have no negative impact on your credit report.

• claim that they can remove accurate negative information from your credit report.

Source: Federal Trade Commission, 2003.

debt to double or triple. What's more, most debt negotiation companies charge consumers substantial fees for their services, including a fee to establish the account with the debt negotiator, a monthly service fee, and a final fee of a percentage of the money you've supposedly saved.

While creditors have no obligation to agree to negotiate the amount a consumer owes, they have a legal obligation to provide accurate information to the credit reporting agencies, including your failure to make monthly payments. That can result in a negative entry on your credit report. And in certain situations, creditors may have the right to sue you to recover the money you owe. In some instances, when creditors win a lawsuit, they have the right to garnish your wages or put a lien on your home. Finally, the Internal Revenue Service may consider any amount of forgiven debt to be taxable income.

If you decide to work with a debt negotiation company, be sure to check it out with your state Attorney General, local consumer protection agency, and the Better Business Bureau. They can tell you if any consumer complaints are on file about the firm you're considering doing business with. Also, ask the office of your state Attorney General if the company is required to be licensed to work in your state and, if so, whether it is.

Part Six

Avoiding Financial Risk

Chapter 30

Gambling, Shoplifting, And Internet Scams

Teens And Problem Gambling

Men and women are attracted to gambling to relieve stress, to escape pressures, and to find excitement. Counselors are seeing an increase in women problem gamblers, along with a rise in teen gambling.

"There has not been much emphasis on the problem of teen gambling," said Renee C. Wert, Ph.D., Coordinator of the Gambling Recovery Program of Jewish Family Service of Buffalo and Erie county, New York. "A mother may give a child a scratch-off ticket, or place a bet on Quick Draw with a child present, but wouldn't give that same child a sip of beer."

The 1996 Prevalence Study by the New York Council on Problem Gambling showed that 86% of New York State teens have gambled at least once in their lives and 75% have gambled within the past year, although all forms of gambling

About This Chapter: This chapter begins with "Teens And Problem Gambling," excerpted from "Problem Gambling on the Rise; Women, Teens Representation Growing," by Eileen A. Hotho, © 2003 Erie County Commission on the Status of Women, Reprinted with permission. "Online Gambling and Kids: A Bad Bet" is from a Federal Trade Commission (FTC) *Consumer Alert*, June 2002. Text under the heading "Shoplifting" is from "Two Types of Shoplifters" and "Why Do Shoplifters Steal?" by Peter Berlin, and reprinted with permission from the National Association for Shoplifting Prevention, © 2004. All rights reserved. For additional information, call toll free at 800-848-9595 or visit http://www.shopliftingprevention.org. "Internet Scams" is from "Public Awareness Advisory Regarding '4-1-9' or 'Advance Fee Fraud' Schemes," United States Secret Service, 2002.

are illegal for teens. As casinos become more plentiful and have a longer history in the community, we can expect teens to try them, according to another study from 1985. That study found that seven years after casinos opened in Atlantic City, 64% of high school students had been able to gamble at a casino at least once.

If teens find access to casino gambling simple, it is even easier for them to buy lottery tickets. A 1996 study in Massachusetts reported that teens attempting to purchase Keno tickets in convenience stores were successful 66% of the time. Most teen gamblers are male, have a job, and their overwhelming preference, according to the Teen Prevalence Study, was for instant scratch-off tickets.

When does a seemingly low-risk fun activity develop into problem gambling? The New York Council On Problem Gambling lists these ten typical warning signs:

1. Gambling to escape worry, boredom or trouble.

2. Suffering from severe mood swings.

3. Believing that life without gambling is impossible.

4. Neglecting personal responsibilities to focus on gambling activities.

5. Fantasizing about "this week's win" to overcome "last week's losses" and dreaming of "the big win."

6. Scheming to borrow money from friends and family.

7. Considering illegal acts, such as prostitution, stealing, and forgery, as a means of financing gambling.

8. Lying to conceal activity.

9. Jeopardizing employment or school work due to gambling.

10. Having self-destructive thoughts because of problems related to gambling.

Problem gamblers often develop physical illnesses such as intestinal disorders, backaches, stomachaches and depression from the stress of hiding their gambling and often increasing debts. Family members of problem

> **✔ Quick Tip**
>
> The Gambling Recovery Program advises the following guidelines for safe adult gambling:
>
> • Never borrow to gamble.
>
> • Be prepared to lose. Winning is fun, but don't count on it.
>
> • Set a limit and stick to it. Leave or stop when you reach your limit.
>
> • Gambling shouldn't be your only way of having fun.
>
> • Don't gamble when you are feeling stressed or depressed.
>
> • Spend only what you can afford to lose.
>
> • Don't let gambling get in the way of your responsibilities.
>
> • Take a break: don't lose track of how much time and money you're spending.
>
> • Don't gamble if you are high, drunk, or stoned.
>
> • Bill money shouldn't be used for gambling.
>
> Source: © 2003 Erie County Commission on the Status of Women.

gamblers also develop many of the same symptoms as they cope with stress and shame related to financial hardships resulting from the gambler's debts.

Gambling recovery programs offer assessment and treatment for problem and compulsive gamblers and those who are close to them. Most insurance carriers cover their services. They often offer an affordable sliding-fee scale for the uninsured or under-insured, based upon income, family size and debts.

Online Gambling And Kids: A Bad Bet

Do kids gamble? The National Research Council (NRC) suggests that not only do most adolescents gamble, but also that they've gambled recently.

The most common types of gambling for kids are reported to be card games and sports betting. But increasingly, kids are gambling on the Internet, where many game operators are operating from servers outside the United States—beyond the jurisdiction of state or federal regulations about the hours of operation, the age of the participants, or the type of game offered.

According to the Federal Trade Commission (FTC), it's easy for kids to access online gambling sites, especially if they have access to credit or debit cards. Indeed, some of the most popular non-gambling websites carry ads for gambling sites, and many online game-playing sites link to gambling sites.

Shoplifting

Because there are two types of shoplifters, two separate approaches are required to deal with the problem.

Professional Shoplifters. These are addicts who steal to buy drugs or hardened criminals who steal for resale and profit as a life-style. These individuals frequently commit other types of crimes and lack any conscience or guilt. The approach here is either a drug treatment program or jail.

Non-Professional Shoplifters. These are the people who make up the majority of shoplifters and who steal for a variety of reasons, mostly related to common life situations and their personal ability (or inability) to cope. They include people who are depressed, frustrated, anxious, influenced by peers, thrill seekers, or kleptomaniacs.

♣ It's A Fact!!
Risks Associated With Kids Gambling Online

- Gambling is illegal for kids. Every state prohibits gambling by minors. That's why gambling sites don't pay out to kids and why they go to great lengths to verify the identity of any winner.

- You can lose your money. Online gambling operations are in business to make a profit. They take in more money than they pay out.

- You can ruin a good credit rating. Online gambling generally requires the use of a credit card. If kids rack up debt online, they could ruin their credit rating—or their parents', if they use their credit card. That can prevent the credit card holder from getting a loan to buy a house or a car, or even from getting a job.

- Online gambling can be addictive. Because Internet gambling is a solitary activity, people can gamble uninterrupted and undetected for hours at a time. Gambling in social isolation and using credit to gamble may be risk factors for developing gambling problems. Gamblers Anonymous (www.gamblersanonymous.org) is a self-help group for problem gamblers. Gam-Anon (www.gam-anon.org) is a self-help program for family members.

Source: Federal Trade Commission, 2002.

Non-professional shoplifting is rarely about greed, poverty, or values. It's about individuals struggling with personal conflicts and needs. These individuals know right from wrong, they know there are consequences and they often have the money to pay, but they continue to steal anyway. These people steal items they often don't need and sometimes don't use. They usually have the money to pay for the item, rarely plan their theft in advance and never try to sell the item for profit.

Research shows that nationwide there are thousands of shoplifters who continually repeat the offense and want to stop, but can't. Their shoplifting has become a habit or even an addiction, and they are too ashamed or afraid to tell anyone, or ask for help. Other shoplifters simply deny they have a problem of any kind. Psychological profiles and admissions by shoplifters revealed that one out of three shoplifters are "at risk" of repeating the offense after getting caught.

While many non-professional shoplifters steal from stores on a regular basis, they usually have no prior criminal record (except perhaps for shoplifting) and are typically the kind of people who don't commit other types of crimes. Their behavior is less related to criminal intent and more the result of situational, emotional, or psychological problems in need of attention. The best approach for non-professional shoplifters is for the community to make available a treatment program at a time when shoplifters will be most receptive to it—that is, when caught and/or prosecuted.

Juveniles Who Shoplift

Shoplifting among juveniles is remarkably similar to adult shoplifting. However, the primary issues related to shoplifting among youth revolve around family, school and peer pressures.

If you were to ask juveniles caught shoplifting, "Why did you do it?" the most frequent reply would be "I don't know." Like adults, the reasons teens shoplift vary, but most commonly it is because they wanted nice things, felt pressured by friends, wanted to see if they could get away with it, or were angry, depressed, confused or bored. Sometimes they are just mad at the world and want to strike back.

While teens, like adults, usually know the difference between right and wrong, when their life becomes too stressful they become more vulnerable to temptation, peer pressure and other things that can lead them to shoplift. This is especially true when they feel unworthy, angry, depressed, unattractive, or not accepted.

Internet Scams

One of the most prevalent Internet scams is called Advance Fee Fraud, known internationally as "4-1-9" fraud after the section of the Nigerian penal code which addresses fraud schemes. The perpetrators of this fraud are often very creative and innovative.

> ♣ **It's A Fact!!**
> Approximately 25% of shoplifters are kids, 75% are adults. And 55% of adult shoplifters say they started shoplifting in their teens.
>
> Source: Excerpted from "Public Education and Statistics," reprinted with permission from the National Association for Shoplifting Prevention, © 2004. All rights reserved. For additional information, call the National Association for Shoplifting Prevention toll-free at (800) 848-9595, or visit http://www.shopliftingprevention.org.

Unfortunately, there is a perception that no one is prone to enter into such an obviously suspicious relationship. However, a large number of victims are enticed into believing they have been singled out from the masses to share in multi-million dollar windfall profits for doing absolutely nothing. There is also a misconception that the victim's bank account is requested so the culprit can plunder it. This is not the primary reason for the account request, but merely a signal they have hooked another victim.

The most prevalent and successful type of Advance Fee Fraud is the fund transfer scam. In this scheme, a company or individual will typically receive an unsolicited letter by mail from a Nigerian claiming to be a senior civil servant. In the letter, the Nigerian will inform the recipient that he is seeking a reputable foreign company or individual into whose account he can deposit funds ranging from $10–$60 million that the Nigerian government overpaid on some procurement contract. The criminals send out mailings en masse, having obtained the names of potential victims from a variety of sources including trade journals, professional directories, newspapers, and commercial libraries. The recipient is usually offered a commission up to 30% for assisting in the transfer.

Initially, the intended victim is instructed to provide company letterheads and pro forma invoicing that will be used to show completion of the contract. One of the reasons is to use the victim's letterhead to forge letters of recommendation to other victim companies and to seek out a travel visa from the American Embassy in Lagos, Nigeria. The victim is told that the completed contracts will be submitted for approval to the Central Bank of Nigeria. Upon approval, the funds will be remitted to an account supplied by the intended victim.

The goal is to delude the target into thinking that he is being drawn into a very lucrative, albeit questionable, arrangement. The intended victim must be reassured and confident of the potential success of the deal. Thus, he will become the primary supporter of the scheme, the "con-within-the-con," willingly contributing a large amount of money to save the venture when the deal is threatened.

The letter, while appearing transparent and even ridiculous to most, unfortunately is growing in its effectiveness. The fraudster will eventually reach someone who, while skeptical, desperately wants the deal to be genuine. Victims are often convinced of the authenticity of Advance Fee Fraud schemes by the forged or false documents bearing apparently official Nigerian government letterhead, seals, as well as false letters of credit, payment schedules and bank drafts. The fraudster may establish the credibility of his contacts by arranging a meeting between the victim and "government officials" in real or fake government offices.

Victims are almost always requested to travel to Nigeria or a border country to complete a transaction. Individuals are often told that a visa will not be necessary to enter the country. The Nigerian con artists may then bribe airport officials to pass the victims through Immigration and Customs. Because it is a serious offense in Nigeria to enter without a valid visa, the victim's illegal entry may be used by the fraudsters as leverage to coerce the victims into releasing funds. Violence and threats of physical harm may be employed to further pressure victims.

In the next stage, some alleged problem concerning the "inside man" will suddenly arise. An official will demand an up-front payment or unforeseen tax or fee to the Nigerian government that will have to be paid before the money can be transferred. These can include licensing fees, registration fees, and various forms of taxes and attorney fees. Normally each fee paid is described as the very last fee required. Invariably, oversights and errors in the deal are discovered by the Nigerians, necessitating additional payments and allowing the scheme to be stretched out over many months.

- In almost every case there is a sense of urgency;

- The victim is enticed to travel to Nigeria or a border country;

- There are many forged official looking documents;

- Most of the correspondence is handled by fax or through the mail;

- Blank letterheads and invoices are requested from the victim along with the banking particulars;

- Any number of Nigerian fees are requested for processing the transaction with each fee purported to be the last required;

- The confidential nature of the transaction is emphasized;

- There are usually claims of strong ties to Nigerian officials;

- A Nigerian residing in the U.S., London or other foreign venue may claim to be a clearing house bank for the Central Bank of Nigeria;

- Offices in legitimate government buildings appear to have been used by impostors posing as the real occupants or officials.

The most common forms of these fraudulent business proposals fall into seven main categories:

- Disbursement of money from wills

- Contract fraud (C.O.D. of goods or services)

- Purchase of real estate

- Conversion of hard currency

- Transfer of funds from over invoiced contracts
- Sale of crude oil at below market prices

Indications are that Advance Fee Fraud grosses hundreds of millions of dollars annually and the losses are continuing to escalate. In all likelihood, there are victims who do not report their losses to authorities due to either fear or embarrassment.

Several reasons have been submitted why Nigerian Advance Fee Fraud has undergone a dramatic increase in recent years. The explanations are as diverse as the types of schemes. The Nigerian Government blames the growing problem on mass unemployment, extended family systems, a get rich quick syndrome, and, especially, the greed of foreigners.

☞ Remember!!

4-1-9 Schemes frequently use the following tactics:

- An individual or company receives a letter or fax from an alleged "official" representing a foreign government or agency;

- An offer is made to transfer millions of dollars in "over invoiced contract" funds into your personal bank account;

- You are encouraged to travel overseas to complete the transaction;

- You are requested to provide blank company letterhead forms, banking account information, telephone/fax numbers;

- You receive numerous documents with official looking stamps, seals and logo testifying to the authenticity of the proposal;

- Eventually you must provide up-front or advance fees for various taxes, attorney fees, transaction fees or bribes;

- Other forms of 4-1-9 schemes include: C.O.D. of goods or services, real estate ventures, purchases of crude oil at reduced prices, beneficiary of a will, recipient of an award and paper currency conversion.

Source: U.S. Secret Service, 2002.

Chapter 31

The Many Faces Of Identification (ID) Theft

Every day you share personal information about yourself with others. It's so routine that you may not even realize you're doing it. You may write a check at the grocery store, charge tickets to a ball game, mail your tax return, buy a gift online, call home on your cell phone, schedule a doctor's appointment, or apply for a credit card. Each transaction requires you to share personal information: your bank and credit card account numbers, your income, your Social Security number, or your name, address and phone numbers.

It's important to find out what happens to the personal information you provide to companies, marketers and government agencies. These organizations may use your information simply to process your order; to tell you about products, services, or promotions; or to share with others.

About This Chapter: This chapter begins with excerpts from "Privacy: Tips for Protecting Your Personal Information," a *Consumer Alert* published by the Federal Trade Commission (FTC), January 2002; the concluding section "If Your Identity's Been Stolen" is also excerpted from this document. "I.D. Theft: What's It All About?" is from the FTC's Office of Business Education, October 2003. "Internet Pirates Are Trying to Steal Your Personal Financial Information," is produced by the Office of the Comptroller of the Currency, U.S. Department of the Treasury, n.d. "Students—Don't Let Identity Thieves Steal Your Future" is from "Identity Theft," produced by the U.S. Department of Education (www.ed.gov), 2004. "Lost Or Stolen: Wallet Or Purse," is from "Getting Purse-onal," *Consumer Alert*, FTC, 2000.

And then there are unscrupulous individuals, like identity thieves, who want your information to commit fraud. Identity theft—the fastest-growing white-collar crime in America—occurs when someone steals your personal identifying information, like your Social Security number, birth date or mother's maiden name, to open new charge accounts, order merchandise or borrow money. Consumers targeted by identity thieves usually don't know they've been victimized. But when the fraudsters fail to pay the bills or repay the loans, collection agencies begin pursuing the consumers to cover debts they didn't even know they had.

ID Theft: What's It All About?

The 1990s spawned this new variety of crooks called identity thieves. Their stock in trade? Your everyday transactions, which usually reveal bits of your personal information: your bank and credit card account numbers, your income, your Social Security number, or your name, address, and phone numbers. An identity thief obtains some piece of your sensitive information and uses it without your knowledge to commit fraud or theft.

Identity theft is a serious crime. People whose identities have been stolen can spend months or years—and their hard-earned money—cleaning up the mess the thieves have made of their good name and credit record. Some victims have lost job opportunities, have been refused loans for education, housing or cars, or even have been arrested for crimes they didn't commit.

Can you prevent identity theft from occurring? As with any crime, you cannot completely control whether you will become a victim. But, according to the Federal Trade Commission (FTC), you can minimize your risk by managing your personal information cautiously and with heightened sensitivity.

How Identity Theft Occurs

Skilled identity thieves use a variety of methods to gain access to your personal information. For example, they get information from businesses or other institutions by:

- stealing records from their employer,

- bribing an employee who has access to these records, or hacking into the organization's computers.

- rummaging through your trash, or the trash of businesses or dumps in a practice known as "dumpster diving."

- obtaining credit reports by abusing their employer's authorized access to credit reports or by posing as a landlord, employer, or someone else who may have a legal right to the information.

- stealing credit and debit card numbers as your card is processed by using a special information storage device in a practice known as "skimming."

- stealing wallets and purses containing identification and credit and bank cards.

- stealing mail, including bank and credit card statements, pre-approved credit offers, new checks, or tax information.

- completing a "change of address form" to divert your mail to another location.

- stealing personal information from your home.

- scamming information from you by posing as a legitimate business person or government official.

Once identity thieves have your personal information, they may:

- go on spending sprees using your credit and debit card account numbers to buy "big-ticket" items like computers that they can easily sell.

- open a new credit card account, using your name, date of birth, and Social Security number. When they don't pay the bills, the delinquent account is reported on your credit report.

- change the mailing address on your credit card account. The impostor then runs up charges on the account. Because the bills are being sent to the new address, it may take some time before you realize there's a problem.

- take out auto loans in your name.

✔ Quick Tip
How Can You Tell If You're A Victim Of Identity Theft?

Monitor the balances of your financial accounts. Look for unexplained charges or withdrawals. Other indications of identity theft can be:

- failing to receive bills or other mail, which signals an address change by the identity thief;

- receiving credit cards for which you did not apply;

- denial of credit for no apparent reason; or

- receiving calls from debt collectors or companies about merchandise or services you didn't buy.

Source: From "I.D. Theft," FTC, 2003

- establish phone or wireless service in your name.

- counterfeit checks or debit cards, and drain your bank account.

- open a bank account in your name and write bad checks on that account.

- file for bankruptcy under your name to avoid paying debts they've incurred, or to avoid eviction.

- give your name to the police during an arrest. If they are released and don't show up for their court date, an arrest warrant could be issued in your name.

What Steps Can You Take?

If an identity thief is opening new credit accounts in your name, these accounts are likely to show up on your credit report. You can find out by ordering a copy of your credit report from any of three major credit bureaus. If you find inaccurate information, check your reports from the other two credit bureaus. Of course, some inaccuracies on your credit reports may be because of computer, clerical, or other errors and may not be a result of identity theft.

Note: If your personal information has been lost or stolen, you may want to check all of your reports more frequently for the first year.

Always manage your personal information with caution and prudence.

- Place passwords on your credit card, bank and phone accounts. Avoid using easily available information like your mother's maiden name, your birth date, the last four digits of your Social Security number or your phone number, or a series of consecutive numbers. When you're asked for your mother's maiden name on an application for a new account, try using a password instead.

- Secure personal information in your home, especially if you have roommates, employ outside help, or are having service work done in your home.

- Ask about information security procedures in your workplace. Find out who has access to your personal information and verify that your records are kept in a secure location. Ask about the disposal procedures for those records as well.

- Don't give out personal information on the phone, through the mail, or over the Internet unless you've initiated the contact or are sure you know who you're dealing with. Identity thieves can be skilled liars, and may pose as representatives of banks, Internet service providers (ISPs), or even government agencies to get you to reveal identifying information. Before you divulge any personal information, confirm that you're dealing with a legitimate representative of a legitimate organization. Double-check by calling customer service using the number on your account statement or in the telephone book.

- Read the privacy policy on any website directed to children. Websites directed to children or that knowingly collect information from kids under thirteen must post a notice of their information collection practices.

- Guard your mail and trash from theft. Deposit outgoing mail in post office collection boxes or at your local post office instead of an unsecured mailbox. Remove mail from your mailbox promptly. If you're planning to be away from home and can't pick up your mail, call the

U.S. Postal Service at 1-800-275-8777 to ask for a vacation hold. To thwart a thief who may pick through your trash or recycling bins, tear or shred your charge receipts, copies of credit applications or offers, insurance forms, physician statements, checks and bank statements, and expired charge cards.

- Before revealing any identifying information (for example, on an application), ask how it will be used and secured, and whether it will be shared with others. Find out if you have a say about the use of your information. For example, can you choose to have it kept confidential?

- Keep your Social Security card in a secure place; don't carry it with you. Memorize your Social Security number and give it only when absolutely necessary. Ask to use other types of identifiers when possible. If your state uses your Social Security number as your driver's license number, ask to substitute another number.

- Limit the identification information and the number of credit and debit cards that you carry to what you'll actually need.

- Keep your purse or wallet in a safe place at work.

Consider Your Computer

Your computer can be a gold mine of personal information to an identity thief. Here's how you can safeguard your computer and the personal information it stores:

- Update your virus protection software regularly. Computer viruses can have damaging effects, including introducing program code that causes your computer to send out files or other stored information. Look for security repairs and patches you can download from your operating system's website.

- Don't download files from strangers or click on hyperlinks from people you don't know. Opening a file could expose your system to a computer virus or a program that could hijack your modem.

- Use a firewall, especially if you have a high-speed or "always on" connection to the Internet. The firewall allows you to limit uninvited access to your computer. Without a firewall, hackers can take over your computer and access sensitive information.

- Use a secure browser—software that encrypts or scrambles information you send over the Internet—to guard the safety of your online transactions.

- Try not to store financial information on your laptop unless absolutely necessary. If you do, use a "strong" password—that is, a combination of letters (upper and lower case), numbers, and symbols.

- Avoid using an automatic log-in feature that saves your user name and password; and always log off when you're finished. If your laptop gets stolen, the thief will have a hard time accessing sensitive information.

☞ Remember!!

- Never provide personal financial information, including your Social Security number, account numbers or passwords, over the phone or the Internet if you did not initiate the contact.

- Never click on the link provided in an e-mail you believe is fraudulent. It may contain a virus that can contaminate your computer.

- Do not be intimidated by an e-mail or caller who suggests dire consequences if you do not immediately provide or verify financial information.

- If you believe the contact is legitimate, go to the company's website by typing in the site address directly or using a page you have previously bookmarked, instead of a link provided in the e-mail.

- If you fall victim to an attack, act immediately to protect yourself. Alert your financial institution. Place fraud alerts on your credit files. Monitor your credit files and account statements closely.

- Report suspicious e-mails or calls to the Federal Trade Commission through the Internet at www.consumer.gov/idtheft or by calling 1-877-IDTHEFT.

Source: Office of the Comptroller of the Currency, U.S. Department of the Treasury.

- Delete any personal information stored on your computer before you dispose of it. Use a "wipe" utility program, which overwrites the entire hard drive and makes the files unrecoverable.

- Read website privacy policies. They should answer questions about the access to and accuracy, security, and control of personal information the site collects, as well as how sensitive information will be used, and whether it will be provided to third parties.

Internet Pirates Are Trying To Steal Your Personal Financial Information

Internet pirates go "phishing." The word is pronounced "fishing," and that's exactly what these thieves are doing: "fishing" for your personal financial information. What they want are account numbers, passwords, Social Security numbers, and other confidential information that they can use to loot your checking account or run up bills on your credit cards.

With the sensitive information obtained from a successful phishing scam, these thieves can take out loans or obtain credit cards and even driver's licenses in your name. They can do damage to your financial history and personal reputation that can take years to unravel. But if you understand how phishing works and how to protect yourself, you can help stop this crime.

Here's how phishing works: In a typical case, you'll receive an e-mail that appears to come from a reputable company that you recognize and do business with, such as your Internet service provider, bank, or online payment service. In some cases, the e-mail may appear to come from a government agency, including one of the federal financial institution regulatory agencies. The e-mail will probably warn you of a serious problem that requires your immediate attention. It may use phrases, such as "Immediate attention required," or "Please contact us immediately about your account."

The e-mail will then encourage you to click on a button to go to the institution's website. In a phishing scam, you could be redirected to a phony website that may look exactly like the real thing. Sometimes, in fact, it may be the company's actual website. In those cases, a pop-up window will quickly appear for the purpose of harvesting your financial information.

In either case, you may be asked to update your account information or to provide information for verification purposes: your Social Security number, your account number, your password, or the information you use to verify your identity when speaking to a real financial institution, such as your mother's maiden name or your place of birth. If you provide the requested information, you may find yourself the victim of identity theft.

How To Protect Yourself

1. Never provide your personal information in response to an unsolicited request, whether it is over the phone or over the Internet. E-mails and Internet pages created by phishers may look exactly like the real thing. They may even have a fake padlock icon that ordinarily is used to denote a secure site. If you did not initiate the communication, you should not provide any information.

✤ It's A Fact!!
A Special Word About Social Security Numbers

Very likely, your employer and financial institution will need your Social Security number (SSN) for wage and tax reporting purposes. Other private businesses may ask you for your SSN to do a credit check, such as when you apply for a car loan. Sometimes, however, they simply want your SSN for general record keeping. If someone asks for your SSN, ask the following questions:

- Why do you need it?
- How will it be used?
- How do you protect it from being stolen?
- What will happen if I don't give it to you?

If you don't provide your SSN, some businesses may not provide you with the service or benefit you want. Getting satisfactory answers to your questions will help you to decide whether you want to share your SSN with the business.

Source: "I.D. Theft," FTC, 2003.

2. If you believe the contact may be legitimate, contact the financial institution yourself. You can find phone numbers and websites on the monthly statements you receive from your financial institution, or you can look the company up in a phone book or on the Internet. The key is that you should be the one to initiate the contact, using contact information that you have verified yourself.

3. Never provide your password over the phone or in response to an unsolicited Internet request. A financial institution would never ask you to verify your account information online. E-mail is not a secure method of transmitting personal information.

4. Use anti-virus software and keep it up to date. Some phishing

✔ Quick Tip

How Can Students Safeguard Themselves From Identity Theft?

The first step to prevent identity theft is awareness of how and when you use your personal information. By keeping close tabs on your personal information, you can reduce your chances of becoming an identity theft victim.

Students applying for or using student loans should also:

• Use caution when using commercial financial aid services over the Internet or telephone. U.S. Department of Education services are free and password-protected.

• Apply for federal student aid at www.fafsa.ed.gov. After completing the Free Application for Federal Student Aid (FAFSA) electronically, remember to exit the application and close the browser.

• Don't reveal your PIN to anyone, even if that person is helping you fill out the FAFSA. The only time you should use your PIN is on secure ED systems.

• Shred receipts and copies of documents with personal information if they are no longer needed.

• Review your financial aid award documents and keep track of the amount of student aid you applied for and have been awarded.

• Report all lost or stolen student identification immediately.

Source: Excerpted from "Reduce Your Risk," U.S. Dept. of Education, 2004.

e-mails contain software that can harm your computer or track your activities on the Internet without your knowledge. Anti-virus software and a firewall can protect you from inadvertently accepting such unwanted files. Anti-virus software scans incoming communications for troublesome files. Look for anti-virus software that recognizes current viruses as well as older ones; that can effectively reverse the damage; and that updates automatically.

5. A firewall helps make you invisible on the Internet and blocks all communications from unauthorized sources. It's especially important to run a firewall if you have a broadband connection. Finally, your operating system (like Windows or Linux) may offer free software "patches" to close holes in the system that hackers or phishers could exploit.

6. Be cautious about opening any attachment or downloading any files from e-mails you receive, regardless of who sent them.

7. Review account statements regularly to ensure all charges are correct. If your account statement is late in arriving, call your financial institution to find out why. If your financial institution offers electronic account access, periodically review activity online to catch suspicious activity.

Students—Don't Let Identity Thieves Steal Your Future

Why should a student, who doesn't have a lot of money or assets, be concerned about identity theft?

Being a student does not safeguard you against identity theft, one of the fastest-growing consumer crimes in the nation. Identity thieves don't steal your money; they steal your name and reputation and use them for their own financial gain. In effect, they steal your financial future.

As a student, you may even be more vulnerable to identity theft because of the availability of your personal data and the way many students handle this data. A recent national survey of college students found that:

• Almost half of all college students receive credit card applications on a daily or weekly basis. Many of these students throw out card applications without destroying them.

- Nearly a third of students rarely, if ever, reconcile their credit card and checking account balances.

- Almost 50% of students have had grades posted by Social Security number.

All of these factors make students potential identity theft victims. In addition, as a student, you may be surprised to learn how many of your daily activities expose you to this crime. For example:

- Do you use your personal computer for online banking transactions?

- Do you use your personal computer to buy merchandise or purchase tickets for travel, concerts, or other services?

- Do you receive credit card offers in the mail? Do you discard these documents before you shred them?

- Do you store personal information in your computer?

- Do you use a cell phone?

- Do you use your Social Security number for identification?

- Do you have a student loan?

You probably answered yes to at least one of these questions about daily

> **✔ Quick Tip**
> **Credit Card Alert**
>
> Pre-approved credit card offers probably flood your mailbox every week. Whatever you do, don't simply throw away these offers; an identity thief can easily pick up a stray application and apply for the card in your name. You should shred these applications before you dispose of them. Credit card companies also entice students on campus with promotional items and free gifts. These offers are risky, providing an opening for identity theft. You should review your statements, and your bank and credit card statements, as soon as you receive them. Thieves can charge thousands of dollars to an account in a very short period of time. Your best protection is to pick up all your mail promptly. Leaving mail lying around your dorm or apartment provides another opportunity for your personal information to be taken and abused.
>
> Source: Excerpted from "Reduce Your Risk," U.S. Dept. of Education, 2004.

transactions. Each of these routine actions places you at risk of being a victim of identity theft because each of these transactions requires you to share personal information such as your bank and credit card account numbers, your Social Security number, or your name, address, and phone number. This is the same personal information that identity thieves use to commit fraud.

If your identity is stolen, you may spend months or even years clearing up the damage thieves have caused to your reputation and credit record. In the time it takes to resolve these issues, you may lose job opportunities and be refused loans for education, housing, or a car. Although you have not committed a crime, been late with a payment, or abused your credit, you are the one who would suffer severe financial consequences as a result of identity theft. As a student or recent graduate, being a victim of identity theft jeopardizes your financial future just as you are beginning to establish your credit record.

Lost Or Stolen: Wallet Or Purse

A lost or stolen wallet or purse is a gold mine of information for a new kind of crook—the identity thief.

Identity thieves can use information found in your wallet or purse—from credit cards, checks, your Social Security card, even health insurance cards—to establish new accounts in your name. That could create an identity crisis that can take months to detect, and even longer to unravel.

If your wallet or purse is lost or stolen, you should:

- File a report with the police immediately. Get a copy in case your bank, credit card company or insurance company needs proof of the crime.

- Cancel each credit and charge card. Get new cards with new account numbers.

- Call the fraud departments of the major credit reporting agencies. (See contact information below.) Ask them to put a "fraud alert" on your account and add a "victim's statement" to your file requesting that creditors contact you before opening new accounts in your name.

♣ It's A Fact!!

- Equifax: www.equifax.com
  1-800-525-6285 (report fraud); 1-800-685-1111 (order a report)
  P.O. Box 740241, Atlanta, GA 30374-0241

- Experian: www.experian.com
  1-888-397-3742 (report fraud or order a report)
  P.O. Box 2104, Allen TX 75013 (order report)
  P.O. Box 9532, Allen TX 75013 (report fraud)

- TransUnion: www.transunion.com
  1-800-680-7289 (report fraud)
  Fraud Victim Assistance Division, P.O. Box 6790, Fullerton, CA 92834-6790 (report fraud)
  1-800-916-8800 (order report)
  P.O. Box 1000, Chester, PA 19022 (order report)

- Ask the credit bureaus for copies of your credit reports. Review your reports carefully to make sure no additional fraudulent accounts have been opened in your name or unauthorized changes made to your existing accounts. In a few months, order new copies of your reports to verify your corrections and changes, and to make sure no new fraudulent activity has occurred.

- Report the loss to your bank if your wallet or purse contained bank account information, including account numbers, ATM cards or checks. Cancel checking and savings accounts and open new ones. Stop payments on outstanding checks.

- Get a new ATM card, account number and Personal Identification Number (PIN) or password.

- Report your missing driver's license to the department of motor vehicles. If your state uses your Social Security number as your driver's license number, ask to substitute another number.

- Change the locks on your home and car if your keys were taken. Don't give an identity thief access to even more personal property and information.

If Your Identity's Been Stolen

Even if you've been very careful about keeping your personal information to yourself, an identity thief can strike. If you suspect that your personal information has been used to commit fraud or theft, take the following four steps right away. Remember to follow up all calls in writing; send your letter by certified mail, return receipt requested, so you can document what the company received and when; and keep copies for your files.

1. Place a fraud alert on your credit reports and review your credit reports.

Call the toll-free fraud number of anyone of the three major credit bureaus to place a fraud alert on your credit report. This can help prevent an identity thief from opening additional accounts in your name. As soon as the credit bureau confirms your fraud alert, the other two credit bureaus will automatically be notified to place fraud alerts on your credit report, and all three reports will be sent to you free of charge.

Once you receive your reports, review them carefully. Look for inquiries you didn't initiate, accounts you didn't open, and unexplained debts on your true accounts. You also should check that information such as your social security number, address(es), name or initial, and employment information. Inaccuracies in this information also may be due to typographical errors. Nevertheless, whether the inaccuracies are due to fraud or error, you should notify the credit bureau as soon as possible by telephone and in writing. You should continue to check your reports periodically, especially in the first year after you've discovered the theft, to make sure no new fraudulent activity has occurred. The automated "one-call" fraud alert process only works for the initial placement of your fraud alert. Orders for additional credit reports or renewals of your fraud alerts must be made separately at each of the three major credit bureaus.

2. Close any accounts that have been tampered with or opened fraudulently.

Credit Accounts. Credit accounts include all accounts with banks, credit card companies and other lenders, and phone companies, utilities, ISPs, and other service providers.

If you're closing existing accounts and opening new ones, use new Personal Identification Numbers (PINs) and passwords.

If there are fraudulent charges or debits, ask the company about the following forms for disputing those transactions:

- For new unauthorized accounts, ask if the company accepts the ID Theft Affidavit (available at www.ftc.gov/bcp/conline/pubs/credit/affidavit.pdf). If they don't, ask the representative to send you the company's fraud dispute forms.

- For your existing accounts, ask the representative to send you the company's fraud dispute forms.

- If your ATM card has been lost, stolen or otherwise compromised, cancel the card as soon as you can. Get a new card with a new PIN.

Checks. If your checks have been stolen or misused, close the account and ask your bank to notify the appropriate check verification service. While no federal law limits your losses if someone steals your checks and forges your signature, state laws may protect you. Most states hold the bank responsible for losses from a forged check, but they also require you to take reasonable care of your account. For example, you may be held responsible for the forgery if you fail to notify the bank in a timely way that a check was lost or stolen. Contact your state banking or consumer protection agency for more information.

You also should contact these major check verification companies. Ask that retailers who use their databases not accept your checks.

TeleCheck—1-800-710-9898 or 927-0188

Certegy, Inc.—1-800-437-5120

International Check Services—1-800-631-9656

Call SCAN (1-800-262-7771) to find out if the identity thief has been passing bad checks in your name.

3. File a report with your local police or the police in the community where the identity theft took place.

Keep a copy of the report. You may need it to validate your claims to creditors. If you can't get a copy, at least get the report number.

4. File a complaint with the FTC.

By sharing your identity theft complaint with the FTC, you will provide important information that can help law enforcement officials track down identity thieves and stop them. The FTC also can refer victim complaints to other appropriate government agencies and companies for further action. The FTC enters the information you provide into our secure database.

To file a complaint or to learn more about the FTC's Privacy Policy, visit www.consumer.gov/idtheft. If you don't have access to the Internet, you can call the FTC's Identity Theft Hotline: toll-free 1-877-IDTHEFT (438-4338); TDD: 202-326-2502; or write: Identity Theft Clearinghouse, Federal Trade Commission, 600 Pennsylvania Avenue, NW, Washington, DC 20580.

Chapter 32

"Risk Management" = Insurance

About Insurance

No one ever intends to have an automobile accident, lose valuable possessions through theft or damage, or become seriously ill, but sometimes through no fault of our own, these things do happen. To help us manage these potential risks of life, we buy insurance, through which we can obtain financial help in emergency situations.

You are probably already covered by several types of insurance without knowing much about it. Here are some of the kinds of insurance you should know about first:

- Health insurance provides coverage for medical care.

- Life insurance insures your life. If you should die, benefits are paid to the person you name as your beneficiary.

- Personal belongings insurance insures you against loss, theft, or damage.

- Automobile insurance covers your automobile and injuries to persons in the event of an accident. Most states require that you carry automobile and liability insurance.

Health Insurance

The United States does not have a government medical plan or health care service that covers the whole population. Instead, most people have private health insurance.

Health insurance can be a costly proposition. If a health premium seems too high for your budget or if, as a healthy young person, you think that health insurance is an unnecessary expense, consider the costs that could be incurred, as outlined below.

> **✔ Quick Tip**
>
> Up to a certain age, depending upon your status as a student and other factors, you may be covered by the health insurance policy of your parents. If you work full time, you may also be covered by a plan through your place of employment. However, most teens and young adults will need to consider how to obtain health insurance for themselves.
>
> Source: U.S. State Department, n.d.

Hospitals, doctors, and other medical costs vary throughout the country, but emergency room care averages more than $200 per visit. Hospital rooms vary in price depending on the hospital and the region of the country, but one overnight stay in a hospital room can cost $200 to $1,000 per day, not including charges for doctors and other medical services. Maternity care and delivery cost between $5,000 and $8,000. Overall, national figures indicate that the average cost for a one-week stay in a U.S. hospital is often as much as $8,000, which is about half the cost of attending some colleges or universities for an entire year.

Are you a college student? Almost all universities and colleges require that students carry health and accident insurance (the cost of which is in addition to the "health fee" generally charged at the beginning of each school term). Most educational institutions recommend a specific student health insurance plan. However, some of these plans are designed to supplement insurance already held by students or their parents. There are countless numbers of health insurance companies and each has numerous plans.

Basic health insurance usually includes doctors' fees (or a percentage of the fee) for major illnesses, as well as hospital and surgical expenses. Minor illnesses or injuries are treated in a doctor's office, and most basic insurance plans do not pay for such care. Most basic health and medical insurance policies specify certain limits, that is, a certain maximum amount the insurance company will pay for certain services. The patient must pay charges in excess of the stated limits.

Major Medical Insurance: This insurance is designed to take care of expenses resulting from a prolonged illness or serious injury. These policies generally involve a "deductible" clause—that is, you pay a certain amount, and the insurance company pays any additional charges or, sometimes, only the major percentage of those charges. Typically, the deductible is $500 to $1000, depending on the policy and the type of coverage. Maximum benefits (the limit the insurance company will pay) vary greatly and generally range from a low of $5,000 (which is not enough coverage) to $1 million or more (which is usually more than most healthy students need). You should purchase insurance that provides at least $25,000 in major medical coverage. If you can afford it, it would be advisable, however, to purchase more coverage.

Life Insurance
How Much Life Insurance Do I Need?

Excerpted and reprinted with permission from the Insurance Information Institute, http://www.iii.org, Copyright © 2005. All rights reserved.

No Dependents: If you are young and plan to have a family in the future, you may also want to consider purchasing life insurance now so that you can lock in a good rate.

Just because you don't have dependents does not mean you don't have responsibilities. For instance, you may be concerned with not being an economic burden to others if you die unexpectedly. You may also want to leave some money behind to close family, friends, or a special charity as a remembrance. In this case, you should purchase enough coverage to pay funeral and burial expenses, outstanding debts and tax liabilities, so that the bulk of your estate goes to your family, friends, or charities.

Your insurance needs will vary greatly according to your financial assets and liabilities, income potential, and level of expenses.

What Is A Beneficiary?

Reprinted with permission from the Insurance Information Institute, http:// www.iii.org, Copyright © 2005. All rights reserved.

A beneficiary is the person or financial institution, (a trust fund, for instance) you name in a life insurance policy to receive the proceeds. In addition to naming a specific beneficiary, you should name a second or "contingent" beneficiary, in case you outlive the first beneficiary.

♣ It's A Fact!!

Health Insurance Plan Exclusions: It is important to read your health insurance policy carefully, especially the section that deals with "exclusions," so that you will know in advance what the insurance company will pay for and what it will not pay for. Below are some areas that are generally not covered by basic health insurance plans:

- Maternity care: You must purchase insurance for maternity care separately and, generally, before pregnancy occurs. Most maternity insurance policies allow only two days' hospital stay.

- Dental services: Dental insurance is usually purchased separately from basic health insurance.

- Eyeglasses: Except in the case of injury to the eye, eye care is generally not covered by basic health insurance.

- Existing conditions: Most insurance companies will not reimburse you for treatment of a condition that existed prior to the effective date of your insurance policy. If you require care for an ongoing medical condition, look closely at any insurance policies you are considering.

- Prescription medications: Many insurance companies do not provide coverage for prescription medications, which can be very expensive. Even if they do provide some coverage, a "copayment" or standard fee (often $10 to $15) is usually required from you for each prescription on a monthly basis.

Source: U.S. State Department, n.d.

If there is no living beneficiary, the proceeds will go to your estate. If there are probate proceedings this could possible delay your loved ones receiving the money. The proceeds may also be subject to estate taxes.

Picking a beneficiary, and keeping that choice up-to-date, are important parts of purchasing life insurance. The birth or adoption of a child, marriage or divorce can affect your initial choice of who will receive the death benefit when you die. Review your beneficiary designation as new situations arise to make sure your choice is still appropriate.

Pay special attention to the wording of your beneficiary designations to ensure that the right person receives the proceeds of your estate. If you write "wife/husband of the insured" without using a specific name, an ex-spouse could receive the proceeds. On the other hand, if you have named specific children, any later-born or adopted children will not receive the proceeds— unless the beneficiary designation is changed.

What Are The Two Types (Term And Permanent) Of Life Insurance?

Reprinted with permission from the Insurance Information Institute, http:// www.iii.org, Copyright © 2005. All rights reserved.

While there a many different types of life insurance policies, they generally fall into two categories—term and permanent.

Term: Term insurance is the simplest form of life insurance. It provides financial protection for a specific time, usually from one to 30 years. These policies are relatively inexpensive and are well suited for goals, such as insurance protection during the child-raising years or while paying off a mortgage. They provide a death benefit, but do not offer cash savings.

Purchasing term insurance is like renting a home. It is a short-term solution. Monthly costs are usually lower, but you will not be building equity. Just as many people rent (while saving to buy a home), individuals who need insurance protection now, but have limited resources, may purchase term coverage and then switch to permanent protection. Others may view term insurance as a cost-effective way to protect their family and still have money to put into other investments.

Permanent: Permanent insurance (such as universal life, variable universal life, and whole life) provides long-term financial protection. These policies include both a death benefit and, in some cases, cash savings. Because of the savings element, premiums tend to be higher. This type of insurance is good for long-range financial goals.

Purchasing permanent insurance is like buying a home instead of renting. You are taking care of long-term housing needs with a long-term solution. Your monthly costs may be higher than if you rent, but your payments will build equity over time. If you purchase permanent insurance, your premiums will pay a death benefit and may also build cash value that can be accessed in the future.

When should I consider term insurance?

Reprinted with permission from the Insurance Information Institute, http:// www.iii.org, Copyright © 2005. All rights reserved.

If you need life insurance for a specific period of time, term insurance should be considered. It provides insurance protection from one to 30 years and is generally the least expensive form of life insurance. If you die during the term of the policy, your beneficiary will be paid the amount of money specified in the policy. If you are still alive at the end of the term, coverage stops unless the policy is renewed. Unlike permanent insurance, you will not build equity in the form of cash savings.

Term insurance can be a useful financial tool for:

- Those who need a large amount of life insurance, but have a limited budget, such as a young couple with children.

- Covering debts that will disappear in time, such as a mortgage or car loan.

- Business owners who want to cover the life of a key employee for a specific number of years.

Keep in mind that premiums are lowest when you are young and increase upon renewal as you age. Some term insurance policies can be renewed when the policy ends, but the premium will generally increase. Many policies require a medical examination at renewal to qualify for the lowest rates. Before deciding on a policy from a specific company, find out what their requirements are. Also, see if you would be able to convert the term policy to a permanent policy later on.

If you think your financial needs will change, you may also want to look into "convertible" term policies. These allow you to convert to permanent insurance without a medical examination in exchange for higher premiums.

Why should I purchase permanent insurance?

Reprinted with permission from the Insurance Information Institute, http://www.iii.org, Copyright © 2005. All rights reserved.

A permanent life policy provides lifelong insurance protection. The policy pays a death benefit if you die tomorrow or if you live to be a hundred. There is also a savings element that will grow on a tax-deferred basis and may become substantial over time. Because of the savings element, premiums are generally higher for permanent than for term insurance. However, the premium in a permanent policy remains the same, while term can go up substantially every time you renew it.

There are a number of different types of permanent insurance policies, such as whole (ordinary) life, universal life, variable life, and variable/universal life. In a permanent policy, the cash value is different from its face value amount. The face amount is the money that will be paid at death. Cash value is the amount of money available to you. There are a number of ways that you can use this cash savings. For instance, you can take a loan against it or you can surrender the policy before you die to collect the accumulated savings.

There are unique features to a permanent policy such as:

- You can lock in premiums when you purchase the policy. By purchasing a permanent policy, the premium will not increase as you age or if your health status changes.
- The policy will accumulate cash savings.

- Depending on the policy, you may be able to withdraw some of the money. You also may have these options:

    1. Use the cash value to pay premiums. If unexpected expenses occur, you can stop or reduce your premiums. The cash value in the policy can be used toward the premium payment to continue your current insurance protection—providing there is enough money accumulated.

    2. Borrow from the insurance company using the cash value in your life insurance as collateral. Like all loans, you will ultimately need to repay the insurer with interest. Otherwise, the policy may lapse or your beneficiaries will receive a reduced death benefit. However, unlike loans from most financial institutions, the loan is not dependent on credit checks or other restrictions.

How Is Life Insurance Sold?

Reprinted with permission from the Insurance Information Institute, http:// www.iii.org, Copyright © 2005. All rights reserved.

You can either buy life insurance as an "individual" or as part of a "group" plan.

Individual Policy: When you purchase an individual policy, you will pick the policy that is right for you and your family. You may purchase it from the same agent or company representative who sells you your home, auto or business insurance policy.

Individual policies can be sold through:

- Insurance agents or brokers
- Directly from the company over the telephone, through the mail or Internet
- Savings banks in some states

If you buy a policy through an agent, you will pay a commission, also called a "load." On the other hand, if you buy the policy directly from the insurance company (mail, phone or Internet)—you will be purchasing a "no load" or "low load" policy. Since there is no sales commission, you will be paying less for the policy. However, not many companies offer "no load" life insurance policies.

Group Policy: You may consider purchasing a group policy from your employer, union or trade association. Associations can sometimes offer highly competitive groups rates, so it makes sense to consider this option when shopping for a policy.

Your employer may also offer life insurance and pay all or some of the cost of the coverage. Although, most plans provided by an employer are term insurance, your state may require a conversion option allowing you to convert the policy to permanent insurance. You would then pay premiums directly to the insurer and retain coverage, if you leave the job. If you pay for the entire cost of the policy yourself, you can usually retain coverage by paying premiums directly to the insurer. An added benefit of purchasing group insurance through your employer is that sometimes the premiums will be deducted directly from your paycheck. This way, the policy will not lapse because you forgot to pay your insurance bill.

How Do I Pick A Life Insurance Company?

Reprinted with permission from the Insurance Information Institute, http://www.iii.org, Copyright © 2005. All rights reserved.

Insurance is a highly competitive business and in most cases, you will have hundreds of companies to choose from. When shopping for insurance, consider:

Price: Premiums vary widely between different companies. Compare prices from at least three companies before buying to make sure you are getting the best value, but make sure you compare similar insurance plans, based on:

- Your age

- Type of policy

- Amount of insurance you are purchasing

Prices may differ among companies because of different features or different levels of service or the financial strength of the insurance company.

Budget: Make sure you can afford the premiums because you will be wasting your money if you are forced to drop the coverage after a few years.

Some state insurance departments publish buyer guides showing what different companies charge. You can also check prices on your own at many of the insurance price-quoting websites or at their toll-free numbers.

Insurer's Stability: In addition to a reasonable price, you want to be confident that the insurance company will be in good health financially to pay your claim if necessary.

Companies that rate insurer's financial stability include:

A.M. Best
Oldwick, New Jersey 08858
908-439-2200
www.ambest.com

Moody's Investors Services
99 Church Street
New York, New York 10007
212-553-0300
www.moodys.com

Standard & Poor's Insurance Ratings Service
55 Water Street
New York, New York 10041
212-438-2000
ww.standardandpoor.com

Weiss Research
4176 Burns Road
Palm Beach Gardens, Florida 33410
800-289-9222
www.weissratings.com

☞ **Remember!!**

Health: In most cases, a full-time student will be covered in the family's health plan until he or she graduates from college, or remains a full-time student up to 23 years of age. However, if the parents belong to a closed-network HMO that doesn't provide non-emergency coverage in the school's area, a separate policy for the student should be considered. Most colleges have a clinic on campus and may offer supplemental insurance as well. If a child gets sick and has to temporarily drop out, parents might want to consider having tuition insurance. Otherwise, even though the child has left school, the family may be on the hook for the tuition.

Source: Reprinted with permission from the Insurance Information Institute, http://www.iii.org, copyright © 2005. All rights reserved.

Service: The insurer you select should offer excellent service. Your agent or company representative should clearly explain all of your options, so you can make the best choice for your needs.

If you have a claim or question, the company should handle it promptly and accurately. Your state insurance department will be able to tell you if the insurance company you are planning to do business with had many consumer complaints about its service relative to the number of policies it sold.

Insurance For Youth

Reprinted with permission from the Insurance Information Institute, http:// www.iii.org, Copyright © 2005. All rights reserved.

Student: When a teenager gets a license, it's probably the first time he or she focuses on insurance. And as young people graduate from high school and head off to college or enter the working world, there are lots of insurance matters for young people out on their own for the first time to think about.

Auto: Teenage drivers represent the highest risk segment of the population and are involved in more serious and fatal accidents than anyone else. From the insurance company's standpoint, high risk requires a higher insurance premium. Teenage drivers can add anywhere from 50 and 100 percent to the cost of a family's auto coverage. Generally, it is cheaper to put a teenage driver on the family policy. Driver education and good student discounts can take the sting out of that to some extent. Many states have graduated driver licensing programs which phase in driving privileges and give teens driving experience under controlled conditions allowing young drivers to demonstrate good driving habits and gain experience. Pick a safe car to drive— the model chosen greatly affects the cost of insurance. If a college student does not have a car during the school year (many schools restrict cars on campus for the first couple of years) and attends a school at least 100 miles from home, tell the insurance company. Rates may be lowered significantly for the period the student is not at home.

Home: There aren't many "student homeowners." But they have "stuff" that needs protection, which usually comes through homeowner or renter insurance. If a student lives at home, or in a college dorm, their personal possessions, including a computer, stereo, television, clothing and such items are covered by the family's policy. If they have any items of exceptional value, it's a good idea to have a separate endorsement on the policy. If a college student lives off campus, the family policy will probably not cover them. They should consider purchasing separate renter insurance.

Life: Life insurance protects a family's way of life. As students approach college, not only are families focused on how to pay for it, they should also be thinking of how to keep things on track if tragedy strikes. Life insurance, whether whole life or term, is one way to ensure that resources will be there for your student to finish college if something happens to one of the family breadwinners. At a minimum, families should think about a limited policy that would cover burial expenses if a child is killed in an accident.

Disability: Disability coverage provides for lost wages in the event you are injured and unable to work. Most part-time jobs do not include such benefits, so disability insurance is unlikely to be provided by employers to students who work while going to school. For parents who are paying for their children's college education, disability insurance would ensure that resources are there should the primary wage earner become disabled and be unable to work.

Long-Term Care: The younger and healthier one is, the less paid for insurance. But long-term care insurance is generally not an insurance priority for a young student unless there are extenuating circumstances.

Renter's Insurance: A Smart Buy

When you rent a home or apartment your first thought may not be about buying insurance. Although your personal belongings are very important to you, it may not seem like you have enough property to insure or you may think you can't afford it. But, in the event of fire, an explosion, bursting water pipes, or theft, could you afford to replace your things? The value of your furniture, electronic equipment, clothes, jewelry and other personal items can add up to more than you think. That's where renter's insurance comes in.

Renter's insurance provides coverage for your personal property while you occupy a dwelling owned by someone else. In a renter's policy you choose the amount of property damage coverage you need based on what it would cost to replace the things you own. With renter's insurance your personal property is protected from many types of perils including those previously mentioned as well as lightning, windstorm, hail, riot, civil commotions, vandalism, falling objects, smoke, and damage from a vehicle.

But, a basic renter's policy provides you with more than just coverage for loss of property at home. You are also entitled to an additional 10 percent of the amount of your policy's coverage limit to cover property away from your home. For example, if you have $50,000 worth of personal property coverage, you will automatically receive an additional $5,000 in coverage on personal property lost, damaged or stolen while it is anywhere else in the United States or Canada.

♣ **It's A Fact!!**
Case Study:
Renter's Insurance

Your rent is $500 per month and your expenses for food and utilities amount to about $500 per month—a total of $1,000 per month. Assume that the renter's policy you purchased provides you with an additional living expenses benefit of $350 per month for six months. After a fire, you and your family must move into a hotel, which costs $700 per month. Your utilities are included but your cost for meals at restaurants is $600 per month. Your total living expense is now $1,300, $300 more than your regular monthly expense. Your renter's policy would pay the difference of $300 for six months.

Source: State of Michigan Office of Financial and Insurance Services, 2003.

In the event that you are forced to find other living accommodations following the loss of your rented apartment or home due to a fire or other peril, a renter's policy also covers your additional living expenses up to a specified limit or for a specific amount of time (e.g., six months) depending on the policy.

A basic renter's policy usually provides you with medical payments coverage for injuries that may occur to someone else in your rented dwelling or which may be caused by you or a family member, and up to $50,000 in liability coverage in case someone sues you for damages caused by you or a family member or which occurs on your property. If, for example, a visitor slips on your rug and breaks a leg, the medical payments coverage in your renter's policy would pay any medical expenses up to the limit in the policy—usually $1,000 per person. If he or she decided to sue you, your liability coverage would provide you with legal protection and pay the cost of a settlement.

There are other important coverages in a basic renter's policy which protect you against many kinds of financial losses. Ask an insurance agent to give you more details and shop around for the lowest price. Renter's insurance is surprisingly affordable. If you rent, renter's insurance is one purchase you cannot afford to do without.

Part Seven
If You Need More Information

Chapter 33

Websites About Money

Banking

American Bankers Association
http://www.aba.com

Credit Union National Association
http://www.cuna.org

Bankrate.com
http://www.bankrate.com

Compare the features of banks across the United States.

Banking Procedures

How to endorse a check
http://www.practicalmoneyskills
.com/english/resources/tutor/
statements/endorse_check.php

How to fill out a bank deposit slip
http://www.practicalmoneyskills
.com/english/resources/tutor/
statements/deposit.php

How to write a check
http://www.practicalmoneyskills
.com/english/resources/tutor/
statements/write_check.php

About This Chapter: The websites in this chapter were compiled from sources deemed reliable. To make it easier to find specific information, they are grouped by topic. All web addresses were verified in May 2005.

How to read your bank statement

http://www.practicalmoneyskills
.com/english/resources/tutor/
statements/bank.php

How to read your credit card statement

http://www.practicalmoneyskills
.com/english/resources/tutor/
statements/credit_state.php

How to record transactions

http://www.practicalmoneyskills
.com/english/resources/tutor/
statements/register.php

Budget Calculators And Spreadsheets

CU Succeed

http://www.cusucceed.net/
resources.php

Consumer's Almanac

http://www.pueblo.gsa.gov/cic_text/
money/almanac/calmanac.htm

Dinkytown.net Financial Calculators

http://dinkytown.net

Indiana Department of Financial Institutions

http://www.in.gov/dfi/education/
links_to_interactive_tool_calcul.htm

Practical Money Skills

http://www.practicalmoneyskills
.com/english/resources/calculators

Downloadable "My Budget Planner"
and a calculator called, "Rework Budget."

Cars

American Bankers Association

http://www.aba.com/aba/cgi-bin/
autoNT.pl

Auto loan calculator.

Automotive.com

http://www.automotive.com

Includes information about crash
safety tests and vehicle recalls.

AutoSite.com

http://www.autosite.com

Includes reviews and ratings; also
offers a loan calculator.

AutoWorld

http://www.autoworld.com

Includes automotive news headlines
and pricing research.

Bankrate.com

http://www.bankrate.com/brm/
auto-loan-calculator.asp

Auto loan calculator.

Car.com
http://www.car.com

Information about car prices and auto loans.

CARFAX, Inc.
http://www.carfax.com

Vehicle history report to help protect against "lemons."

Cars.com
http://www.cars.com

Information about car prices and a loan calculator.

Edmunds
http://www.edmunds.com

Car prices and a loan calculator; with "Tips and Advice" on buying, selling, or owning an automobile.

The Insurance Institute for Highway Safety
http://www.hwysafety.org

Vehicle ratings and safety test results.

Kelley Blue Book
http://www.kbb.com

Car prices with vehicle ratings and advice for buying a new or used car; also includes motorcycles, personal watercraft, and snowmobiles.

NADA
http://www.nada.com

Consumer area offers information about car prices, including classic cars and motorcycles.

Used Car Advisor
http://www.used-car-advisor.com

Includes a section for teens.

USF Federal Credit Union
http://www.creditunion.usf.edu/wizards/autocalc.html

Auto loan calculator.

Consumer Issues

Better Business Bureau
http://wwwbbb.org

Call for Action, Inc.
http://www.callforaction.org

A nonprofit network of consumer hotlines.

Consumer Action Handbook
http://www.savingscoalition.org

National Association of Consumer Agency Administrators
http://www.nacaa.net

For information on state-specific consumer legal questions.

Consumer World

http://www.consumerworld.org

A searchable public service site with links to 2000 consumer resources such as product reviews, bargains, and agencies.

Credit Cards And Other Loan Information

Bankrate.com

http://www.Bankrate.com/brm/rate/cc_home.asp

Cardratings.com

http://www.cardratings.com

CardTrak

http://www.cardweb.com/cardtrak

Cardweb.com

http://cardweb.com

Federal Reserve Board

http://www.federalreserve.gov/../pubs/SHOP/default

"Choosing a Credit Card" and links to additional information.

Springboard

http://www.ncfe.org/index.htm

Credit information and help from the Center for Financial Education.

Credit Reports (Online Ordering)

Equifax

http://www.equifax.com

Experian

http://www.experian.com

TransUnion

http://www.transunion.com

Financial Aid For College

Collegeboard.com

http://www.collegeboard.com/pay

Information about college costs, scholarships, financial aid applications, education loans, and college financing.

Federal Student Aid

http://www.studentaid.ed.gov

Information on student aid from the federal government.

FinAid

http://www.finaid.org

"How to" guidance on getting student financial aid.

Savingforcollege

http://www.savingforcollege.com

Information about Section 529 (prepaid) and other college savings plans.

Students.gov

http://www.students.gov

A federal information portal, including tips on planning and paying for education with additional information on career development

Junior Achievement, Inc.

http://studentcenter.ja.org

Information about education, business, and career development to help you become 'workforce ready.'

Interactive Financial Sites

CBIC SmartStart

http://www.cibc.com/ca/youth

Financial advice with a section focused on needs of kids aged 13–18.

Consumer Debit Resource

https://www.consumerdebit.com

Click on "About Checking" for interactive information about how to write checks, use a check register, deposit money in your account, review your statement, and balance your account.

Consumer Jungle

http://www.consumerjungle.org

Covers credit cards, transportation, living on your own, telecommunications, and e-commerce fraud.

ItAllAddsUp.org

http://www.italladdsup.org

The National Council on Economic Education site for teens. Five interactive lessons show the fundamentals of budgeting, saving and investing, preparing for college, buying a car, and credit.

Jump$tart.org

http://www.jumpstart.org/
realitycheck

A student online calculator that tells you how much income you will need to support the lifestyle you want, lists a few jobs that fall into your desired pay scale, and describes the level of education you will need.

LifeSmarts.org

http://www.lifesmarts.org

Internet competition that tests knowledge of consumer issues; run by National Consumers League.

Sense & Dollars

http://senseanddollars.thinkport
.org

Maryland Public Television interactive website.

U.S. Securities and Exchange Commission

http://www.sec.gov/investor/tools/quiz.htm

Take this "Money $marts" test to see what you know about stocks, bonds, and other investments.

Job And Career

Bureau of Labor Statistics

http://www.bls.gov

Exploring career information; click on topics of interest including "Wages, Earnings, and Benefits." One important source of career information is *The Occupational Outlook* at http://www.bls.gov/oco/home.htm.

Career Colleges and Technical Schools

http://www.ed.gov/students/prep/college/consumerinfo/index.html

Information from the U.S. Department of Education about career-training after high school.

Career Key

http://www.ncsu.edu/careerkey

Use self-assessment tools to identify areas of interest and learn about required skills for various career choices.

Career Talk

http://www.careertalk.com

Advice on various job-seeking topics; suggestions for preparing for different types of interviews.

Cool Works

http://www.coolworks.com/teen-jobs

Information about work at parks and camps; also "Teen Resources" section.

Federal Trade Commission

http://www.ftc.gov/bcp/conline/pubs/services/votech.htm

Suggestions about choosing a career or vocational/trade school; also with information about filing a complaint if you are not satisfied with a vocational or correspondence school.

GotAJob.com

http://gotajob.com

Click on "Brain Food" for information about getting a job and working, including writing a resume and cover letter or preparing for an interview.

JobHunt

http://www.job-hunt.org

Job search advice includes information about how to make on-line job searches safer.

JobHuntersBible.com

http://www.jobhuntersbible.com

Information about using the internet for a job search.

JobStar Central

http://www.jobsmart.org

Includes links for resume-writing tips and career guides.

Junior Achievement, Inc.

http://www.ja.org

Help for new entrepreneurs; JA explains its mission as building a "bridge between education and business."

The Monster Board

http://www.monster.com

In addition to job search functions, offers career advice.

MyFuture.com

http://www.myfuture.com

Information about military careers.

Snag A Job

http://www.snagajob.com

Job search site with a focus on hourly and part-time jobs; also, interview tips and resume help.

Studentjobs.gov

http://www.studentjobs.gov

A joint project of the U.S. Office of Personnel Management and the U.S. Department of Education's Student Financial Assistance office.

Teens4Hire

http://www.teens4hire.com

Job search information and advice for teens.

U.S. Department of Labor

http://www.dol.gov/dol/topic/training/youth.htm

Youth job training resources, including links to information about Job Corps, Youth Opportunity Grants, Apprenticeship, and other government-sponsored youth career programs.

Money Problems

American Financial Services Association (AFSA) Education Foundation

http://www.afsaef.org

CampusBlues.com

http://www.campusblues.com/moneyprob.asp

Consumer Credit Counseling Service

http://www.cccsintl.org

Debtors Anonymous
http://www.debtorsanonymous.org

Gamblers Anonymous
http://wwww.gamblersanonymous
.org

National Association for Shoplifting Prevention
http://www.shopliftingprevention
.org

Taxes: Forms And Information

U.S. Internal Revenue Service
http://www.irs.gov

Offers information about federal taxes, including filing requirements, refunds, and downloadable tax forms.

Teen Financial Resources

Jump$tart
http://www.jumpstart.org

An organization working to improve financial literacy among K–12 students.

Kiplinger, "Money Smart Kids"
http://www.kiplinger.com/columns/
kids/archive.html

Archived "Money Smart Kids" articles about money management; topics include things like budgeting, cell phones, credit cards, and saving for college.

The Mint
http://www.themint.org

Information for kids about earning, spending, saving, and tracking money; also includes a glossary of finance terms.

Motley Fool
http://www.fool.com

Click on "Fool's School" for basic investment information.

NTRBonline
http://www.ntrbonline.org

NTRB (National Teen Resource Bureau) presents articles and links, written and collected by teens for teens.

YoungBiz
http://www.youngbiz.com

Stories about "treps"—teen entrepreneurs who've started "fresh, funky and financially rewarding" businesses.

YoungMoney

http://www/youngmoney.com

Articles on money management, comparison shopping, consumer protection, careers, and more.

Other Sites

Bureau of Economic Analysis

http://www.bea.gov

Recommended for those interested in U.S. economic statistics, includes tables summarizing gross domestic product (GDP) and state personal income.

Federal Citizen Information Center

http://www.pueblo.gsa.gov

Information on consumer topics.

Public Broadcasting Service (PBS)

http://www.pbs.org/newshour/on2/budget.html

"Managing Your Money" article, with links to articles about jobs, money for college, and credit.

Social Security Administration

http://www.socialsecurity.gov/history

Multimedia history of Social Security in the United States.

Soundmoney

http://soundmoney.publicradio.org

Website for the American Public Media broadcast.

Treasurydirect

http://www.treasurydirect.gov

Invest in Treasury securities online.

Chapter 34

A Directory Of Financial Organizations

American Bankers Association
120 Connecticut Ave., N.W.
Washington, DC 20036
Toll-Free: 800-BANKERS
Website: http://www.aba.com

American Financial Services Association (AFSA) Education Foundation
919 Eighteenth St., N.W.
Washington, DC 20006
Phone: 202-466-8611
Fax: 202-223-0321
Website: http://www.afsaef.org
E-mail: info@afsaef.org

Better Business Bureau
4200 Wilson Blvd., Suite 800
Arlington, VA 22203-1838
Phone: 703-276-0100
Fax: 703-525-8277
Website: http://www.bbb.org

Center for the Study of Services
733 15th St., N.W., Suite 820
Washington, DC 20005
Toll-Free: 800-213-7383
Phone: 202-347-7283
Website: http://www.checkbook.org

About This Chapter: The organizations listed in this chapter were compiled from resources deemed reliable. They are listed alphabetically. All contact information was verified in May 2005.

Consumer Action
717 Market St., Suite 310
San Francisco, CA 94103
Phone: 415-777-9635 (Consumer Complaints)
Fax: 415-777-5267
Website: http://www.consumer-action.org
E-mail: info@consumer-action.org

Consumer Debit Resource
AboutChecking and Education
Consumer Outreach
8501 N. Scottsdale Rd, #300
Scottsdale, AZ 85253
Toll-Free: 800-428-9623
Fax: 602-659-2197
Website: http://www.consumerdebit.com

Consumer Federation of America
1424 16th Street N.W., Suite 604
Washington, DC 20036
Phone: 202-387-6121
Website: http://www.consumerfed.org

Credit Union National Association
P.O. Box 431
Madison, WI 53701-0431
Toll-Free: 800-356-9655
Fax: 608-231-4127
Website: http://www.cuna.org

Debtors Anonymous
General Service Office
P.O. Box 920888
Needham, MA 02492-0009
Phone: 781-453-2743
Fax: 781-435-2745
Website: http://www.debtorsanonymous.org
E-mail: webmaster@debtorsanonymous.org

Gamblers Anonymous
International Service Office
P.O. Box 17173
Los Angeles, CA 90017
Phone: 213-386-8789
Fax: 231-386-0030
Website: http://www.gamblersanonymous.org
E-mail: isomain@gamblersanonymous.org

InCharge Education Foundation
2101 Park Center Dr. Suite 310
Orlando FL 32835
Phone: 407-291-7770
Website: http://
education.incharge.org

Insurance Information Institute
110 William Street
New York, NY 10038
Phone: 212-346-5500
Website: http://www.iii.org

JumpStart Coalition for Personal Financial Literacy
919 18th Street, N.W., Suite 300
Washington, DC 20006
Toll-Free: 888-45-EDUCATE
Phone: 301-725-9707
Website: http://www.jumpstart.com

Junior Achievement, Inc.
JA Worldwide
One Education Way
Colorado Springs, CO 80906
Phone: 719-540-8000
Fax: 719-540-6299
Website: http://www.ja.org

Myvesta
P.O. Box 8587
Gaithersburg, MD 20898-8587
Phone: 301-762-5270
Website: http://www.dca.org

National Association for Shoplifting Prevention
380 North Broadway, Suite 306
Jericho, NY 11752
Toll-Free: 800-848-9595
Phone: 516-932-0165
Fax: 516-932-9393
Website: http://
www.shopliftingprevention.org
E-mail:
nasp@shopliftingprevention.org

National Consumers League
1701 K St., N.W., Suite 1200
Washington, DC 20006
Phone: 202-835-3323
Fax: 202-835-0747
Website: http://www.nclnet.org
E-mail: info@nclnet.org

National Council on Economic Education

National Council on Economic Education
1140 Avenue of the Americas
New York, NY 10036
Toll-Free: 800-338-1192
Phone: 212-730-7007
Fax: 212-730-1793
Website: http://www.ncee.net
E-mail: sales@ncee.net

National Endowment for Financial Education

5299 DTC Boulevard, Suite 1300
Greenwood Village, CO 80111
Phone: 303-741-6333
Website: http://www.nefe.org

Index

Page numbers that appear in *Italics* refer to illustrations. Page numbers that have a small 'n' after the page number refer to information shown as Notes at the beginning of each chapter. Page numbers that appear in **Bold** refer to information contained in boxes on that page (except Notes information at the beginning of each chapter).

Federal Reserve Bank of Atlanta, check
books publication 139n
Federal Reserve Bank of Boston, banking
basics publication 123n, 139n, 149n,
155n
Federal Reserve Bank of Dallas,
publications
economics 3n
entrepreneurs 215n
Federal Reserve Bank of New York,
electronic banking publication 183n
Federal Reserve Board, Web site address
382
Federal Reserve Board of Governors
publications
checking accounts 155n
credit cards 289n
credit management 271n
savings accounts 123n
Federal Reserve System, described 6
Federal Student Aid, Web site
address 382
Federal Trade Commission (FTC)
see US Federal Trade Commission
fees, defined 291
FICA see Federal Insurance Contributions
Act
FICA tax, defined 249
FinAid, Web site address 382
finance charges
computation method 305
credit cards 294–97, 300–301
described 295
minimum, defined 305
financial aid, information 209
financial literacy, overview 23–24
financial planning, money savers 29–30
financial records
overview 11–15
retention 13
"Financing College" (Teen Consumer
Scrapbook) 271n
"Fiscal Fitness: Choosing A Credit
Counselor" (FTC) 319n
fiscal policy, defined 261
float, described 190–91
FLSA see Fair Labor Standards Act
Food and Drug Administration (FDA)
see US Food and Drug Administration

fraud
checking accounts 168–70, **169**
examples **281**
4-1-9 schemes **343**
Internet scams 340–43
loans 279–87
merchandise returns 50–52
travel offers **35**
free checking, described 157
free gifts
advertising 32–33
myths **62**
"Frequently Asked Questions: The
Teen Entrepreneur Guide to Owning
a Small Business" (Small Business
Administration) 203n
fringe benefits
defined **240**
described **245**
FTC see US Federal Trade Commission
"FTC Releases Consumer Fraud Survey"
(FTC) 279n
"Full-Time Students and Taxes" (IRS)
257n
full warranty, defined **69**

G

Gamblers Anonymous
contact information 390
Web site address 386
gambling
online **338**
overview 335–38
recovery programs **337**
"Get Rid of Debt!" (Edmondson) 319n
"Getting Purse-onal" (FTC) 345n
Glass, Amy 224
goal setting
assistance 20
described 18
GotAJob.com, Web site address 384
government checks, described 148
grace period
credit cards 300
defined **128**, **291**, **305**
gross income, defined **265**
group policy, described 371
guarantees, described 69–70